by Jerry Kovarsky

Foreword by Stephen Fortner
Editor in Chief, *Keyboard* magazine

To Stefan

Happy Christmas "2019"

Well I hope you're not too much of a dummy
to learn Tee Hee!!

DUMMIES
A Wiley Brand

love Mum
xxx

Keyboard For Dummies®

Published by: **John Wiley & Sons, Inc.,** 111 River Street, Hoboken, NJ 07030-5774, www.wiley.com

For general information on our other products and services, please contact our Customer Care Department within the U.S. at 877-762-2974, outside the U.S. at 317-572-3993, or fax 317-572-4002. For technical support, please visit www.wiley.com/techsupport.

Wiley publishes in a variety of print and electronic formats and by print-on-demand. Some material included with standard print versions of this book may not be included in e-books or in print-on-demand. If this book refers to media such as a CD or DVD that is not included in the version you purchased, you may download this material at http://booksupport.wiley.com. For more information about Wiley products, visit www.wiley.com.

Library of Congress Control Number: 2013948009

ISBN 978-1-118-70549-0 (pbk); ISBN 978-1-118-70731-9 (ebk); ISBN 978-1-118-70566-7 (ebk); ISBN 978-1-118-70563-6 (ebk)

Manufactured in the United States of America

C10006871_121118

Contents at a Glance

Table of Contents

Foreword

When the folks at Wiley first approached me about adding a title on playing keyboards to their hugely popular *For Dummies* family of reference books, I was delighted. The concept, they said, was to be different than the excellent *Piano For Dummies* (first published in 1998). It was to go beyond how to play the piano and cover all the ways in which modern electronic keyboards make learning music fun, enrich the lives of players of all levels of ability and aspiration, and give professionals powerful creative tools not offered by the traditional piano or organ.

I was particularly inspired because this was very much the same challenge faced by *Keyboard* magazine (originally called *Contemporary Keyboard*) at its inception in 1975. Then, electronic keyboards and synthesizers were a nascent and esoteric thing — sci-fi starships piloted by a crew of rock-and-rollers, academics, avant-garde composers, and committed enthusiasts. Now, they're enough of a known quantity that — although technology never ceases to evolve — they really do offer something for everyone. Which sort of instrument is best for you? How do you take full advantage of its features? How do the two somewhat-different experiences of pushing buttons and playing notes integrate to produce musical fulfillment? How can all this technology actually help you *play better* as opposed to being a crutch? That — and much more — is what this book is all about.

Just after that first phone call with Wiley, a little guy with wings and a harp — make that a keytar — appeared on one shoulder, and a red guy with horns and an unusually pointy tuning fork appeared on the other. "Write this book," said the red guy. "Think of the prestige, the fame, the red carpet!" "Puh-leeze," retorted the winged guy, "the only carpet is the one you'll get called on for blowing the deadline because you're already so busy running a magazine. You and I both know that Jerry Kovarsky is *the* one to write this. Call him. *Now*." Fortunately for all of us, the winged guy then shot a bolt of lightning from his keytar, and the only other thing I heard from the red guy was his tuning fork ringing (a tritone, of course) as he vanished in a puff of smoke.

Indeed, I can think of no better guide for your first journey into keyboards than Jerry Kovarsky. He's as talented a traditional keyboardist as he is a technologist, so he understands that technology is there to serve the music. He was there at the dawn of MIDI, the digital language at the core of every electronic musical instrument since the early '80s. Though he has held high-level product management gigs for Casio and Korg — two companies that have long been at the forefront of creating fun and affordable musical instruments — even their competitors always considered him an asset thanks to his tireless passion for educating people about music technology in general. Last but not least, his technical know-how, integrity, and get-it-done attitude have earned him the trust and friendship of many of the keyboard world's brightest stars, including prog-rock godfather Keith Emerson and the late, great George Duke.

I hope that *Keyboard For Dummies* launches you into a lifetime exploration of creating cool sounds, playing your favorite tunes, and even composing some of your own. If you're hungry for more after working through this book, head to www.keyboardmag.com to check out our online content and subscribe to the print edition of *Keyboard* magazine. There, you'll find music lessons from today's top players, how-to articles from experts including Jerry, and interviews with stars who put keyboards at the center of their music making. Now, dig into this book and start putting these instruments at the center of yours!

Stephen Fortner
Editor in Chief, Keyboard *magazine*

Introduction

*I*t used to be simple; you could say, "I play the piano" or "I play organ." That was pretty much it. Through the last few decades, thanks to technological advances, the world of keyboards has exploded. Now so many options are available that when you press down on those familiar black and white keys, any sound may come out. A small portable keyboard can have the sound of a nine-foot concert grand piano, and that baby-grand-piano-looking instrument can produce the sounds of a full orchestra and a rock band to boot! Anything is possible in the world of electronic keyboards today, and you don't have to rob a bank to get a single keyboard that can do what took cape-wearing rock stars a circle of gear to do in the late '70s.

And therein lies the reason behind *Keyboard For Dummies.* No one has adequately tackled this subject, explaining what all the keyboard options are and how to choose and use them. When I was approached to write the book, the task was more than a little daunting. I know the subject matter well; my whole career has been in keyboards — playing them, teaching with them, developing and marketing them, and enjoying them. But this field is such a wide area to cover, from simple little toys up through a wide variety of home and stage keyboards. So my goal is to make technology easy to understand, clearly explain the many types of keyboard available, and help you dive in and use and enjoy the features of these various instruments. I have only two requirements for covering an instrument in this book:

- ✔ It has the aforementioned black and whites keys
- ✔ It has a power cord or runs on batteries

Show me those two things and I'm in.

About This Book

Keyboard For Dummies makes sense of this wide world of electronic black-and-white-key instruments. I explain all the types of keyboards available today, grouping them into logical categories. You gain a basic understanding of how they work, what each is good for, and how to choose the right one for your needs.

I cover the basics of music so I can share some playing tips, and I introduce the fundamentals of synthesis so you can tweak your sounds and effects when you need to. You get into the basics of computer integration and even discover how to play songs by ear. My goals are to make things clear, interesting, informative, unintimidating, and most of all, fun! I don't care what type of music or which keyboard family is your favorite. I try not to let my personal taste color any of my writing. Though perhaps my age slips through now and again; I can't try to be any younger (or older) than I am.

Covering such a wide array of keyboards and topics means that not every chapter relates to your specific needs. *Keyboard For Dummies* is written so you can dive in to any chapter that interests you; you don't have to read it from front cover to back. In particular, you can skip over shaded sidebars and anything marked with a Technical Stuff icon. These bits are interesting but provide more information than what you absolutely need to know to understand the point at hand. But I think that if you're interested in keyboards, you'll find every chapter of some interest to at least expand your horizons about the possibilities that are out there.

Reading is all well and good, but I'm talking about sound and music here. I love this quotation, often attributed to comedian Martin Mull: "Writing about music is like dancing about architecture." I couldn't agree more, so I provide plenty of online audio examples that take the words and concepts in this book and translate them into sonic reality for you to absorb and enjoy.

Within this book, you may note that some web addresses break across two lines of text. If you're reading this book in print and want to visit one of these web pages, simply key in the web address exactly as it's noted in the text, pretending as though the line break doesn't exist. If you're reading this as an e-book, you've got it easy — just click on the web address to be taken directly to the web page.

Foolish Assumptions

I've made some assumptions about who you, the reader, are. If any of these is true about you, this book is for you:

- ✔ You're a beginner to music, keyboards, and technology and want guidance from the ground floor up, including tips to help you purchase the right keyboard for you and use its features to the fullest.

- ✔ You're a good pianist who wants to explore keyboard technology.

- ✔ You just love music and keyboards.

✔ You're a parent or other adult shopping for a keyboard for a child and need suggestions on what types and features are best for youngsters to practice with.

✔ You're curious and want to learn.

Icons Used in This Book

Throughout the book I use icons to help break up the text and to draw attention to points I'm making. Here's what each icon means:

 This icon highlights helpful info that will enhance your keyboard skills. It may be a shortcut or another way of doing things. Think of it as a friend, adding to the information at hand.

 This icon identifies important tidbits you should squirrel away for later use.

 Potentially damaging or dangerous issues carry the Warning icon. Take them seriously.

 At times, I go into greater background detail than what you need to grasp a basic topic, and I use this icon to identify that extra information. It isn't essential reading, but gives you a deeper understanding of a subject.

 I've sprinkled a lot of audio examples throughout the text to bring all the subject matter in this book to life. When you see this icon, it indicates that you can find an online audio track related to what you're reading about.

Beyond the Book

In addition to the book content, you can find a free online Cheat Sheet that includes a glossary of common keyboard terminology, a helpful list of must-have and good-to-add accessories, and a who's who of keyboard companies. Go to www.dummies.com/cheatsheet/keyboard to access this handy reference material, and then print it out and keep it by your side when purchasing, studying, and playing your keyboard.

You can also access additional free articles that cover information I simply couldn't fit into the book. You'll find information on sixth and seventh chords, the General MIDI (GM) soundset, and entertaining educational features included on some keyboards. I also offer lists of songs that showcase each type of keyboard. You can find them at www.dummies.com/extras/keyboard.

Finally, www.dummies.com/go/keyboard is home to the more than 100 audio tracks that accompany this book. Head there to listen to me demonstrate the sounds of instruments, play all the exercises provided, use various keyboard features, and much more. Sometimes I even talk!

Where to Go from Here

You don't have to read *Keyboard For Dummies* in any particular order; I've written it to be modular, so jumping around is perfectly fine. You can turn to the table of contents, find the section you're most interested in, and get started. That said, starting with Chapter 1 will give you a great overview of what this book covers.

If you don't have a keyboard and want to learn about what's out there, be sure to read Chapters 2 and 3. Want to know more about music and playing basics? Skip right over to Part II. If you have an arranger keyboard or anything with automatic accompaniment, be sure to check out Chapters 10 and 11. Interested in synthesis? Chapter 14 is for you. Eventually, you'll want to read them all; I wrote this book to be a resource that you can keep coming back to for (hopefully) years to come. Enjoy!

Part I
Getting Started with Keyboards

In this part . . .

✔ Meet the many kinds of keyboards that have been played throughout the years and the various types that are available today. They fall into logical families that help you to make sense of all the options.

✔ Determine what your music-making needs are and decide what type of keyboard is the best choice for you.

✔ Settle your keyboard into its optimal home. After it's there, a few common-sense safety precautions and bits of upkeep will help keep it in tiptop shape.

Chapter 1

Living in a Keyboard World

You've probably seen images and scenes of people wielding the power and majesty of playing a keyboard:

✓ Young genius Mozart driving his peer Salieri mad with his effortless brilliance (no, I wasn't there; I saw the movie *Amadeus*)

✓ Early rockers like Jerry Lee Lewis and Little Richard banging away like men possessed

✓ The ever-so-detached cool of the jazz pianist, playing with head close to the keys, cigarette dangling from his lips, lost in concentration

✓ Prog-rocker Keith Emerson stabbing knives into his Hammond organ and riding it across stages, and then, for a break, strapping onto a spinning grand piano *and playing,* in the ultimate feat of showmanship

✓ Countless music videos in the '80's featuring bands behind stacks of synthesizers or dancing around wearing strap-on keyboards (and sporting interesting haircuts to boot.)

✓ Singer-songwriters like Billy Joel, Elton John, Alicia Keys, John Legend, and Carole King spinning their tales of life and love from behind massive grand pianos

All these images (and more) have caused many a young boy and girl to embark down the road of playing keyboard. And many baby boomers and successful businesspeople have returned to this love after carving out their careers and want to pick up where they left off.

Beyond the familiar black and white keys, though, keyboards can be wildly different instruments, and looking at the front panels may not give you much of a clue as to what's inside. This chapter gives you an overview of what keyboards are and just what you can do with them. ***Remember:*** I provide online audio tracks throughout the book to help demonstrate the topics at hand, including the discussions introduced in this chapter.

If what you're interested in is the acoustic piano, I recommend *Piano For Dummies* by Blake Neely (Wiley). It's a wonderful guide to all things piano.

Distinguishing Basic Keyboard Characteristics

The first thing to realize is that all keyboards aren't the same. They may make different types of sounds by different methods of sound production and are meant to do different things for the needs of different players. The following sections help you navigate this potentially confusing terrain.

Examining keyboard designs throughout the years

I divide keyboards up into the following types based on how they produce their sound to make the differences among keyboards easy to understand; you can read more in Chapter 2:

- **Acoustic instruments:** These instruments require no power to make their sound, so I don't cover them here. But they include the acoustic piano, the harpsichord, and old pump pipe organs and such. Each produces its sound in different ways and sounds distinctly different from the others. And their sounds are certainly included in your electronic keyboard.

- **Electro-mechanical instruments:** These options produce their sounds mechanically or acoustically and then have amplifiers and electronics to make the sound louder. The classic Rhodes and Wurlitzer electric pianos fall into this group, as well as the funky Clavinet (clav) and the mighty Hammond organ. These sounds are important to know because they're included in almost every keyboard you try out today.

✔ **Electronic instruments:** Keyboards in this group produce their sounds by electronic means, either analog or digital, and are what this book covers most in-depth. Electronic keyboards use a variety of technologies to produce their sounds. Brochures and websites throw around terms like *sampling, analog synthesis, DSP,* and *modeling,* along with hundreds of seemingly meaningless acronyms. In Chapters 2 and 14, I describe and compare all these methods of sound production.

Touching on key weight

Those black and whites may look the same at first glance, but keys (or the key mechanism) can vary greatly from instrument to instrument. The first main distinction is whether the keys are weighted. *Weighted* keys give the feel of playing an acoustic piano. These keys may seem harder to play, but they offer you much more control over your *dynamics,* or ability to play more softly and loudly.

Non-weighted keys are often called *synth-action;* they're lighter to the touch and can be faster to play. The next step up is *semi-weighted* keys, which are firmer, more solid light-touch keys.

I discuss key weighting in greater detail in Chapter 2. The quality can vary from model to model and brand to brand, so it's an important aspect to consider when buying a keyboard; be sure to check out Chapter 3 as well.

Join the family: Grouping keyboards

Electronic keyboards fall into well-established families or categories of instruments. Each has a relatively standard set of features and is meant to be used for specific musical needs and playing situations. Within each family, you encounter entry-level models that are more basic and then step-up models that add to the quality and number of sounds, the number of features, the size and quality of the keyboard feel, and so on. The main keyboard "food groups" are as follows:

✔ **Digital pianos:** Acoustic piano wannabes or replacements.
✔ **Stage pianos:** Digital pianos intended for the performing musician, with additional sounds and pro features.
✔ **Portable keyboards:** Fun, lightweight, and full of features to help you sound better.

✔ **Arrangers:** Keyboards with sophisticated backing features to produce the sound of a full band from your simple chord input.

✔ **Organs:** Instruments dedicated to reproducing the sound, features, and feel of the legendary Hammond B3. They may include some additional sounds such as pipe organ, combo organs, and even other keyboard and synth sounds.

✔ **Synthesizers:** Keyboards that allow you to make your own sounds and adjust the sounds provided. They can sound the most electronic and imaginative but now often include imitative and natural sounds as well.

✔ **Workstations:** Basically, synthesizers with onboard recording systems to allow you to create complete works of original music. Very advanced and feature-rich.

✔ **Controllers:** Keyboards that don't make sound themselves but are used to trigger sounds from your computer and other keyboards. These options use the MIDI standard to communicate with the sound-producing devices. (Head to Chapter 17 for details on MIDI.)

Chapters 2 and 3 are your keys (pun intended) to getting more info on all these families of instruments. Deciding which one is right for your needs can be confusing, but I help you organize and prioritize your needs, thinking through what you want to do, where you want to do it, and what you can afford, in Chapters 3 and 18.

Speaking the Musical Language

Perhaps you can pick up simple melodies by ear and hunt and peck with a few fingers to play the notes, but eventually you're going to want to develop your skills more. Learning to read musical notation opens up a way to communicate so much about playing any type of keyboard. It allows you to read the examples in this book and others; to buy sheet music and songbooks of your favorite piano pieces, artists, and songs; and to tackle instructional courses. Chapter 5 is your friendly and easy-to-follow introduction to the language of music. Developing your finger facility and strength takes you from fumble to finesse. Chapter 6 gets things rolling and will have you playing with good posture and fingering technique in no time.

Some forms of print music use what are called *chord symbols* to indicate notes that can be played beneath a melody. They're usually intended for guitar players to strum along, but the keyboardist can also use them to enhance his playing. A form of print music called a *fake book* provides only a melody and chord symbols, so you need to know your chords to follow along. And you need to understand chords to use certain backing features of some keyboards. Read up on chords in Chapter 7.

Making the Most of Your Keyboard's Basic Features

You can just turn on your keyboard and start playing, and you'll have a great time. But these are electronic keyboards, and they do so much more than that. Your keyboard is brimming with features and cool capabilities, like any self-respecting tech product these days is. I don't know of any that offer video games or let you video chat with your friends, but you never know what may come to pass!

Working with sounds

Some keyboards offer a small grouping of sounds; simple digital pianos may have 16 or so. But most offer at least 100 and sometimes thousands. Finding them, selecting them, and understanding whether they're simple single sounds or complex combinations of instruments stacked on top of each other or split between your hands takes some study. Chapter 8 breaks that all down and provides step-by-step instructions.

Exploring effects

What you hear coming out of a keyboard is actually more than just a sound; it almost always has some extra sonic treatment called *effects* added to it. Effects are audio treatments such as reverb, chorus, EQ, and delay, and they add to the spaciousness, color, and tonality of each sound. Even in simple keyboards, you have the choice whether to use them, and many keyboards allow you to vary the settings of their effects to produce different results, sometimes completely changing what effect a sound uses. Chapter 9 has the details.

Getting into automatic playing features

Many of today's keyboards have some functions that can do some playing on their own (with your guidance, of course). You can sit back and let the keyboard do some of the work. The most common features are

- ✔ **Drum rhythms:** All portables and arrangers and many high-end digital pianos offer an on-demand drummer to add some groove to your performance. You can select the choices from the front panel, add fancy transitions called *fills,* and sometimes select progressively busier variations. Some stage pianos, synths, and workstations also offer these grooves, although they may be lurking within the arpeggiator feature (which I discuss in a moment). Visit Chapter 10 to find out more about getting your groove on.

- ✔ **Auto-accompaniment:** How about having a full backing band ready to play whatever style of music, song, or chords you think of? Portables, arrangers, and some high-end digital pianos can do that and more. If you haven't been around keyboards and music for some time, you may not realize just how good the backing bands on today's keyboards have become. In a word: amazing! But like anything in life, you get back what you put into it, so read Chapter 11 to bone up on all the ways you can lead your band to even greater heights and realism.

- ✔ **Arpeggiation:** With *arpeggiation,* you hold a few notes or a chord, and the keyboard repeats them over and over in a dizzying array of possible patterns — from simple up and down repetitions to pulsing grooves to complex rhythmic patterns. An arpeggiator is often what produces the fancy riffs you hear in pop and dance music. Many of the more advanced options can also produce realistic guitar strumming, harp flourishes, and even drum grooves. Chapter 12 has an introduction to this cool tool.

Delving into More-Advanced Digital Features

If you think of yourself as tech-savvy, you're probably looking for even more from this book, and I'm ready for you. Many of the keyboards have pretty advanced features — some that you would've thought you needed a computer to do. The following sections dive deeper into these digital waters.

Stepping into the virtual recording studio

Keyboards now commonly include some form of recording so that you can play and then listen back to yourself. Two forms of recording are available today:

- **Audio recording**: This method is the recording of the actual sound you produced. It's what you listen to from a CD, an MP3 player, or your favorite online music streaming service.
- **MIDI recording**: *MIDI* is the *Musical Instrument Digital Interface* standard, a fancy name for a digital way that musical products can talk to each other. It's not the sound you hear but rather a way of communicating the gestures, moves, and settings of your electronic device as you played it.

Each format has its own terms, capabilities, and benefits, and musicians at every level use each of them. Chapter 13 breaks them both down and helps you see what you and your keyboard can do in terms of creating and sharing your music with others. If you want to know even more about MIDI, check out Chapter 17 as well.

Shaping the sounds you play

So many of today's keyboards offer control over the sounds that are included, whether that's adjusting them a little bit or completely changing them, warping them, or building them from the ground up. For many musicians, creating the sound is as important as the music they play with it. The art of making sounds is usually called *programming* a keyboard, or *sound design*. If you've heard the terms *waveform, oscillator, filter, envelope generator,* or *LFO,* you know that they're the building blocks of this creative art. And Chapter 14 is your entry into this highly rewarding aspect of using an electronic keyboard.

Checking out the computer connection

Thanks to the development of MIDI, keyboards can connect to computers and tablets for a broad array of activities and enjoyment. In Chapter 17, I introduce you to all these categories of software, from recording and sound editing to playing additional sounds that are running on your computer to working with virtual teachers. This exciting world is the cutting edge of music making and study.

Practicing with and without Help

Whether you prefer to study keyboard playing with an electronic teacher or just want to hack out songs you love on your own, I have you covered.

Lurking inside many portable keyboards and digital pianos are patient music teachers, waiting to help you learn a few tunes and build your musical skills. They never yell, won't slap your wrists with a ruler, and are willing to go over things as slowly and as many times as you need. In Chapter 15, I explain and demonstrate both the Casio and Yamaha ways of giving you virtual keyboard lessons and provide practical advice on how to get the most out of them.

But sometimes you hear a song and you just want to sit down and play it right away at your keyboard. Why wait until you can buy the music or go to your next piano lesson? Learning to play by ear and to figure out songs from recordings is a great skill to develop. Some can do it naturally, but for most people, it takes some work. I have worked very hard at developing that skill, and I'm happy to share my best tips with you in Chapter 16.

Chapter 2

So Many Keyboards, So Little Time

* *

In This Chapter

▶ Defining the differences among acoustic, electro-mechanical, and electronic keyboards

▶ Describing key feel and polyphony

▶ Meeting the many types of electronic keyboards available

▶ Debating the pros and cons of acoustic and electronic keyboards

* *

*A*t first glance, keyboards seem like they must all be the same. After all, each offers the familiar groupings of black and white keys, right? In truth, other than the fact that you place your fingers on the same keys to produce the same notes, the world of keyboards is vast, and each instrument is played somewhat differently from the others. They feel different, they're different sizes and weights, and they can vary significantly in cost. Some keyboards produce one sound, others offer a few sounds, and others may produce thousands of different sounds.

If you've watched your favorite artist or band perform, you've often seen a keyboard player behind a couple of keyboards or perhaps surrounded by a large circle of them (cape and wizard hat optional). Or you've seen a band with two, three, or even more keyboardists, each with a couple of keyboards piled up. Perhaps you've wondered why they had so many: Is it a macho reaction to the guitar player with that wall of amps? A nerd fantasy run amuck? Or do they actually require multiple keyboards to produce what you're hearing and enjoying? I think all of the above are true to some extent, but the final option is the actual serious answer.

In this chapter, I pull back the curtain on the wide variety of keyboards that exists. I help you understand the basic technology of how they make their sound(s), what makes each one special, and what each is best for. I explain how digital pianos reproduce the acoustic for far lower cost, smaller size, and less required upkeep. You discover what touch sensitivity is and how that dynamic control over volume behaves differently on the various types of keyboards. Finally, I help you recognize when only the real acoustic instrument will do.

Identifying Different Types of Keyboards

The first step in helping you understand the vast array of keyboard instruments is to break them down into some logical groupings based on how they're designed and how they operate. The following sections outline these groupings: acoustic, electro-mechanical, and electronic. The keyboards you'll be looking at today are likely electronic, but knowing and understanding all these offerings is a good idea.

Acoustic keyboards

An *acoustic* instrument produces its sound mechanically, without the need for electricity, speakers, or any form of electronics. It's made from natural materials such as wood, metal, fabric, or even animal skin. So when you think of acoustic instruments, you think of acoustic (steel or nylon string) guitar, the upright bass, a conga drum, and so on. In the world of keyboards, the main acoustic instruments are the acoustic piano, the harpsichord, the clavichord (not the Clavinet!), the celeste, and the earliest pipe organs. (Think about it: Bach certainly didn't have access to electricity!) Figures 2-1 through 2-3 show the big three from this group: the acoustic piano, the harpsichord, and the pipe organ, respectively.

Figure 2-1:
Acoustic
grand piano.

Photograph courtesy of Yamaha Corporation of America

Figure 2-2:
The harpsi-
chord.

Figure 2-3:
The pipe
organ.

The piano (and to an extent, the clavichord) strikes a string with a type of hammer to produce a musical pitch. The harpsichord plucks a string to do the same. The celeste uses a hammer to strike a metal bar to produce a bell-like tone. And the pipe organ runs pressurized air (called *wind*) through a pipe to produce a sustaining musical tone. Each instrument has different-sized objects attached to each individual key to produce all the pitches needed to play a piece of music. So even though you see the same layout of black and white keys on the keyboard, what happens when you press a key down is very different inside the instrument.

Listen to Tracks 1 through 5 to hear examples of each of these acoustic keyboards.

In the world of acoustic instruments, the size of the instrument itself determines the volume or amount of sound the keyboard can produce. Larger/longer strings, bigger pipes, and a bigger body help the keyboard produce more sound. In the case of a piano, a wooden soundboard inside the case resonates to help amplify or increase the volume of the vibrating string(s). So a smaller spinet piano can't produce as loud a sound as a nine-foot concert grand piano, in large part because of the size of this wooden soundboard.

Electro-mechanical keyboards

An *electro-mechanical* instrument is one that combines an acoustic/mechanical sound generator with some additional electronics, usually to help amplify or increase the volume of the sound produced. So the initial sound, both the tone and pitch, is determined by an acoustic mechanism (usually a string or metal object being plucked or struck in some fashion). All these instruments include a *pickup per string/tone* (a device that translates sound vibrations into an electrical signal) and an amplification system for you to hear their sound, which means they require electricity to operate. And without the sounds' being fed into an onboard or external speaker, you wouldn't be able to hear them.

These instruments are so popular that they remain the core group of sounds (along with the acoustic piano) reproduced in all electronic keyboards to this day. So getting more familiar with their features and sound is an important part of your keyboard education.

The most common of these instruments include the Rhodes electric piano (sometimes called the Fender Rhodes and often alluded to as a *tine* piano), the Wurlitzer electric piano (often referred to as a *reed* piano), and the Hohner Clavinet (commonly called *clav* for short), pictured in Figures 2-4 through 2-6, respectively. Slightly less common but still popular were the Hohner Pianet and the Yamaha CP-70/80 electric grand pianos.

Figure 2-4:
Rhodes MK1
suitcase
electric
piano.

Photograph courtesy of Ken Rich/Ken Rich Sound Services

Figure 2-5:
Wurlitzer
electric
piano,
model 200A.

Photograph courtesy of Ken Rich/Ken Rich Sound Services

Photograph courtesy of Ken Rich/Ken Rich Sound Services

Figure 2-6:
Hohner D6
Clavinet.

Tracks 6 through 12 provide examples of each of these electric pianos and electro-mechanical instruments.

The Hammond organ (the most common models are the B-3, C-3, A-100 and L-100) is also an electro-mechanical instrument, producing its sound through a tonewheel method. Figure 2-7 shows the classic B-3 with a Leslie speaker cabinet, its most common means of amplification.

Another distinctly different electro-mechanical instrument is the Mellotron, which played back taped recordings of sounds (amplified through electronic means) when a key was pressed. So although its original tone isn't produced acoustically, it's produced from a mechanical mechanism: a tape playback system (think back to eight-track tapes if you're old enough to remember those).

Listen to Tracks 13 and 14 to hear examples of the Hammond organ and Mellotron.

Photograph courtesy of Hammond Suzuki USA

Figure 2-7:
Hammond
B-3 with
Leslie
speaker.

Electronic keyboards

Electronic keyboards produce their sounds completely by some electronic or digital means. They may contain tubes or resistors, chips, and circuit boards inside — no vibrating strings or spinning elements involved. The early combo organs from the '60s, such as the Vox Continental (shown in Figure 2-8) and the Farfisa Compact, are common examples of electronic keyboards used in pop and rock music of that day. Throughout the '50s and '60s, electronic console and theatre organs were the main home keyboards other than an acoustic piano.

In the late '60s/early '70s, the Moog synthesizer started to be used in rock, pop, and other types of music. Figure 2-9 shows the Moog modular system that Keith Emerson used for the classic solo on "Lucky Man." Other brands soon followed, such as ARP, Sequential Circuits, Oberheim, EML, EMS, and Korg. These instruments are all examples of *analog electronics*, where electronic voltages move between components and are manipulated to produce the desired sound. Many of these famous analog synthesizers are still sought after and used today because each had its own characteristic sound and features. Analog synthesizers remain so popular that a number of companies are making new models today, from the simple to the highly complex.

Figure 2-8:
Vox
Continental
combo
organ.

Photograph courtesy of Korg USA, Inc., and David Jacques

Figure 2-9:
Keith
Emerson's
mighty
Moog
modular
system.

Photograph courtesy of Tony Ortiz, Archivist for Emerson, Lake & Palmer

A *synthesizer* is an electronic keyboard whose primary purpose is to provide the user access to the tools and functions to create and vary the sound produced. I use the term to make that distinction from other electronic keyboards that offer only preset sounds or have limited access to sound shaping/creation.

Check out Tracks 15 through 17 for examples of the Vox and Farfisa organs as well as a Moog synthesizer.

The mid-'80s saw the development of the digital keyboard and synthesizer that has continued through today. These products are really dedicated computers running software designed to do a specialized task: make musical sounds. Most use custom chips and circuits and won't run your favorite shoot-'em-up games or connect to the Internet, but some do repurpose a computer to become a complete music studio. Some of the most famous digital keyboards/synths are the Yamaha DX7, the Korg M1 music workstation, the E-mu) Emulator sampling keyboard, and the Casio SK-1. All the keyboards I discuss in the next section are electronic, and they're by far the most common type you find today. Figure 2-10 shows a modern-day electronic keyboard.

Figure 2-10: The Korg Krome, a modern digital synthesizer/ workstation.

Photograph courtesy of Korg USA, Inc.

Appreciating How Digital Keyboards Make Their Many Sounds

Today's keyboards are pretty amazing; press a button and any sound can come out. Known keyboards such as acoustic piano, electric piano, and organs? Check. Saxes, flute, trumpet, trombone, violin, and cello? Check. Rock guitar, bass, drums, and even crowd applause? Check. Soaring synth leads, burbling electronic blips and bleeps, and swooshing and sweeping sound effects? All that and more!

Did you ever wonder how they make all these different sounds? Digital keyboards aren't all the same; they produce their sounds many different ways. Here are the major methods they use (check out Chapter 14 for how to use these methods to shape sounds):

- **Digital synthesis:** *Digital synthesis* is a broad category indicating that the manufacturer has designed a special method of making sound, using a computer chip to produce artificial tones that can be varied and manipulated into many different sounds. Don't be put off by my use of the term *artificial;* these instruments can produce wonderful sounds and often can provide expressive imitations of real-world instruments. *Frequency modulation* (FM) is a form of *algorithmic synthesis* that Yamaha used to produce many highly successful synths like the DX7, and it's still used today in some products. Casio had what it called *phase distortion* (PD) in its CZ range of synths, and Kawai used a digital technology called *additive synthesis* in its K-series synths, to name just a few.

- **Sample-playback:** *Sampling* is the process of digitally recording the sound of a real-world object and being able to play it back and further manipulate the recording. *Sample-playback* can sound much more realistic than other forms of synthesis because it's using the real sound as opposed to a re-creation or imitation of an instrument's sound. Sampling first appeared in keyboards in the '80s, and instruments such as the E-mu Emulator, the Ensoniq Mirage, the Fairlight CMI, and Akai samplers became very popular. Because digital memory was very expensive in those days, the sounds were good but not yet great. Costs have come down over the years, and today keyboards (and computer software) that use sample-playback can produce highly nuanced and very realistic sounds.

- **Physical modeling:** *Physical modeling* is another form of digital synthesis, but it specifically focuses on studying how a real-world instrument creates its sound and then re-creates each piece or component of the original device down to its materials, behaviors, and responses. For example, to replicate a drum's sound, you'd look to the materials the head and body are made from, the size of the body or shell, and so on, and how that part of the instrument would change over time after being activated or react depending on how it was struck. Stringed, woodwind, and brass instruments; drums; and mallet instruments are all areas that have been explored using this approach.

In the world of keyboards, the most common instruments modeled in this fashion are the clav, the tine (Rhodes) and reed (Wurlitzer) electric pianos, and especially the tonewheel (Hammond) organ (often called *clonewheels*). This form of synthesis gives you very detailed control over all aspects of the sound and in some instruments lets you create new designs that don't exist in real life. Roland has done some very interesting things in this regard for the acoustic piano (in V-Piano), allowing you to imitate changing the strings' material and length, the hammer's size and material, and other futuristic manipulations. In software, a company called Modartt is doing similar things with its Pianoteq line of titles.

✔ **Virtual analog:** *Virtual analog* is similar to physical modeling but has grown into a category of its own; the initial goal was to re-create the complete layout and character of an existing (usually analog) synthesizer. Virtual analog is a very popular segment, and models exist in both hardware and computer software forms. The designer studies and often re-creates each element at the component level and attempts to re-create the sound, response, and complete feature set of a given classic synthesizer. From there, she often adds new features and expands the capabilities of the synth to bring it into the modern age. Many companies make new, imaginative synths with this method, creating an instrument with the types of parameters and capabilities of the classics along with their own ideas, often bringing together forms of digital synthesis along with the modeled analog synthesis.

Considering Key Feel and Response

The design, feel, and touch of the key mechanism (commonly called the *key action*) used on modern keyboards can vary a great deal. Understanding how key actions work and what each offers can help you differentiate among the various types of keyboards and models offered. The following sections introduce a couple of important key action characteristics.

Touch sensitivity

Key actions come in two main classes: dynamic (touch-sensitive or velocity-sensitive) and non-dynamic. The term *dynamics* in music refers to changes in loudness or volume.

A *velocity-sensitive* key action responds to how firmly or softly you play the key, transferring that energy to the sound-producing mechanism to allow you to play many different volume levels from soft to loud. *Non-dynamic keyboards* have keys that are simple on/off switches that cause the sound to play. You create dynamics by using a foot pedal, not by varying the touch of your fingers on the keys.

The acoustic piano is velocity-sensitive and can produce an incredibly wide range of dynamics. The Rhodes and Wurlitzer electric pianos and the clav are also velocity-sensitive, although they have narrower ranges of dynamics. The pipe organ, all combo/console/theatre organs, and the harpsichord, on the other hand, aren't velocity-sensitive. For example, the harpsichord's quill always plucks the string the same way, so the dynamics don't change. Early analog synthesizers used organ keyboards, so they too were non-dynamic.

Later high-end analog synthesizer models added touch sensitivity; examples include the Yamaha CS-80, Sequential Circuits Prophet T8, and Moog Polymoog and Polymoog Keyboard. But the advent of digital synthesis and MIDI made velocity-sensitive synthesizers and keyboards much more common. (The earlier section "Appreciating How Digital Keyboards Make Their Many Sounds" has information on digital synthesis; flip to Chapter 13 for the lowdown on MIDI.)

Velocity-sensitive synthesizers have two sensors, as shown in Figure 2-11; the first is at the top of the key, where the key sits when at rest. The other is at the bottom of the key action, where the key reaches when pressed down fully. The system uses these sensors to measure how quickly the key moves from the top to the bottom and then translates that speed or value into a dynamic level. The idea is that the harder you press a key, the faster it actually moves downward. So soft touch is actually a slow depression of the key, and hard touch is a faster movement.

The terms *velocity-sensitive* and *touch-sensitive* are often used interchangeably, but *velocity sensitivity* is the truly correct term for today's electronic keyboards because it's how MIDI translates the playing force into different values.

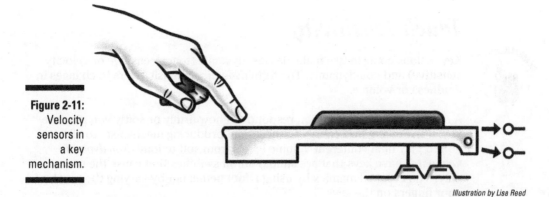

Figure 2-11:
Velocity sensors in a key mechanism.

Illustration by Lisa Reed

Key weight

A few types of keys are available to be used on keyboards, some lighter and others heavier to the touch.

Key weight has nothing to do with the dynamics of the key mechanism discussed in the preceding section. Any type of key can be velocity-sensitive, regardless of which of the following weight classes it falls into:

- **(Fully) weighted:** A *weighted* or *fully weighted* key imitates the mass of the piano key action. Both acoustic piano keys and high-end digital piano keys are made of wood with a coating or veneer on top, as shown in Figure 2-12. The keys have a certain amount of weight to them, so your finger exerts more energy to make them move. This resistance gives you more feedback when you're trying to play dynamically, and that allows for more nuanced control of soft dynamics. (That control is why serious pianists prefer weighted keys). The key has a slightly protruding top front lip and is enclosed on the front surface.

- **Semi-weighted:** *Semi-weighted* keys provide a middle ground between weighted and non-weighted key mechanisms for synth actions. Some manufacturers add some weight to the non-weighted synth key or plastic piano-shaped key (usually by gluing a metal bar to the underside of the key) to increase its mass and make it feel a bit more solid to the touch. It usually has a spring in the mechanism to provide resistance to your touch.

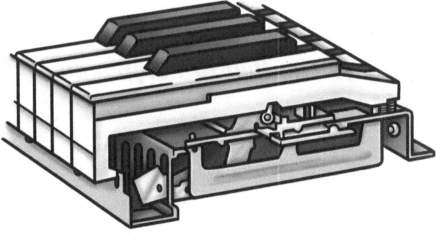

Figure 2-12:
Piano-style
weighted
key action.

Illustration by Lisa Reed

✔ **Non-weighted:** *Non-weighted* or *synth-action* keys are the lightest, simplest action. They often have some spring in the mechanism to add some slight resistance — just enough to keep them from feeling loose and uncontrollable. Simpler plastic keys used on combo organs and synthesizers have little mass, or resistance, to them, so they can be played very easily and often more quickly. Figure 2-13 shows that key design. This key is made entirely of plastic and looks more like a diving board with no front edge. Non-weighted keys are preferred by non-pianists and for playing organ, clav, and synth sounds, which aren't called upon to reproduce that wide a range of dynamics. Yes, they're played dynamically, but not to the same degree as is expected from the acoustic piano.

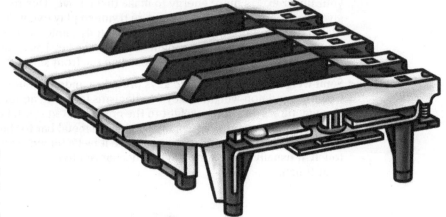

Figure 2-13: Synth-style key action.

Illustration by Lisa Reed

Paying Attention to Polyphony

After you start to explore electronic keyboards, you need to understand and consider polyphony. *Polyphony* means "many voices," and in music it means having multiple tones or parts playing at the same time. In an instrument, it's the ability to play more than one note at a time and is called being *polyphonic*. A trumpet, a flute, a saxophone, and even the human voice can sound only one note at a time, so they're *monophonic*.

The guitar has six strings, so it's considered six-note polyphonic. The acoustic bass has four strings, so it's — yup — four-note polyphonic. Acoustic and electro-mechanical keyboards have as much polyphony as they have keys. So the piano is considered 88-note polyphonic!

However, this one-to-one key-to-polyphony ratio isn't true of electronic keyboards because the key isn't attached directly to the sound-producing mechanism (for example, a string). Rather, a chip or circuitry inside the keyboard produces the sound, and the power of those electronics is what determines how many notes you can play.

In keyboards, some analog synthesizers are monophonic because in the early days, building a polyphonic synthesizer was very expensive. With the advent of digital technology, today's electronic keyboards generally seem to have big numbers for their polyphony; you see specs that state 32, 64, 100, 128, and up to 256 voices or notes of polyphony. However, various factors can quickly reduce the amount of polyphony truly available:

- ✔ Playing a piano sound for a couple of bars with the *damper* (or *sustain*) pedal down uses up a *lot* of notes in a short time.

- ✔ Some instruments use two voices to produce a stereo sound, so you cut the polyphony in half when playing one of them. The same issue applies when playing a *layered* sound (two sounds at the same time, such as piano and strings). At minimum, you're using two voices for each note played, and this number can double or quadruple depending on how the sounds are designed.

- ✔ If your keyboard is playing a drum rhythm or producing auto-accompaniment patterns as you play, they too require notes of polyphony to sound.

What happens when you run out of polyphony? The designers of electronic keyboards are very smart; what they usually do is "rob" or stop sounding the oldest sustaining note. So as you keep playing piano with the sustain pedal down, your earliest-played notes start to shut off, one by one, until you let off the pedal and start again. This way, you always hear the most recent notes as you play them, and only the notes that are already fading away are robbed. If a lot of voices are required to play a single layered or complex sound, this stealing of voices happens more quickly, and is more noticeable.

So when you're checking out a keyboard, reading the specs may not be enough. Yes, more polyphony is always better, but you have to figure out whether what a keyboard offers is enough for you depending on what features you plan to use regularly. Try playing your favorite songs, go for the layered sounds, or turn on any rhythms or accompaniment offered. Listen as you play for any noticeable note-stealing. Remember that this effect is most noticeable in solo, exposed playing. If you'll be playing in a band, you may not notice it as much, and that's a good thing. I discuss choosing the right keyboard for you in Chapter 3.

Meeting the Major Electronic Keyboard Food Groups

The majority of keyboards produced today are electronic. The term *electronic keyboards* covers the complete range of sounds and key feel possible, and a number of keyboard families can be grouped together based on the types of sounds they make, their general physical layouts and interfaces, their intended purposes, and other criteria. In the following sections, I organize them all and explain their basic features and common use.

Virtually all electronic keyboards today include the Musical Instrument Digital Interface (MIDI), which I discuss in Chapters 13 and 17. I mention it here sometimes in the context of any special features or applications of it.

Digital pianos

Digital pianos form the largest category of electronic keyboards, which makes sense considering that the acoustic piano is the most popular keyboard of all time. These electronic keyboards are designed to provide the touch and sound of the piano, and the category ranges from relatively inexpensive lightweight models to large re-creations of a grand piano shape with many additional features. The 88 keys are usually weighted to give some mass and resistance to the touch to mimic the wooden keys of a real piano. (I discuss key weight in more detail in the creatively titled "Key weight" section earlier in the chapter.)

Most models use sample-playback as their method of producing sound, and as you go up in price, you get better-quality sound thanks to more memory allotted for the samples/recordings, as I describe in Chapter 3. The digital piano usually provides some other sounds, often including some variations of the acoustic piano (such as bright piano, warm piano, and so on), some type of electric piano, perhaps a harpsichord, and some form of organ (pipe and possibly sampled tonewheel). A string ensemble is also common. Many models allow you to layer two sounds on top of each other; the most common use of this option is to play piano with strings blended together.

The digital piano is considered a home instrument, and most models include some form of onboard speakers so you can hear them without any other gear required. But they always have a headphone output, which is great for silent practice. To provide realistic piano performance, the digital piano always comes with a sustain pedal, and mid- and higher-priced models usually include all three pedals to replicate the true piano experience.

Style and finish become a selling point of the home digital piano. Many models are offered in a variety of faux-wood finishes and colors to match your décor or taste, and the style usually aims to mimic the look of their acoustic brethren, such as spinet and upright pianos or baby grands.

Digital organs

The digital organ basically reproduces the touch, sound, and layout of a classic Hammond *tonewheel* organ. It often uses modeling technology to reproduce all the characteristics of that complex sound engine. Many other keyboard types have tonewheel organ sounds, but these sounds are usually sampled, so they can't provide the real, interactive experiences of producing tonal variations by sliding in and out the nine drawbars that produce the various harmonic overtones. Each drawbar is like a volume control to mix these various harmonics together, with virtually limitless combinations possible.

The term *tonewheel organ* describes the system of tone production invented by Laurens Hammond for his instrument. In that design, 96 individual metal wheels spin in front of a magnet and pickup, each producing a pure tone. The pitch of the tone is determined by the number of notches cut into each wheel and the wheel's rotational speed.

The keyboard on a tonewheel organ isn't weighted. Each key has a smooth front edge/lip and solid front panel and is commonly called a *waterfall* key (shown in Figure 2-14). The smooth edge makes it easy to slide your hand up and down the organ keys, producing what's called a *palm smear,* without pain or damage.

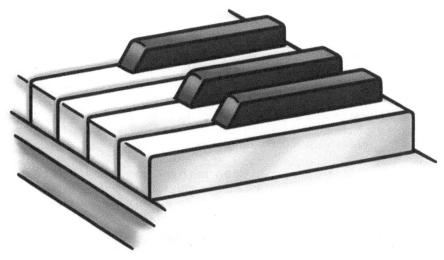

Figure 2-14:
Waterfall
key action.

Illustration by Lisa Reed

The tonewheel organ is usually played through a rotary speaker cabinet (called a Leslie after its inventor, Don Leslie), so these digital models have a built-in effect to replicate that sound. I discuss the design of the Leslie speaker in greater detail in Chapter 9.

Additional controls include a percussion effect that adds a *transient* (short click) to the note attack and a chorus/vibrato circuit that adds some pitch variation to the sound. In a digital organ, all these controls are presented on the front panel.

The original organs almost always had two keyboards (called *manuals* in organ-speak), but the digital versions come in both dual and single manual versions. Many keyboard players do fine with one manual, usually playing this keyboard alongside another instrument that is more of a piano or synth.

Some models of digital organ include other essential keyboard sounds such as acoustic piano, electric piano, clav, and so on, and some keyboards are hybrids that combine multiple types of sound engines into one performance keyboard. They're designed for the performing keyboardist who needs the most sound in the smallest space but still wants the dedicated interface of the tonewheel organ.

Stage pianos

A *stage piano* is designed for both aspects of its name: It's focused on reproducing the piano experience as well as the needs of the keyboardist playing live in a band. It's designed to be moved around often and is less concerned about looking like a real piano and more concerned with being rugged and reliable for live performance.

The key mechanism of a stage piano is similar to a mid- to upper-end digital piano, with a decent 88-key weighted action. Of course, the better the weighted action, the heavier the keyboard is, so some models trade off the amount of resistance/feel to shed some pounds. A stage piano is often used to play other sounds and even control other MIDI devices. Therefore, the best models may offer what is called *aftertouch,* or the ability produce other effects on the sounding note(s) by pressing down on a key and into a rubber sensor strip underneath the key mechanism.

Positioned first and foremost as a piano, stage pianos offer good-to-excellent sample-playback piano sounds and performance. Large memory/long samples, multiple velocity points, and other sampled nuances are common. I explain more about these technologies in Chapter 3.

Unlike the home digital piano, a stage piano focuses much more on the quality of the various electric pianos, clav, strings, some synth, and even organ sounds. It always offers the ability to split the keyboard and layer multiple sounds and usually has memory locations reserved for these types of setups.

The front panel interface of a stage piano is usually more complicated than the average home digital piano. But at the same time, the most important functions, such as selecting sounds, are clearly highlighted or laid out with bigger buttons. This visibility is important because these keyboards have to be seen under moody stage lighting and accessed quickly during a performance.

Portable keyboards

Portable keyboards usually fall in to the range of entry-level to slightly more advanced instruments that combine basic sounds with some fun and/or simple learning features (see Chapter 15) and onboard accompaniment (Chapter 11). They're geared more toward beginners and are very affordable. The portable electronic keyboards first came to prominence in the '80s and were pioneered by Casio and Yamaha, as they still are today. This category of keyboards has really developed in recent years and now offers a surprising amount of features and value for the money.

Most portable keyboards use regular sized, non-weighted synth action keys, not weighted keys like a piano does. Key ranges come in 49- and 61-key lengths, sometimes offering up to 88 semi-weighted keys, none with aftertouch (which I describe in the preceding section).

The sounds are produced by sample-playback technology and tend to be decent but pretty basic. Portable keyboards don't have a lot of memory for the samples, so don't expect pro quality; however, the sounds are surprisingly good for the money and not at all what you may be expecting if you've had a portable from the '80s or even the '90s. What they may lack in quality they certainly make up for in quantity; these keyboards usually offer between 400 and 800 sounds! Along with real instrument sounds and some general-purpose synth sounds, these keyboards often have some fun sound effects and other noises that can be fun for kids (and kids at heart) to play with.

Synthesizers

All too often, electronic keyboards are referred to as synthesizers (or synths for short). My definition of the word *synthesizer* is "an electronic instrument with the primary purpose of creating and shaping sound and the parameters to do so." So a digital piano that has some simple sound tweaking settings isn't a synth. If I were to add one additional characteristic to my list, I'd say that a synth goes beyond the emulation of acoustic instruments and electro-mechanical keyboards; it's an instrument for people who enjoy the imaginative and creative possibilities of new and fresh sounds.

Sound can be created from analog, digital, sample-playback, or modeled technologies, and sometimes these technologies are combined in a single instrument. The earliest analog synthesizers had various modules of electronics. To help create sounds, the front panel and overall interface of a synthesizer have dedicated controls for the most important parameters for sound creation: Knobs and sliders are most common, although switches, buttons, ribbons, pads, and other controls may be available.

Over time, digital technologies, storage memory, and many more advancements came along. But many of the basic concepts and terms have remained the same. I mention these basic parameters because they're some of the common terms you see labeled on the front panel of a synth (and I discuss them in greater detail in Chapter 14):

✔ An *oscillator* produces the basic waveform or sound. A special type of oscillator called a *low frequency oscillator* (LFO) modulates another parameter to create *vibrato* (pitch fluctuation), *wah-wah* types of sound (filter fluctuation), and *tremolo* (volume fluctuation).

✔ A *filter* shapes the tonal character of the oscillator by blocking certain frequencies from passing or by accentuating them.

✔ An *amplifier* or *amp* adjusts the level of the sound.

✔ An *envelope generator* modifies the levels of a signal over time. This function is commonly applied to both the filter and the amp, but you can also use it to change pitch over time and other characteristics.

Synthesizers today come in many shapes and sizes; some have mini keys and are relatively inexpensive, while others have full-sized keys but are only monophonic and have shorter key ranges (sometimes only 24 or 37 keys). Still others offer more polyphony and 49- and 61-key ranges. Some synths even offer 88-key weighted keys because they include acoustic and electric piano sounds along with their vast range of imaginative sounds. Few offer aftertouch sensitivity.

Workstations

A *workstation* is a synthesizer that has some form of onboard recording included. So a workstation is always a synthesizer (because it allows you to create new sounds), but a synthesizer isn't necessarily a workstation (because it doesn't necessarily have an onboard *sequencer,* or recording function). Simple, right?

Synthesizer workstations use digital forms of sound-production, be they sample-playback, digital synthesis, modeling technology, or combinations of all these. User-sampling is sometimes included, so you can record your own sounds, sound effects, or load in sounds that others make. Dedicated sampling keyboards/modules became popular in the late '80s and the '90s and often included sequencers. But over time, they were absorbed into the synth workstation concept and also migrated to the computer because of its abundant, cheap memory, its disk space, and its visual interface.

The workstation tends to be a jack-of-all trades because it combines sound creation, music recording, and live performance features into one box. Many musicians buy one for the sound, regardless of whether they need all the other features, because often a manufacturer's best-in-class model is a workstation; the synth version of the same sound-producing technology is usually somewhat stripped down (lower-quality key action, smaller display, and so on) to reduce the price. Workstations usually come in 61-key synth action and 88-key weighted action key lengths, and the upper-end models usually offer aftertouch. Some brands offer 73- or 76-key versions.

The workstation gets a bad rap as a recording platform in some circles because computer audio/MIDI recording systems have far outclassed its capabilities. But sometimes just turning on one dedicated system is easier and more intuitive for capturing a quick idea. And a workstation is an all-in-one, so it's far easier to take around with you. Thanks to the universality of MIDI, you don't have to make an either/or choice; you can use the workstation by itself or connect it to your computer and use those tools as well.

Arrangers

An *arranger* keyboard is an instrument that combines a wide variety of sounds with an automatic accompaniment system, which produces the sound of a full backing band from simple chords you play. They usually come in 61-key synth action configurations (sometimes 76) and rarely offer aftertouch.

Many portable keyboards also have this feature, so what makes a product an arranger is the quality of the sounds, the inclusion of other pro features, and the general build quality of the case and onboard speakers. Really, the dividing line between portables and arranges typically comes down to price. Anything higher than $500 or so is probably being called an arranger. Arranger keyboards usually use sample-playback technology to produce their sound, although some also offer a form of organ modeling as well.

The concept of automatic accompaniment was first introduced in home and theatre organs from the '50s and '60s and moved into digital keyboards in the early '80s. The basic idea is that by playing only minimal parts with your left hand (to feed the automatic accompaniment system) you can sound like you're playing with a complete band of musicians who know every song you do!

The backing parts include what rhythm pattern is used, what sounds are in the backing band, and how the parts are mixed in volume. These setups may produce the music of a certain musical genre, such as jazz swing, disco, pop ballad, or '60s rock, or they may even get specific enough to emulate a single song as done by a famous artist.

An arranger keyboard is considered *the* professional keyboard across much of Europe and throughout the Middle East, so it has many advanced features for live performance including mic input, vocal effects, and even onscreen lyric display so you'll never forget the words to a song again!

Many arranger keyboards offer onboard song players (both MIDI and audio), and usually include a MIDI sequencer. They're sometimes positioned as being a better form of music workstation for songwriting because they include a full backing band ready to play whatever song ideas you feed in, as opposed to an empty place where you have to play all the parts yourself.

This all sounds too good to be true, right? Why would anyone want anything other than an arranger keyboard? The one main downside of arrangers is that the front panels of these instruments tend to be very crowded and complicated because they have to fit in so many features. So finding/selecting sounds can be a bit more difficult, and with more buttons, the chance that you'll press the wrong one in the heat of performance increases.

Controller keyboards

With the advent of MIDI in 1983, the concept of the sound module was born. Because MIDI allowed you to connect multiple keyboards and trigger them all from one master keyboard, you didn't need every other sound source to always have keys on it. You just needed a box that had the sounds you wanted. This setup saved you space and cost. Over time, a new class of keyboard arose out of this situation: the *controller* keyboard, a MIDI keyboard that usually produces no sound by itself but rather is designed to control other keyboards, modules, and (increasingly) music software instruments and applications.

A controller keyboard may come in any length; the most common are 25-, 49-, 61-, and 88-key lengths. Most 88-key models are semi-weighted or fully weighted; the others are usually non-weighted. Few offer aftertouch sensitivity. A whole class of mini- and micro-sized controllers has developed to serve the mobile musician looking to carry her whole music studio with her wherever she goes.

Besides keys for triggering notes, controller keyboards need to be able to send various types of MIDI messages to the receiving device. Selecting sounds is of course essential, as are some wheels, knobs, sliders, and/or switches to add some expression or variations to the sound, much like the knobs on a synthesizer. Velocity-sensitive drum pads have become common on most mid- and upper-end controllers.

Controller keyboards are often used not only to play sounds but also to operate the MIDI and audio recording software used on computers so that the controls also serve to mix track levels, position sounds in the stereo field, solo and mute tracks, and other recording console functions.

In the context of this book, controller keyboards are probably not the droids you're looking for. I mention them only for completeness of describing the available categories of keyboard in the market today. That said, if you plan to get some simple music software for your computer, whether it's for you or a child, you may find that buying a small controller keyboard is a good additional choice so you can locate it very close to the computer and take it with you if you use a laptop or tablet computer. (For more thoughts on buying a keyboard for a child, check out Chapter 3.)

Deciding Whether to Plug In

The world of electronic keyboards is so vast and capable. But as good as technology has gotten, some aspects of acoustic and electro-mechanical instruments haven't been, and perhaps won't ever be, re-created on an electronic keyboard. Understanding the pros and cons of each type is helpful so you never feel misled by a salesperson. The following sections explore the differences between acoustic and electronic pianos/keyboards to help give you the full story.

When only the real acoustic thing will do

The acoustic piano is a highly evolved, complex mechanical thing that is beloved in every culture. As good as digital equivalents have become, a few aspects of the originals remain out of reach:

- **Multiple key strikes/restrikes:** When you play a key repeatedly on an acoustic piano, the previous note doesn't stop ringing, and the vibrating string doesn't come to a complete halt between strikes. The second (and third, and so on) strike of the same key in quick succession seems to add to the vibrations in a pleasing fashion and doesn't sound like fresh strikes happening from silence. Repeated strikes on digital pianos always sound like a new, clean strike of the note.

- ✔ **String/note interaction:** When more than one note is played at a time and the dampers are off those strings, the striking of the new notes being played cause the currently vibrating/sustaining strings to react in different ways and at different volumes. (This is a simplistic explanation of phenomena called *sympathetic vibrations* and *string resonance*, which are outside the scope of this book.) Digital pianos and software are starting to try to replicate these behaviors, but they've taken only baby steps in this regard. The richer the music you play, using more notes and harmonies with a lot of sustain pedal, the more easily you can hear the difference between a good grand piano and the best digital equivalent.

- ✔ **Refined touch/control of dynamics:** Advanced and accomplished concert pianists have spent decades working on their touch and control of dynamics on the best acoustic grand pianos. They can control not only the volume but also the tone of the instrument through their touch. And those skills just don't successfully translate to the digital instrument. Some feel you can get close, especially when you're only listening to the performance. But for the player trying to express herself in such a skillfully nuanced fashion close isn't close enough.

These discrepancies are why a serious classical performer or student aiming for a career in concert performing requires the acoustic instrument. Likewise, few top-class jazz pianists will ever be satisfied with a digital instrument for their recordings and live performances. Many may use electronics as an additional sound color and for studio purposes but not for their most important playing.

The piano isn't the only instrument that brings players to this deciding line. As I mention earlier in this chapter, the tonewheel organ is a complex instrument, with a unique multicontact key mechanism and richly interactive sound generator. Every instrument (even the same model and year of manufacture) sounds a little different because of aging and care (or lack thereof), and many top players play only the real instrument. The same standard holds true for clavs and analog synths; you still see an artist like Stevie Wonder performing with a real clav on top of his synth workstation keyboard.

And of course, appearance is everything. For many artists and bands, having the real instrument is a badge of honor. They want to use the original instrument to show they respect it, they have discerning taste, or they're just cool. And that's okay!

Advantage, electronics!

There are two sides to every story, and electronic keyboards have plenty of unique advantages that make them appealing. Here are a few things to consider in favor of the digital instrument:

- ✔ **Never needs tuning:** Acoustic pianos sound wonderful when they're in tune. Depending on where you live and what room you keep your piano in, it may stay in tune — for as long as a few months. Piano tuners recommend getting an instrument tuned at least twice a year (at an average cost of $100 to $150), but in my experience, the tuning starts to drift after a few months, and the instrument then needs some attention. Concert pianists require the piano to be tuned before every performance. Temperature, humidity, and especially changes in those conditions cause an acoustic piano to go out of tune, as do vibrations (such as from wheeling around a piano on a dolly). Digital pianos/keyboards use recordings of the notes and never go out of tune.

- ✔ **Sounds better than what you paid:** When you buy an electronic keyboard, the piano sound you get was likely sampled from a very expensive grand piano (often costing more than $50,000!). Now, what did you pay for that keyboard again?

- ✔ **Weighs less/is easier to move around:** An upright piano usually weighs around 700 pounds, and a grand piano can easily weigh 1,000 pounds. A real Hammond organ weighs over 300 pounds, not including the Leslie speaker, which weighs 150 pounds. By contrast, a home digital piano may only weigh 60 to 100 pounds, and portable keyboards usually weigh less than 15 pounds. Even an 88-key pro stage piano usually weighs less than 50 pounds. Which would you rather move?

- ✔ **Provides variety of sound:** An acoustic or electro-mechanical keyboard usually produces one tone — maybe a few variations at best. Any electronic keyboard is going to offer a number of completely different sounds, so you're always getting multiple instruments (often hundreds) in one.

- ✔ **Allows private practice:** Electronic keyboards always have a headphone output, so you can play to your heart's delight without disturbing your family or neighbors. If you haven't yet mastered your latest piano piece, you may welcome the privacy so that others can't hear your mistakes or incessant repetition of that one measure over and over again.

- ✔ **Takes up less room:** A digital keyboard is almost always smaller than its equivalent acoustic or electro-mechanical brethren, often significantly so. If space is an issue for you, you'll appreciate the digital.

- ✔ **Has MIDI:** MIDI offers so many benefits and opportunities for composition and recording, and integrating a keyboard with a computer/tablet/smartphone.

Chapter 3

Choosing the Right Keyboard for You

In This Chapter

▷ Understanding the needs of each skill level

▷ Considering what type of music you'll play and with whom

*I*f you're just starting out playing or have put in very little time studying so far, you don't need the top-of-the-line model in your chosen category of keyboard. (I cover keyboard types in Chapter 2.) Likewise, if you're pretty accomplished, you may be tempted to just go for the most keyboard your budget can afford, but price shouldn't be the only criteria for your choice. Sure, the salesman (if you're shopping in a store) will likely ask you how much you want to spend, but you need to establish some other criteria that will affect your happiness long after you pay off that credit card bill!

So what are the other important criteria to look at? In this chapter, I guide you through the various considerations you should evaluate to decide what's the right choice. Reflecting honestly about your skill level and where you think you want to go with your playing is a good first step. Making sure your choice offers you the sounds and features for your favorite styles of music is a must. And buying a keyboard for a child requires factoring in some extra guidelines.

Looking at What's Important for the Beginner

There's nothing wrong with recognizing that you're a beginner. Perhaps you took a few lessons many years ago and have now decided you want to get back to the joy of making music for fun and relaxation. That's great! You're likely a beginner and should be proud of that. (Sorry, being able to play The Kingsmen's "Louie Louie" or Harold Faltermeyer's "Axel F" [the theme from *Beverley Hills Cop*] doesn't make you an accomplished player. And it just may get you kicked out of your local music store if you keep coming in and playing them for hours on end.)

Maybe you never took a lesson or even touched a keyboard except for using the one on your computer to send a few e-mails and post pictures of your cat. Now you want to start to play the musical keyboard for fun or to get involved with your church or school. Wonderful! Playing music is a great way to let off a little steam, to express yourself, and to experience the joy of artistic creation.

Perhaps you've bought (or inherited) a rather old, beat-up acoustic piano and have only been taking lessons for a little while. You're doing okay with your lessons, but your piano sounds bad, won't hold a tuning, or takes up too much room in your home, so you're considering moving into the electronic realm.

Whatever your beginner story, here's a small list of things I recommend you consider when choosing an electronic keyboard:

✔ **Piano features:** The first fork in the road that you must consider when selecting a keyboard is whether you want to play primarily acoustic piano sound and styles of music. If so, you need to be sure that whatever you're looking at offers that sound; most keyboards today do, and you'll be surprised to see that even some organs and programmable synthesizers do. The basic piano features you need in this situation are

  • **A weighted key mechanism:** As I discuss in Chapter 2, only a weighted key action gives you the true piano feel experience.

  • **At least 61 keys (5 octaves):** Remember that an acoustic piano has 88 keys (a little more than 7 octaves). For beginner lessons, you play in only one to three octaves, but you'll be expanding your reach farther in no time.

  • **At least one pedal to help you sustain your notes:** This feature is called a *damper pedal* on an acoustic piano but may be called a *sustain pedal* or just a *momentary pedal* depending on your model. It may come with the unit, but you may have to purchase it as an option instead.

✔ **A variety of sounds:** I'm a firm believer that every beginner should get a keyboard that offers more than one type of sound regardless of whether he has a piano-centric musical taste or goal. Being able to hear what you play with different tones keeps your playing and practicing experience interesting and fresh. I'm not talking about having the right sound for a style of music; I just mean you should have some variety.

✔ **A metronome or drum rhythms:** To develop your playing, you need a steady time-keeper to help get your rhythm solid. A *metronome* is the device students use for this purpose. Back in the day, it was a wooden, wind-up box that had a metal wand that swung back and forth, clicking as it went, but metronomes migrated to being electronic years ago. In your keyboard it can be as simple as a steady click or beep that you can set the speed of; you can also use built-in drum rhythms to not only keep your time steady but also make your practice and performance more polished-sounding and fun. You can buy these features separately, but getting a keyboard that already includes them is much simpler. I talk more about these features in Chapter 10.

✔ **Other aids for study or learning:** If you're planning to study or take lessons or you want some help in learning to play, you should consider having a simple onboard recorder, which allows you to record and then listen back to your playing. Evaluating what you're doing is so much easier as an observer than as a participant. I discuss this feature more in Chapter 13.

Some keyboards offer onboard lessons or helpers to learn included songs, which can be a great way to have a patient teacher always on call. Chapter 15 covers these systems in depth. Finally, having MIDI (the Musical Instrument Digital Interface) on your keyboard enables you to connect the keyboard to a personal computer or tablet device for fun and learning. Pretty much every keyboard made since the mid-'80s offers MIDI, so I just mention it here to let you know it exists. I give more details in Chapter 17.

✔ **Accompaniment features:** Some keyboards can provide extra band members to play along with you. You can simply add an extra hand for your piano playing or go all the way up to the sound of a full group of players: drums, bass, other chord parts, and fancy extras. Taking advantage of these features can deliver a very full sound without a lot of playing technique or effort. Accompaniment can make your practice time more interesting by letting you hear your pieces in different settings and give you the experience of playing along with other musicians. I talk more about this feature in Chapter 11.

I'm Good; I Want More! Graduating to More Pro Features

You've been playing for a while now; perhaps you've taken lessons for years or just have put in a lot of time on your own. You may have been playing only the acoustic piano or organ until now and want to expand your horizons. Or you've had the same electronic keyboard for many years and aren't up on all the new models, features, and possibilities available. Never fear; the following sections highlight some of the top features you should be looking into.

Getting the piano-centric experience

If you're ready to take your piano-based performance to the next level, modern keyboards offer all kinds of advanced and expressive options. In the following sections, I lay out some additional considerations that help you mimic the acoustic piano sound and feel as closely as possible.

Ample polyphony

As you progress to playing more notes and chords, especially while using the damper/sustain pedal, you will often have a lot of notes sounding at once. So you want a keyboard that has a large number of voices or notes that can sound at the same time. Otherwise, notes stop sounding so new notes can play. This spec is called *polyphony,* and I discuss it in detail in Chapter 2. Good numbers to look for are higher than 100.

Characteristics of the keys

When you're an intermediate player, the touch and quality of the key feel become more important. Your fingers are likely stronger, and you can play a more weighted key action, which gives you better control over your touch and dynamics. But you need to check how quickly the key returns back up to be ready to play again; some weighted keyboards can feel a bit sluggish in this regard.

Accomplished players often use the introduction to Billy Joel's "Angry Young Man" to test this response time.

Other key-based attributes include the following:

- ✔ **Touch curves:** Does your keyboard offer different *touch curves* (also called *velocity curves*)? This feature translates the force you play a key with into instructions for how the sound plays back. With one curve, you can very easily go from very quiet to loud; another curve may require much more force before you get up into the louder range. You can also turn off touch sensing completely so that your keyboard accurately plays like an organ or harpsichord, with no touch dynamics. This variation in touch response is critically important and can fool you into thinking the key touch is harder or softer than it really is. And that's a good thing; by changing the touch setting of a keyboard that just feels okay to you, you can transform the instrument into the perfect partner for your musical expression. So explore this feature before passing judgment on the feel of a particular keyboard.

- **Graded hammer action:** Many digital piano-type products offer what's called a *graded action* or *graded hammer action,* which feels heavier at the bottom and gets progressively lighter as you go higher. This design is to simulate the feel of a top quality acoustic grand piano.

- **Surface feel:** Some pianos offer a different surface feel to the keys themselves instead of using the somewhat slippery molded plastic of most electronic keyboard keys. The white keys of an acoustic piano are usually a simulated ivory surface (real ivory use was outlawed decades ago), and the black keys are ebony. Yup, that Stevie Wonder song *was* a play on words about a piano! So better quality piano-centric keyboards will use some sort of material or treatment to offer a less slippery feel to the keys.

- **Sostenuto pedal:** An acoustic piano has three pedals; the middle pedal, called the *sostenuto pedal,* becomes important as you study more classical piano pieces. If that is your goal, be sure your instrument has this function either as a dedicated (preprogrammed) middle pedal or as an assignment you can make to a second, optional pedal.

- **Key resistance and spacing:** Make sure the black and white keys offer the same resistance. Variation in resistance may not be noticeable at first touch/play, but I've played many lower-end and mid-level keyboards where the black keys are shorter than usual and feel stiffer than the white keys. They're harder to control dynamics from and are especially hard to play when you have to slide your hand forward on the keys for certain chord shapes and musical passages. While I'm on this issue, be sure your fingers fit comfortably between the black keys; if you don't have enough space between keys, and your finger binds a bit, you end up sounding sloppier because your finger causes the adjacent black keys to sound at times you didn't intend them to.

Improved/expanded piano samples

Devoting more memory for the piano samples is the most common and important improvement to your piano sound that comes with spending more money on a keyboard, or getting one that is focused primarily on being a piano. This additional memory can be used in the following ways:

- **Sampling more notes per octave:** Manufacturers have to trade off how long their recordings of each note are with how many notes they record from the piano. Common practice is to record every third note, for example, stretching each recording a note or two above and below the original note to fill in the spaces. More memory means manufacturers can avoid this stretching of samples and record every note of the piano's 88-key range. Try playing each note in succession from the bottom to the top to listen for this aspect of the sound. Do you notice any obvious changes every few notes? That's a sure sign of stretched or skipped samples.

✔ **Including longer piano samples:** Increased sample length is the most obvious improvement you notice when trying out a better piano sound. Play and hold a single note and listen to the sound. If the sound has a good attack but quickly develops a short, buzzy sound or goes from a rich sound to a very simplistic, pure tone, it is using a small amount of memory. What's happening here?

Listen carefully and analyze most sounds; after the attack, the sound usually settles in and either keeps sustaining at the same level (an organ, wind and brass instruments, or vocals), or starts to decay (drum hits, plucked strings, or struck strings). To conserve memory when sampling, each recording plays through the initial attack, and then a portion of the next recorded area is set up to repeat for as long as the key is held down. This process is called *looping* the recording, and the repeating section of the recording is called the *loop*. The sound can still fade away while the loop is playing back, so the piano note still decays naturally, as do guitars, basses, and other decaying sounds.

Using more memory for each sample allows the loop to be placed later in the recording, and to be longer. These techniques ensure that the loop sounds pure and consistent with the sound that came before it. (Check out the nearby sidebar "In the loop on looping" for more details.) Some instruments are doing away with loops completely, recording the full attack and natural decay of each note of the piano for the most realistic sound possible. Unlooped samples require a lot of memory, so they're offered only on more expensive electronic keyboards or in software instruments

Listen to Track 18 to hear examples of very small memory/looped piano notes as compared to longer samples with later loops and unlooped notes.

✔ **Sampling multiple velocity levels:** Another way manufacturers improve piano sounds with more memory is to offer recordings of the keys being played at multiple velocity levels. *Velocity* indicates how hard the keys are struck, from very soft all the way up to very forcefully. Without getting too technical about it, suffice it to say the sound of the instrument is very different depending on this touch, and the more levels that a keyboard has recorded/offers, the better. If you play a single note over and over again at different strengths, you can begin to hear velocity switching. Simpler systems just play back the same sample louder or softer and may make it a bit darker at soft levels and brighter as it gets louder. But it's obviously the same recording being played back each time. In multilevel sampled pianos, you can hear a darker, more rounded tone at the lower strike levels and notice the sound getting louder, brighter, more harmonically rich, and more "pointed" in its overall shape as you play harder. If these switches are done poorly, you hear an obvious jump in the level, brightness, or some obvious character point when going from level to level. This jump isn't desirable, and you should listen carefully for it. A good instrument shouldn't have any glaringly obvious jumps.

Check out Track 19 to hear examples of a single velocity layer piano being played at various strengths, and then of a multiple velocity layer with obvious switch points. Finally, you hear a smoothly switched example, which is the most desirable.

✔ **Adding multiple brand samples:** Some manufacturers upgrade their piano-centric offerings by providing samples of more than one brand/ model of piano. You can't always know which model they're offering (because of legal issues brought on by using the brand names themselves), but the two most common makes sampled are the German Steinway and the Japanese Yamaha. Other popular brands sampled are the Austrian Bosendorfer and the Italian Fazioli. Each piano has its own character and qualities, and having more than one type in your keyboard helps as you play different styles of music and play in different settings. Some keyboards even offer a sampled upright piano, which has a very different quality compared to a grand.

Increasing sound nuances

Current keyboard technology can add more nuances to the sound of a sampled piano. Many of these distinctions may be subtle, but they're worth looking for/asking about.

✔ *Release samples* are the sound of the key being let go and the felt damper returning down to stop the string from vibrating. They add character to the note, and after you've gotten used to hearing them, taking them away/ turning them down can make a sound more plain and simplistic.

✔ *Damper resonance* is a term used to describe the sound of all the strings and the whole inner body of the piano ringing/vibrating when you hold down the sustain pedal. Normally, felt dampers are pressed up against the string(s) for each note of a piano, and when you play a key only that key's damper moves away to let that note ring/that string vibrate. Figure 3-1 shows this part of the piano's mechanism.

For each key that is depressed, the corresponding felt damper raises off the string(s) so they can freely vibrate. When they key is released the damper returns to rest on the string, stopping the vibrations.

But when you press down on the sustain pedal, all the dampers lift away from the strings so that the played notes cause all the other strings to vibrate ever so slightly. The notes you actually played will be strong and clear, but all the others provide a slight, pleasing ambience to the sound. You can most clearly hear this effect by playing notes up very high on the piano repeatedly, first without pressing the damper pedal and then with the damper pedal held down. The sound changes from a dry character to a more open, spacious sound like you're playing in a larger room with some subtle echoes happening.

Tracks 20 and 21 illustrate examples of release samples and damper resonance on a sampled piano instrument.

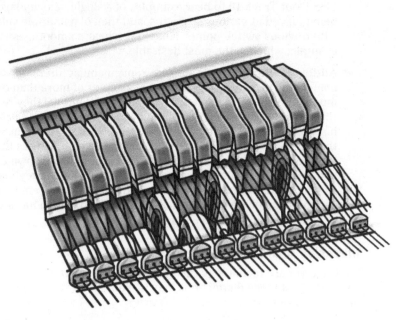

Illustration by Lisa Reed

Figure 3-1:
The piano
damper
mechanism.

In the loop on looping

As I note in the nearby section "Improved/expanded piano samples," a keyboard with more memory has more options for looping each recorded note. Such a keyboard can allocate the amount of memory used in two ways: how much of the original recording is used before the loop occurs and how long the section of the recording used for the loop itself is. Having more original recording before the sound goes into the loop is desirable for decaying sounds such as the piano. It sounds more real, and you don't notice the loop as much because it occurs as the sound is already fading in volume. You can train your ears to hear the loop when auditioning those sustained single notes on a piano sound. Listen for how quickly after the attack the sound transitions into the sustained, and often noticeable, loop.

Loop lengths can be very short in simple sounds, such as a nylon guitar or the upper notes of a piano. But for the lower notes of a piano, which take much longer to settle in after the attack, or for complex sounds such as a string section or distorted electric guitar, the length of the looped section of audio becomes very important. To put it into piano terms, the length of time a note takes to decay to full silence ranges from 20 to 25 seconds on the low end to only ½ to 1 second at the top.

If you play a note or sound and after the attack it turns into a shrill, harsh, buzzing tone, you're hearing a short loop. This short loop sound is undesirable, but it was quite common in keyboards from the late '80s through most of the '90s, when memory was still very expensive. Nowadays, memory options have improved greatly, and for the primary sounds that are important in a keyboard, these shortcuts shouldn't be obvious. But for the secondary sounds and extras, you'll still hear short loops, and you have to decide whether it's acceptable to you.

A note about organ "touch"

If you're an organ player, the best key actions start sounding the moment you depress a note rather than using the typical electronic keyboard method of sounding when the key reaches the bottom of its movement down. The organ isn't a velocity sensitive instrument, so it doesn't need the capacity to measure the force that you pressed a key to provide dynamic control. So the most natural organ performance on a keyboard triggers from the top of the key movement. This setting may be one that you have to turn on, so be sure to ask/check for it.

Both of these additions are best appreciated in solo playing and in small ensembles like a duo or trio. Even playing along with a busy or loud drummer often masks these subtle characteristics.

Going beyond the piano: Sound options and considerations

You want to consider a number of other features of a keyboard beyond its piano capabilities before making your purchase. And that doesn't include issues about the brand's support and promotion of the instrument, which can be just as important. Keep the following in mind:

- ✔ **Does the keyboard offer the right variety of high-quality sounds?** You want to listen to the quality of the other sounds that are important to you. How realistic and expressive are they? Does the keyboard have enough variety of the specific sound group(s) that you care about? If you like playing Clavinet (clav) and you get only one sound, you won't be happy with that compared to the wide variety of tones the real instrument can produce.

  If organ is an area that's important to you and you're not buying a dedicated organ "clone," this question is especially important; you should thoroughly explore a keyboard's organ sound variety to see whether the drawbar settings you require are included before deciding. Not sure what's important to you? Check out the later section "Determining the Type(s) of Music You Want to Play" for tips on sounds associated with various genres of music.

- ✔ **Are any additional sounds available for free or for purchase?** If so, are they just new settings for the same basic sounds, or can you add all-new samples and synthesis engines to expand the possibilities? Adding sounds may be software-based or may involve adding a hardware board or card to the unit. Does the company support this feature with new sounds available for free or for purchase? Do other companies support it? Is an active online user community doing this?

✔ **Are the sounds adjustable at all?** If you're fussy about your sounds, you may want to change some aspect about them — perhaps just adding a different effect or slightly shortening or lengthening the release of a note when you let go of a key. But your keyboard needs to have some level of basic editing for you to be able to do those things. Find out whether the model you're looking at has editing capability and empty or rewritable locations to save your edits to. I talk about effects in Chapter 9 and simple sound editing in Chapter 14.

If you're well-versed in sound editing, then you want to study the voice architecture and editing capabilities to see whether the keyboard has all the things you want. Does it offer a computer- or tablet-based editor? Usually these functions offer a more graphic-rich interface and may provide additional editing features such as ability to copy parts of sounds, librarian functions for organizing and rearranging the onboard sounds, and possibly sound conversion capabilities between models.

Other features to consider

Moving beyond the sound and feel of the keyboard, you should spend time looking into these important helpers to be sure they offer the variety and features you need:

✔ **The metronome and drum rhythms:** For the more advanced player, the variety of rhythms offered becomes more important. Does the keyboard provide enough choices and variations for the styles of music offered to cover your musical needs? A common issue I find is that a groove matches what I need but the drums are playing on the hi-hat and I need an open cymbal sound, or vice versa.

Does the keyboard offer anything besides 4/4 grooves? You'd be surprised how little attention manufacturers pay to a good variety of 3/4 or waltz-time grooves, not to mention playing in odd time signatures like 5/4 and 7/4. Remember to look into this point before you make your purchase. (If these fractionlike numbers don't make sense to you, this feature isn't something you likely need to worry about. If you're interested, though, you can read more about time signatures in Chapter 5.)

If changing between variations within a rhythm style without stopping is important to you, check out arranger keyboards.

✔ **The accompaniment features:** The variety and variations of accompaniment styles are very important considerations if that's a feature you're looking for. Make sure a keyboard offers depth of variety in the areas that are important to you.

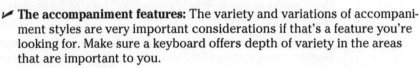

Can you add more styles to the keyboard? And if so, does the company support this feature itself with new offerings? How many other companies/people support your model with new styles? Is an active online user-community doing this?

✔ **The right controllers/pedals:** Make sure whatever keyboard you're considering purchasing has the pedals and controls you need. For example, if *bending pitch* (emulating the soulful string bends that blues and rock guitar players do) is important to you, you need a pitch bend wheel. Also check to see whether the keyboard offers both *momentary/toggle pedals* (more properly called *switches*) and *sweep-type pedals* (sometimes called *expression* or *C/V pedals*). If you want to control volume with your foot or rock a wah-wah effect back and forth, you need to use the sweep-type pedal. Confirm whether a keyboard lets you use a pedal for a certain function you need, such as changing the rotary speaker speed for an organ sound.

Determining the Type (s) of Music You Want to Play

Certain instruments have become so indelibly associated with a style or genre of music that just their images evoke particular sounds. When you see an accordion, you think polka music. See an image of a guitar player in front of a stack of speakers, and you think of rock and roll. See a banjo, and you . . . row faster! Oh, and think of bluegrass music.

So when you're considering the right variety of sounds as I suggest in the earlier section "Going beyond the piano: Sound options and considerations," thinking about the styles of music you want to play is helpful. Doing so helps you to check off the list of desired/required sounds you want in your new keyboard to be able to play those styles of music convincingly. To help kick-start that process, I list some of the most popular genres of music followed by their most essential sounds:

✔ **Rock/blues:** Bright acoustic piano, electric grand piano, reed and tine electric pianos, tonewheel and vintage '60s organ, clav, "harder" synth sounds, string ensemble, tape strings/Mellotron, brass and reed ensembles, tenor and baritone sax, medium distorted harmonica, medium to distorted electric guitar, muted distortion guitar, fingered and picked electric bass, drums, cowbell. Lots of cowbell.

✔ **Pop/ballads:** Wide range of acoustic piano, reed and tine electric pianos, tonewheel organ, vibes, medium to softer synth sounds, vocal and synth pads, string ensemble, brass and reed ensembles, flute, solo sax, muted trumpet, clean to medium electric guitar, acoustic 6-string and 12-string guitar, nylon guitar, acoustic bass, fingered and fretless electric bass, drums, percussion.

✔ **R&B/funk/hip-hop:** Wide range of acoustic piano; reed and tine electric pianos; clav; tonewheel organ; vibes; medium to softer synth sounds; simple lead synth sounds; vocal and synth pads; string ensemble; solo strings; brass and reed ensembles; solo sax; flute; muted and open trumpet; clean to medium electric guitar; wah guitar; muted guitar; nylon guitar; acoustic bass; fingered, slapped, picked, and fretless electric bass; drums; electronic drums; percussion; record scratch sound effects.

✔ **Country/folk/bluegrass:** Wide range of acoustic piano; honky-tonk piano; reed and tine electric pianos; clav; tonewheel organ; accordion; vocal and synth pads; string ensemble; solo strings; fiddle; solo sax; harmonica; clean to medium electric guitar; 6-string and 12-string guitar; banjo; mandolin; Dobro; pedal steel guitar; autoharp; zither; acoustic bass; fingered, picked, and fretless electric bass; drums; percussion; washboard.

✔ **Broadway/jazz/big-band:** Acoustic piano, electric piano, tonewheel organ, vibes, ensemble strings, solo and ensemble brass, solo and ensemble woodwinds, mixed brass and woodwind ensemble, harmonica, scat vocals, clean electric guitar, acoustic bass, fingered and fretless electric bass, drums, percussion.

✔ **Electronic dance:** Processed acoustic piano (house piano, compressed piano, and so on); synth electric pianos; vintage '60s organ; clav; wide range of synth sounds; string ensemble; brass and synth brass ensembles; medium to distorted electric guitar; muted distortion guitar; ethnic plucked stringed instruments; synth bass; drums; electronic drums; percussion; synth sweeps, blips, and sound effects; spoken vocal phrases and effects; ethnic samples and loops; orchestral hits.

✔ **Classical/liturgical:** Acoustic piano, tonewheel organ, pipe organ, harpsichord, celeste, bells/chimes, xylophone/marimba, solo and ensemble strings, solo and ensemble brass, solo and ensemble woodwinds, nylon guitar, harp, tympani, crash cymbal, snare drum, bass drum, percussion.

I also discuss sounds as they relate to styles of music in Chapter 8.

Considering Your Keyboard's Location

An important consideration when choosing your new keyboard is where and how you plan to use it. If you're going to place it in a location (such as your music room, your church, or a school auditorium) and never move it, size and weight aren't really an issue. In public situations, you want to consider what the case looks like and whether the keyboard comes with a nice stand. If a lot of people are going to be viewing the keyboard from the back or side, the cosmetic design becomes an important criteria, as may a covered bottom. (This cover was called a *modesty panel* back in the church organ days for obvious reasons.)

If you don't have room to always leave the keyboard set up, however, you need to consider size and weight and how they affect the hassle of storing it and setting it up, particularly if you're going to be moving it from room to room or transporting it between locations for performances.

Onboard speakers or line outputs become very important if you'll be playing your keyboard in a public location where others need to hear it. Make sure the quality and power of the onboard speakers is appropriate for the venue — will they fill the room with enough sound or do they need help? If the venue is a bright, outdoor one, you need to consider whether you'll be able to see an onboard display. Some displays wash out very easily under bright lights or are hard to read from different angles.

Playing Well with Others and Alone

Some features can become more important based on the situation(s) you'll be playing your keyboard in; features that are helpful for solo work may not mean much for a band member. I have spent decades developing electronic keyboards and have learned a lot from my customers, artists, and others in the industry. I'm happy to share some of these tips and observations with you in the following sections to help you make the best choice for your needs.

An onboard music rack or stand can be helpful in lots of performance situations because most require you to read some music. Playing classical music in particular often involves reading from large scores, so you need to consider whether the supplied rack will hold the size and bulk of the music you'll be using. Forward-thinking musicians are starting to use tablet computers as their music readers, and those are more likely than huge paper scores to fit on the average supplied keyboard music rack.

Going solo

You can find two main schools of solo keyboard performance: the solo pianist and the one-man band.

As a *solo pianist,* you basically play piano, piano layered with strings or a warm synth sound, and perhaps some electric piano. So the best-quality sounds with all possible nuances work well. Your sound is very exposed so even subtle aspects like damper resonance and key-off samples can be heard and enjoyed. Having some backing rhythms is nice because they add to your performance while still allowing the solo piano approach to shine. You will be playing in small rooms or as background music a lot, so onboard speakers can usually carry your performance, making your setup much easier. If you're a singer-songwriter and will be playing in clubs with sound systems, you don't need much beyond your keyboard, a stand, and your pedal(s), plus maybe a microphone input with some dedicated reverb for your voice. A number of stage pianos and arranger keyboards offer this feature.

The one-man band is more of an outgoing entertainer; you're playing a wide variety of music, talking, and likely singing, and you need to come off like a complete band. The professional arranger is best choice of keyboard for this work, for sure. You can put together this type of show with a workstation keyboard, but doing so requires much more time and effort developing the backing tracks to play all the songs you'll need to cover. Only the fussiest and most advanced keyboardists are likely to go that route. Choosing the right arranger keyboard for you comes down to quality and variety of sounds, accompaniment patterns, mic input, keyboard feel, and perhaps vocal harmony features.

Accompanying vocalists

Having a transpose function can be very helpful if you are playing in a duo or small group with a vocalist. A singer often needs to change the key of a song to stay in the most comfortable range. And because males and females have different vocal ranges, they almost never sing a given song in the same key as each other.

Learning how to play a song in more than one key is a more advanced musical skill, so why not let technology help you out? A *transpose* function shifts the tuning of the keyboard so you can keep playing in the key of C on the keys, but the notes that come out will be moved up or down by an amount you specify. So by simply selecting a transpose value, you can now play in any key you require with no change in your playing. Thank you, technology!

If this option is important to you, check out your potential keyboard candidates to see how easily you can access this feature; is it right on the front panel, or do you have to go wading through a lot of menu pages? Can you easily turn off the function so you're back to normal tuning/operation? Does the feature show or tell you that you're currently transposed? Pianists have told me stories about starting a song and getting angry or confused stares from a singer, only to realize that they were still transposed from the last song and had forgotten about it. Having to stop and start again because "it's the keyboard player's fault" can be very embarrassing.

Performing classical music with others

A great piano sound and perhaps pipe organ and harpsichord are obviously your main sound choices when playing classical music with others. But many musicians have told me stories of how they had to help augment a given classical or church ensemble to cover the parts of a missing or sick member and were the hero of the day when their keyboards could reproduce the solo string, woodwind, or even percussion instrument that was required. This benefit is certainly something to consider if your music choices will include all these instrument types.

Onboard speakers are another good feature because you don't need to be very loud when playing classical, and the sight of an electronic keyboard in this type of ensemble can already be a cause of some concern. Carry in an instrument amplifier or speaker system, and who knows what the reaction will be.

Jamming in a pop, rock, or jazz band

Playing in a band usually means you have to cover many more sounds than just typical keyboard sounds. Be sure to evaluate the synth, string, brass, and vocal sounds carefully so you ensure that you can cover all the styles of music needed.

You often have to cover more than one part, so split and layer features are important. You should be able to store these multisound parts and recall them easily. (Chapter 8 has more on splitting and layering sounds.) Having a special live mode where you can arrange sounds in order so you can change them easily during a song is also very helpful. This way, you can mix and match single sounds and multipart sounds in an easy list to select from. Many performers like to use a foot pedal to advance through these lists so their hands can stay on the keyboard at all times. (Or one hand playing, one hand on your favorite beverage; who am I to judge?)

Having the ability to keep one sound sustaining while you change to your next sound is becoming more common, or at least more in demand from players. With this feature, current notes keep sounding while the new sound loads in the background; only when you play new notes do you hear the new sound, so you can get a seamless (not choppy) transition between sounds. This function, called names such as *patch remain, smooth sound transition, seamless sound change,* and so on, is certainly worth asking about.

Band work is the most common place where you see players using more than one keyboard. The most common reason for this arrangement is the feel of the keys. Playing piano on an unweighted synth action isn't very satisfying; trying to play tonewheel organ on a weighted keyboard is equally difficult and can be downright painful when you attempt to do the palm slides up and down the keys that are common in organ playing. Likewise, playing rhythmic clav and fast synth parts is much easier on the unweighted keys. (I discuss key weight earlier in the chapter.)

A second issue is that a single keyboard may not be able to provide enough key range per part for the split and/or layered parts you need to cover. A two-keyboard approach becomes the right answer. How to choose what type of keyboards depends on whether you are primarily a pianist who needs extra sounds, an organist who needs extra sounds, or perhaps an electronic music performer who needs a variety of instruments. Here are some of the most common approaches/combinations:

- Piano/stage piano on the bottom with an all-purpose synth/workstation on top

- Piano/stage piano on the bottom with an organ on top

- Weighted action workstation on the bottom with synth action synth/ workstation on top

- Weighted action workstation on the bottom with organ on top

- Organ on the bottom (sometimes dual manual organ) with stage piano on top

- Organ on the bottom (sometimes dual manual organ) with all-purpose synth/workstation on top

Purchasing a Gift for a Child

When considering what keyboard to buy for a child, I can address a few common scenarios to help guide you:

- ✔ For a very young child, you likely just want to offer a fun, interactive experience. The keyboard should be smaller and portable so you can store it away when the kid isn't using it and can take it on family trips. The world of portables is the right place to search. Lighted keys, interactive games, and a variety of sounds are all good features to have.

- ✔ For getting a child started on piano lessons at an early age, a lower-cost digital piano or portable digital piano can be a good choice compared to a low-end acoustic piano.

- ✔ For a child between the ages of 8 and 12, many of the full-sized portables and digital pianos are great options. Having a variety of sounds and onboard rhythms adds to the interest and fun factor.

- ✔ For a teen who has been playing piano for a few years, getting a lower-end workstation or synth may be the way to go; it provides the sounds and features that let him play the popular music he enjoys and even consider jamming with his friends or starting a band. This age is when you have to account for the "coolness" factor; the look and brand appeal start to become important.

  Another good choice for the fledgling hipster is a true synthesizer; some lower-priced models are very popular, and some even run on batteries so they're easily portable. Synthesizers help promote the fun in exploring and playing keyboards, which is important for keeping kids from being pulled away from music by the many other time-soaking temptations of modern life.

At any age, if you're going to be providing the child with piano lessons, consider that the teacher will want a weighted action, at least one pedal (damper/sustain), and at least a five-octave range (61 notes). For serious piano study, the teacher is going to want a dedicated piano product and will look askance at anything that doesn't attempt to re-create the complete piano experience.

Doing Your Due Diligence

When you have some idea of what kind of keyboard you want, take full advantage of the helpful online information at your fingertips. The following sections discuss some steps you should take when you're doing your homework.

Visiting various manufacturers' websites

Have a plan before you start. Here's my basic checklist:

- ✔ **Read the promo copy for the category and/or models you want to investigate.** Yes, it's going to hype the product and its benefits like crazy, but try to read through the sales pitch and see what the instrument actually does.

- ✔ **Check the specs to be sure the instrument has the features/size/weight you need.** You may encounter a lot of tech talk, but I often find that only the spec list gives me the info I need about the presence of connectors (inputs, outputs, pedals, and such) and more-detailed features I'm looking for.

- ✔ **See whether the manufacturer offers any frequently asked questions about that model or category of keyboards.** FAQ lists answer many common questions.

- ✔ **Listen to the demos and watch the videos.** *Tip:* Odds are these clips are all going to be available on popular video sites such as YouTube and SoundCloud as well, so if a manufacturer's website is hard to navigate or you want to easily compare different products/brands, you may find doing a search on those outside sites to be a better research experience.

- ✔ **See whether manufacturers are running any promotions.** Knowing whether a brand is running a national sale, rebate, or value-added promotion before you hit the stores is always good.

Reading the manual

Reading the manual is simply the best way to research the features and capabilities of a keyboard beforehand. Almost every manufacturer provides its manuals for download from its website in PDF format. I don't expect you to read the manual from cover to cover, but some targeted research can help you understand whether a product does what you want and how complicated the processes are.

Manuals may come in multiple documents:

- ✔ **Owner's manual:** The *owner's manual* is the main document that explains the complete functionality of the product. It's the how-to guide for the product and the first document I suggest you study.

- ✔ **Quick guide:** A *quick guide* can help you get started on the simplest/ most common tasks. It isn't the best one to do your research from, but knowing it exists is a plus if you buy that model.

- ✔ **Reference guide:** A *reference guide* is the more technical document that describes every parameter, function, and technical concept in greater detail. It's more of a what-is than a how-to document. Sometimes manufacturers move the more complicated aspects of a product over into this document, so you may need to look to it for some answers.

- ✔ **Other documents:** Some manufacturers make a separate document (a *data list* or *voice name list*) to describe the sounds, effects, and songs a keyboard provides. This document can be a very helpful for finding out whether a keyboard has the sound(s) and/or effects you want, for example.

Looking for user groups for the brand(s) or category you're interested in

Researching within a user group can be invaluable, exposing issues and teaching you work-arounds that the manufacturer doesn't discuss. Typing the brand name and "user group" into your search engine quickly leads you to various groups of owners and interested parties. I never trust any one search to be definitive, so I usually try some variations of the search terms as well: Put quotation marks around the terms ("[brand] user group"), which returns only results of the exact search term. Try "usergroup" with no space. Try a few different search engines. Check Facebook and Yahoo Groups as well.

After you find a group, search for your model of interest or any questions you may have. I can promise you that you're not the first person to visit that site looking for the information you want, so a search is the best first step; the users may be tired of answering the same basic questions over and over again. You may need to join the group before you can search using its tools.

Here's a simple way around having to join a group to search its content. In your search engine, type "site:" and then the URL of the user group's website, with no space after the colon. Then add your question or terms. The engine will only search that website, narrowing the search and bypassing the site's internal mechanism.

You can also find user groups devoted to the general category of instrument you are looking for. Here are a few I frequent:

- ✔ **Piano and digital piano centric:** www.pianoworld.com/forums. I especially like the Digital Pianos — Synths & Keyboards sub-forum.

- ✔ **All-around keyboards:**

  - http://forums.musicplayer.com/ubbthreads.php/ forums/18/1/The_Keyboard_Corner. This one's a bit more geared toward professionals and is very into tonewheel organs.

  - www.keyboardforums.com.

- ✔ **Arranger keyboards:** www.synthzone.com/forum/ubbthreads. php/category/5/The_Arranger_Keyboard_Forums. I especially like the General Arranger Keyboard forum.

Checking out reviews for the model(s) you're interested in

Product reviews fall into three categories:

- ✔ **Commercial music magazines:** The most popular ones are *Electronic Musician, Keyboard, Future Music, Pianist,* and *Sound On Sound* (SOS). Most have both print and online subscriptions and often release content into public viewing after a certain number of months.

- ✔ **Online reviews:** Some online-only outlets discuss and review products; my favorites include GearJunkies.com, HarmonyCentral.com, and SonicState.com. These are all pretty tech-oriented sites, so they cover synths and workstations the best.

- ✔ **User reviews:** A number of music retailers allow their customers to post reviews (good and bad) about products. I'm not going to list names because I don't want to give unfair sales advantage to any businesses, so be sure to search around. Harmony Central also has a long history of posting user reviews. Take a look at YouTube as well; a growing number of users/owners post their own video reviews of products, including tips and tricks for using the keyboard.

Chapter 4

Setting Up and Caring For Your Keyboard

In This Chapter

▶ Finding a good spot for your instrument

▶ Getting the keyboard (and its miscellany) out of the package and assembled

▶ Making electrical and audio connections

▶ Maintaining your keyboard

So you've chosen the right instrument for your needs and have brought it home to start making music. Where will you be able to focus on playing, practicing, and enjoying making music without distraction (and without distracting others)?

In this chapter, I discuss how to set up your keyboard, how to safely move it around, and how to keep it in tip-top shape. I also acquaint you with the various types of connections (and connectors) that allow you to plug in headphones for private enjoyment or hook up to other gear to hear your keyboard in open air. I talk a little bit about electrical safety and some best practices when using powered electrical gear. Finally, I guide you on how to get help when you have a problem.

Deciding On the Right Spot

When the time comes to settle your keyboard into its new home, you may not have a lot of location choices; if you have a small home or apartment, your options may be limited. They may even be nonexistent, such that you're going to have to keep the keyboard in a closet and only bring it out when you want to play. That's okay; the important part is that you're getting involved in playing music! With a little forethought on the possibilities and requirements, you can figure out where the best place in your home is for your new keyboard.

Locating near needed connections

The most obvious requirement is that your new keyboard needs to be plugged into an electrical outlet. Ideally, you want to choose a location near one so you don't have the power cord stretching across areas where people need to pass or where it may prove too tempting to young children or pets.

Not only does the keyboard need to fit in the chosen area, but you also need enough room to get up and down easily and to move your arms and feet freely. You can check this clearance out ahead of time by sitting on a chair in the prospective area and playing air keyboard (moving your arms left to right) and tapping your feet. If you've knocked over a lamp, pulled out the plug to your TV, and elbowed a family member in the process, you may want to rethink that location!

If you want to connect your keyboard to another speaker/amplifier, you need room for that device as well; it should be able to be pointed toward you so most of the sound is coming right at you, not drifting into your landlord's living room or your new baby's nursery. If you're going to connect the keyboard to your computer speakers or home stereo, you should be located as close to the device as possible so your cables aren't easily tripped over by passerby. I don't think your warranty covers pulling the keyboard to the floor from tripping over the wires.

Surveying sound considerations

Sound issues are often the least-considered part of this process. Your keyboard offers the chance for silent practice, and you intend to be using headphones all the time. No worries, right? Not quite. Most headphones don't cut out all the outside sound, so you'll likely still hear things happening around you. Sitting near where folks will be watching TV, playing video games, or just loudly socializing will be distracting to you. You're better off finding a quieter, more private part of the dwelling to set up in.

Less obvious are the noises that you'll be making that may disturb others. No, I'm not talking about the moaning, grunting, and out-of-tune singing that may accompany your playing, although maybe you *should* consider that. Few keyboards are completely silent when played; the keys themselves make some noise, and if you're using a digital piano, stage piano, or other weighted key instrument, it will certainly make noise. (Head to Chapter 2 for info on weighted key actions.) This constant knocking/thumping sound, like an army of mice in combat boots running around, can be very annoying to others in the same room. So being able to isolate yourself a bit from the most popular room/part of the house is a good idea.

When you're using the keyboard's onboard speakers or connecting to another amplification system, you need to consider whether the keyboard/ speakers are up against a common wall with a neighboring apartment or a room where someone would need quiet while you want to play. If you have no choice but to locate there, just realize that you'll need to use your headphones during the hours when you'd most likely be disturbing others.

Avoiding distractions

When you play your keyboard, it should be your primary focus. You want to pay attention to that activity and get lost in the music, which can be hard to do with a TV screen or a window to your neighbor's yard in your peripheral field of vision. You need to consider the potential distractions a keyboard location presents that can keep you from focusing intently on your music making.

If you're a parent buying an instrument for your child to study/take lessons on, especially consider what visual distractions the location will provide. Asking a child to concentrate on practicing while she's looking out a window at all her friends playing in the next yard just isn't going to work out. Likewise, locating the keyboard in direct sight lines of the family TV is a bad idea. Ideally, you should put the instrument in a quiet room against a solid wall. If you're concerned that your child won't focus on her playing, locate the keyboard close enough that you can see or check in a few times during her session, but not so close that your looking in is a distraction.

Unboxing Your New Toy

In the excited rush of opening up your new instrument, you may actually miss some important in-box element of your purchase. And the last thing you want is to injure yourself before you even get a chance to play. In the following sections, I offer a few pointers that have come from both my personal experience and years of customer service.

Safety first! Opening the box carefully

Smaller keyboard boxes may involve flaps that insert into slots, with some tape over the seams. But many larger boxes have been stapled shut, with tape then placed over the seams. Scratching or cutting yourself on these staples is all too easy if you pull apart the box and leave the staples in place. I strongly suggest you use some small pliers to completely remove the staples before opening the flaps.

Likewise, be careful when using scissors or box cutters to slice through the tape. If you start cutting before you remove the staples, the blade may jump up and cut you in the process. You may also want to cover your hands altogether; as a pianist, I'm super paranoid about my hands and fingers, so I wear gloves when unpacking larger boxes.

What's inside? Going down the checklist

Your keyboard comes wrapped in some type of plastic bag or material and has molded foam end caps on both ends to protect it and hold it in place in the box. What many people often miss is that some important accessory may also be located in the end of the foam insert; they just throw the foam aside or even throw it away, only to notice later that something they need is missing. So look carefully at both end pieces.

Besides the keyboard itself (including the stand assembly if it's a home digital piano), you should be looking for the following items (not all will apply to your chosen model; check the beginning of your owner's manual for more information):

- ✔ **Power cable or external power supply:** Larger keyboards often just use a cable to connect the keyboard directly to a wall outlet, but many keyboards use a smaller adapter or *wall-wart* type of power supply. Some of these connectors are two-piece affairs, with the larger, rectangular piece plus a second cable that connects between it and the outlet (much like you see with some laptops).

- ✔ **Owner's manual or operation guide:** Your keyboard package includes some sort of documentation (traditionally a printed hardcopy) to help you operate it. These instructions may be a complete owner's manual or just a brief getting-started guide to help you with only the most basic tasks. These booklets commonly show up in a clear bag, which may also include a warranty card and perhaps a CD- or DVD-ROM. This disc likely contains most of your needed documentation — the owner's manual, a deeper *parameter guide* (which explains each and every function and parameter of the product), a voice/sound name list, and other documents.

   Note: To keep costs down, many manufacturers are moving toward including fewer printed materials and providing lengthier documentation as an electronic PDF file. On a Mac, the included program Preview can open this file type, but otherwise you need a free program called Adobe Reader to be able to open and view these documents on your computer. Go to www.adobe.com/reader to download this free application.

   Products often change during their lifespans, adding new features and fixing mistakes in documentation. A newer version of your keyboard's document(s) may be available for download from the manufacturer's website.

✔ **Warranty card:** A *warranty card* registers your ownership of the product with the manufacturer, ensuring your coverage for repairs/problems during a set time period the company offers. In the United States, you aren't actually required to fill in/return this type of card to be eligible for warranty coverage. Your proof of purchase (a store receipt is best) guarantees your coverage of whatever the manufacturer offers. The European Union offers even stronger consumer protection without the need for filing forms with the manufacturer.

Many manufacturers offer extended warranty time periods (usually double the regular time) if you go to their websites to fill out your warranty info. This extension is a great benefit to you, and it's free, so I recommend you check into this possibility and take advantage if it's available. You can always choose to ignore most of the marketing info, uncheck any of the prefilled "e-mail me!" boxes, and just put in your basic profile/contact info.

✔ **Additional hardware:** If you've bought a home digital piano with an included stand assembly, the screws, wing nuts, and other hardware connectors are in a separate bag somewhere in the box. Look carefully for any such items in the foam inserts and even taped to the inside of the box.

✔ **Included sustain/damper pedal:** If your keyboard is supposed to come with a pedal, that pedal will usually be in a white cardboard box within the shipping box. Sometimes these free pedals are only small flat switches, so the box can be small and easily overlooked.

✔ **Additional cables:** Some keyboards come with a USB cable for connecting the instrument to your computer for MIDI and/or audio functionality. Although you may not require that capability right away, if it was promised to you, be sure to locate the cord. (When you're ready to connect for MIDI, check out Chapter 17.)

✔ **"Free gifts" with purchase:** Manufacturers sometimes include software trial versions from partner companies, free magazine subscriptions, or other promotional items. These may be included in the clear plastic bag with the documentation/warranty card or may be loose in the box.

✔ **Bundled goods from the retailer:** Some retailers put together special bundle promotions, where they add other goods (such as headphones, a carrying case, a stand, music books or software, and so on) to your package price. These items are always packed in one or more separate packages and either are given to you at the time of purchase or shipped at the same time. If your keyboard is being delivered, look carefully for markings such as "Box 1 of X", "Box 2 of X," and so on to be sure that your carrier gives you all the boxes that are part of your order. Your shipping notice from the company should define how many boxes to expect.

Setting Up Your Keyboard

Any stand you use with your keyboard probably requires some assembly. But if you're working with a home digital piano or very large arranger keyboard that comes with a custom stand as part of the package, I suggest you connect the instrument to a power source to make sure it's working okay before you assemble the stand and place the keyboard on it. You'd much rather find out you've got a bum keyboard before you put together the stand, especially a complicated one with lots of doodads. No one wants to build the stand only to realize you have to take it all apart to have the instrument looked at.

You can easily look up the weight of your new keyboard to be sure the stand can hold it, but you also need to consider the amount of force and constant vibration that playing the keyboard is going to exert. A small child or delicate player isn't going to produce much extra pressure on the stand, but if you're planning to play some bangin' rock and roll, highly rhythmic funk, or dramatic classical pieces, you should seriously consider the sturdiness of your stand. The cheapest stands are an X design (shown in Figure 4-1), with a simple cross brace underneath. These types are okay, but they're not as sturdy and solid as a design that has four (or more) actual legs underneath (also shown in Figure 4-1). Check to see whether the keyboard/stand combo easily rock backs and forth (which you don't want).

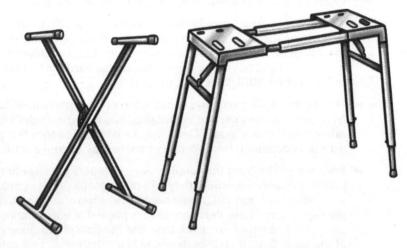

Figure 4-1:
Common
stand
designs.

Illustration by Lisa Reed

Stand height is another important consideration. Good piano technique requires that your arm is basically level from the elbow across to the hand, so position your stand accordingly (keeping in mind the height of the keyboard itself as well). Angling your hand downward or upward causes stress and can tire and even hurt your wrist muscles. When sitting, the chair, stool, or bench you use often determines what height the stand needs to be set at. However, you can adjust the height on fancier piano benches and many computer desk chairs. I've even sat on a small cushion to raise me up in a computer chair, and it's actually quite comfortable!

When standing, the straight forearm rule applies, with the added issue that you're more likely to cause the keyboard to vibrate or even move with your forceful playing (and dancing around!). Be sure that your stand doesn't bounce too much or move around and that all connections are hand tightened securely.

You may opt to use some other surface — such as a table, desk, or counter — rather than a stand. Be sure to place some padding or a towel beneath the piano before putting it on a surface that can scratch easily; the instrument may have some unfinished edges or screws protruding. And think carefully about your seating plans; you want to make sure you're observing the proper arm position even with your unconventional surface.

Hook Me Up: Taking Care of All Sorts of Keyboard Connections

Your keyboard is electronic, so you're going to have to hook up some things before you can play. Even with just a little portable, you need to insert batteries to get started. The following sections cover the most common connections you'll encounter.

Making the electrical connection

Electricity is a powerful source of energy, and you need to be respectful of it and careful when using it. Most people know not to stick their fingers, their tongues, or pointy objects into an outlet, but not everyone thinks carefully when plugging in power cables or adapters.

You should always have the power cable or power adapter plugged into the keyboard before you connect it to the power source. Don't let your finger slip over to the prong or tip of the plug when pushing it in. Look to see whether the plug has one prong larger than the other (to ensure you're grounded properly) before plugging it in.

Plugging a lot of devices into one outlet can be a fire hazard. Consider distributing them around to other outlets or even parts of your room/house if possible. You can buy multioutlet plugs that attach to the normal dual-outlet boxes found in the wall, giving you four or even six outlets. If you want to use one of these, be sure to secure it to the wall outlet with the long screw provided.

Many people choose to use a multioutlet strip that sits on the floor instead of crowding the wall outlet. I like this approach because adapters and wall-warts often cover up adjacent outlets; plus, they can be heavy and even fall out of the wall. I recommend you invest in an outlet strip that offers *surge suppression* or *surge protection*. This feature protects your gear from sudden spikes in the power that may damage your electronic keyboard.

That said, a strip-based surge protector won't protect you if your house is struck by lightning; you need much more expensive and advanced gear for that level of safety. If a strong thunderstorm is reported in your area, unplug your valuable electronic devices (and appliances) until the storm passes.

Firing up your keyboard

Hopefully, you've already turned on your keyboard once while setting up the stand (as I note in the earlier section "Setting Up Your Keyboard") just to briefly test its function. Now you're ready to really get the electricity flowing so you can use your instrument for actually playing.

This book is a much more informative and fun read than the usual owner's manual that comes with a keyboard. Believe me, I've read a lot of them in my career! That said, I can't hope to explain each and every electronic keyboard available and how they work. So reading this guide isn't a substitute for reading the manual that came with your product. I strongly suggest you at least browse through the opening section of your manual regarding connections and first-time use before officially starting up your keyboard. It's okay; I'll wait here patiently while you do that now.

I'm assuming here that your keyboard has built-in speakers. If it doesn't, jump to the later section "Music to my ears: Working with headphones" or "Attaching to musical instrument amplifiers and other ¼-inch jack devices" before continuing this section. You can come back here after you've made the right connections.

Follow these steps to safely get your keyboard going:

1. **Plug in any pedals you have.**

   Look carefully on the back panel to be sure you're plugging the pedal into the right jack. Read up more about this hookup in your product's owner's manual or getting started guide.

2. **Find the Main Volume control and turn it all the way down.**

   This control may be labeled just Volume or Output. I always recommend taking this step when turning on an electronic instrument; some cheaper ones make a popping sound when you first turn them on, and no one wants to listen to that, especially through headphones or amplified through another system.

3. **Locate the power switch or button; turn it on and wait for the keyboard to fully boot up.**

   The on/off control may be on the front panel, around the back of the unit, or even on the side. Remember, some units take a few moments to fully wake up and be ready to play.

4. **Play a single note over and over while you raise the volume to your desired level.**

   I usually keep the volume up at around ¾ of its range, but your choice may differ depending on your surroundings.

5. **If your keyboard has built-in demos or songs, get one of those playing, step back a bit from it, and listen while adjusting the volume.**

   This step is a good way to enjoy your first listen to your new instrument in your home surroundings. Set the volume too loud, and you may find you start rattling pictures on the wall or disturbing some other item. Either batten down the offending vibrating object or lower the volume.

Music to my ears: Working with headphones

Perhaps your keyboard doesn't have onboard speakers, or you just want to enjoy some private practice time. Every electronic keyboard offers a headphone output for that purpose. (Often, if a keyboard does have onboard speakers, plugging a headphone in will automatically turn off the speakers. Smart, huh?) The following sections introduce various kinds of headphones and help you connect your headphones to your keyboard.

Breaking down headphone varieties

You can use a number of different headphone types. Check them out in Figure 4-2.

- ✔ **On-the-ear/earpad headphones:** These headphones sit on your ears/earlobes and have some foam or cushioning covering the speakers for comfort. The sound quality coming out is typically good to very good, but they won't block out much of the surrounding sound. They also leak more sound, so others can listen in to what you're hearing

- ✔ **Over-the-ear headphones:** *Over-the-ear* headphones sit over your whole ear and have a closed design that keeps the sound in and reduces external noises. They reproduce bass frequencies better than on-the-ear designs.

- ✔ **Earbuds:** These options sit inside the center of your outer ear, held in place by the curves of your ear or sometimes a hook that goes around your ear. Their quality can vary wildly, from very cheap and poor sounding to very good. They don't tend to reproduce bass frequencies as well as over-the-ear choices and intentionally don't block out too much sound (for safety when wearing them in public).

- ✔ **In-the-ear headphones:** These specialized earbuds actually fit into the ear canal and can offer superb sound, bass frequency reproduction, and noise isolation. They can feel uncomfortable at first, though, and may take a little getting used to.

Headphones bring the sound very close to your ears (and in the case of in-the-ear varieties, right into the ear canal), so you should be careful about listening at high volumes. Many of the warnings advise against loud listening "for long periods of time," but I say "at all." Your hearing is precious and can easily be damaged by loud sound/music. Try to set the volume as low as you can while still hearing and enjoying it rather than as loud as you can before causing pain/bleeding!

Plugging in your headphones to your keyboard

Headphones and headphone outputs use two types of connectors. Here, I correctly call the receptacle on your keyboard that accepts the headphone a *jack* and the connector at the end of the cable a *plug*. However, note that these terms are sometimes used interchangeably in other sources. Here's the breakdown:

- ✔ The most common musical instrument/audio connector is called a ¼-inch plug or *phone plug*. Figure 4-3 shows the shape of this connector. It's the largest plug used and makes a great connection because of its long shaft. It's available in mono and stereo versions, so be sure you have the stereo version, indicated by dual black rings near the tip of the plug.

On-the-ear

Over-the-ear

Figure 4-2:
Popular
headphone
types.

Earbuds

In-the-ear

Illustration by Lisa Reed

Stereo allows the sound to come out of both speakers of your headphones; *mono* comes from only one side or the other, which you don't want.

✔ Figure 4-3 also shows the increasingly common 3.5-millimeter plug, also called a *mini-plug* (and also called a ⅛-inch plug even though ⅛ inch doesn't quite equal 3.5 millimeters; don't ask!). This smaller option is used where space is at a premium. It's the most common plug size for mobile phones, media players, and most earbud headphones. It makes a good connection but can be a bit fragile, so always be careful not to tug on the cable or put pressure on this connection. Make sure you have the stereo version.

Your headphones may well have a different-sized plug from your keyboard's headphone output. Adapters that can convert between these two sizes are very common and easily found at your local music store, electronics store, or online.

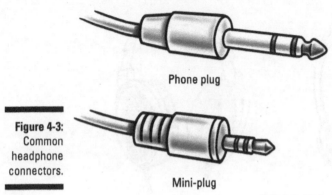

Phone plug

Figure 4-3:
Common
headphone
connectors.

Mini-plug

Illustration by Lisa Reed

Armed with the right headphones and cable/connector, you can now plug in the phones to your keyboard. I recommend doing so before you put them over your ears. You can never be too safe about your hearing!

Doing without onboard speakers and headphones

If your keyboard doesn't have onboard speakers and you want to share your playing with others (or you just don't want to wear headphones), you can connect your instrument to a number of different devices or speakers. The main requirement is that the other device must have a power source that isn't your keyboard; your keyboard's output signal isn't strong enough to drive basic speakers. Luckily, almost every device you're likely to choose from (whether it's a home theater/stereo, a computer or MP3 player's speakers, or an amplifier) fits that bill.

Here's a general rule for turning electronics (such as your keyboard) and audio gear on and off when connected to a separate amplifier, powered speaker, or whatever: With both devices off, always turn on the sound-producing item first (the keyboard, MP3 player, and so on). Then turn on the amplifier/powered speakers second. This order ensures that any pops or wake-up sounds the device makes don't go out your speakers, possibly harming them or your hearing. When shutting down, always turn off the amplifier/powered speakers first, followed by the sound-producing item. Just remember, first on, last off.

Connecting to your home stereo

All home stereo systems include some form of additional input, usually labeled as an aux or auxiliary input and sometimes tape input. Home stereo audio/video gear commonly uses a different type of connector called an *RCA plug.* Figure 4-4 shows this option, which has a small, thin plug connector surrounded by a metal shield. These plugs are mono, which means you need two cables to connect to your home stereo/theater device if you want to hear your keyboard coming out of both speakers.

Figure 4-4:
RCA plug.

Illustration by Lisa Reed

This plug is commonly used in home stereo and home theater audio/video products. It makes a great connection because of its metal shield, which fits securely over the jack on the device you're plugging into.

Here are the most common situations for connecting:

- ✔ If your keyboard has two ¼-inch line outputs labeled L/Mono and R (left/ mono and right), you need two cables that have male mono ¼-inch plugs on one end and male RCA plugs on the other. (The terms *female* and *male* are used to describe jacks and plugs in the obvious way.) These are very common, easily found items.

- ✔ If your keyboard has a single stereo 3.5-millimeter jack (labeled as an output), you need a special type of Y cable that has a male stereo 3.5-millimeter plug on one end and splits out into two cables with male RCA plugs on their ends.

- ✔ If your keyboard offers no jack labeled as an output, you can use the headphone jack to connect to your stereo. If it's a 3.5-millimeter jack, follow the advice in the preceding bullet. If it's a ¼-inch jack, you need a cable with a male stereo ¼-inch plug on one end that breaks out into two male RCA plugs on the other. This Y cord is less commonly found in general electronics stores but readily available in musical instrument stores and online.

Many Y cables are very short, and it's possible (although not optimal) to use a stereo 3.5-millimeter or ¼-inch (depending on your jack) plug to two female RCA jacks and then buy two longer male RCA to male RCA cables to make up the distance.

Your best bet is always to use a cable long enough to make the connection without requiring adapters or additional connectors. These items can weaken the signal and make noise. Brick-and-mortar stores may have limited selections of cable lengths, so if you can't find the right cable length in a store, I suggest you shop online. Many companies offer a much wider variety of cable types and lengths on their websites than any storefront carries. And many of the familiar-name stores offer a wider selection on their websites than they carry in the store.

When you're armed with the correct cables, here's how to connect them:

1. **Make sure both devices are turned off and their volumes set to 0.**
2. **Connect the L output of your keyboard to the L aux in and the R output of your keyboard to the R aux in.**
3. **Turn on the keyboard first, waiting until it has fully powered up before moving on.**
4. **Set your home stereo to aux and then power it on.**
5. **Bring the keyboard's volume up to around 50 percent.**
6. **While playing some notes on the keyboard, slowly bring up the home stereo volume to around 10 to 25 percent.**

   If you need a little more volume, go back to your keyboard and raise its output slightly.

Using your computer speakers

Computer speaker systems can range from sounding okay to very good, and many include a *subwoofer* (a special speaker placed on the floor to reproduce low frequencies) that can add to the richness of your sound. These speakers usually accept a single stereo 3.5-millimeter plug. The easiest connection is if you have a stereo 3.5-millimeter output or headphone jack on your keyboard. Then you only need a long cable with a stereo 3.5 millimeter plug on each end. If that isn't available, here are the two other common scenarios:

✔ The next easiest connection is to use the stereo ¼-inch headphone output. This option requires a male stereo ¼-inch plug on one end with a male stereo 3.5-millimeter plug on the other.

✔ You can use the two ¼-inch main outputs if you really want to, but this strategy is the least desirable of those presented here. To go this route requires a Y cable that joins two mono ¼-inch plugs into a single male stereo 3.5-millimeter jack. This connection is more complicated than needed, trust me.

After you've got everything connected, follow the instructions from the pre-ceding section for powering on and setting volume.

Attaching to musical instrument amplifiers and other ¼-inch jack devices

For the sake of simplicity, I lump together musical instrument amplifiers, powered speakers, and mixers and speakers (PA systems) in this section. All these devices use ¼-inch jacks for their inputs. The main distinction for you is whether the device is stereo or mono. Many keyboard and guitar amplifiers you find in a musical instrument store are mono. If you have only one powered speaker, you'll be playing in mono.

Your keyboard always sounds better when connected in stereo, but if you have to, you can listen to it in mono. Some better keyboard amps are stereo devices; even if they have only one cabinet, they still have dual speakers inside. These amps are better for keyboards than a mono keyboard, or guitar, amplifier. In the case of powered speakers, you can always buy and use two separate speakers to fully reproduce the stereo image your keyboard delivers.

To connect in mono, you should use the line output labeled L/Mono. This output treats the internal signal properly for listening in mono, so you don't lose any of the frequencies or information. This output is almost always a ¼-inch jack, so use a common male ¼-inch to male ¼-inch instrument cable, sometimes referred to as *unbalanced* or *guitar cables.*

Some smaller portables and digital pianos with onboard speakers don't have line outputs, so your only choice is the headphone jack. In this case, you need a cable that has the matching connector to your headphone jack (male ¼-inch or 3.5-millimeter) with the mono ¼-inch plug on the other end. It doesn't really matter whether the headphone plug is stereo because you won't be reproducing that imaging anyway. You more commonly find a mono ¼-inch or 3.5-millimeter plug to the mono ¼-inch plug you need for the amp/powered speaker.

If you need to use a PA system (possibly in your church, a school, or a small coffeehouse), you connect your ¼-inch line outputs to two channels of the mixer, which always has ¼-inch jacks. Therefore, two normal line/instrument cables will do. Be sure to locate a control called *pan* and set one channel all the way left and the other all the way right so your sound comes out of both speakers in true stereo. Some mixers have stereo channels, which simply means that one channel can accept two ¼-inch inputs and doesn't need the individual pan control(s). It will have one knob called *balance,* which should be kept straight up.

Protecting Your Investment: Care and Upkeep

Your electronic keyboard doesn't require much maintenance; that's one of the major advantages of it over an acoustic or electro-mechanical instrument. That said, it's not indestructible, so in the following sections, I detail a few things you should know about keeping it safe and in good shape.

One of the most important things to remember while playing, cleaning, moving, or just displaying your keyboard is that water and electronics aren't good friends! Don't douse your instrument with water while cleaning or keep any drinks, vases, or calming waterfalls near it. Be on the lookout for children and overly zealous house/party/club guests carrying beverages near your prized possession. If anything liquid does spill on the keyboard, turn the instrument off immediately, unplug it, and wipe up the spill with a soft cloth. If you fear any liquid got inside the case, don't use the keyboard again until a skilled technician can look inside and assess the possible damage.

Avoiding temperature extremes

Electronics don't operate well in extreme temperature conditions, period. I doubt you're going to be playing your keyboard at midday in the Mojave Desert or jamming outside in the middle of winter, but other situations can still expose it to extreme temperature conditions.

The most common scenario is leaving it in your car when you move it to bring it to a friend's house or to a place you're going to play (church, school, club, or whatever). Closed cars can get very hot in the summer and very cold in the winter, so try not to leave the keyboard in these conditions for a long period. Get to where you're going and take the keyboard out of the car right away. Don't leave it in the car overnight; always bring it into the building.

Be especially careful about the display and other plastic parts, which can disfigure easily in extremely hot, direct sunlight. If you're playing outside, try to ensure that the stage area is under some shade, whether that's from a building, a tree, or some kind of tent or umbrella.

If the keyboard has been exposed to very cold conditions, allow it to come back to room temperature before turning it on. Feel the front panel or case to judge when it has warmed up enough. These changes of conditions can also cause some condensation to build up on the case or inside the unit. Be sure to wipe off any you see.

Combating dust with a keyboard cover

A little dust or dirt on the outside of the case looks sloppy, but the real problem occurs when that grime gets into the buttons, switches, and sliders; inside the case; or stuck between the keys. These items can all quit working reliably when blocked by these contaminants.

Acoustic pianos and some digital pianos have a folding or sliding lid to cover the keys. Always keep this cover closed to protect the keys when you aren't playing.

If you plan to leave your instrument in the open and it doesn't have a built-in cover, I recommend protecting it with a nice-looking cloth or towel. Better yet, you can buy a dust cover; look online for companies (such Gator, Kaces, Keywear, LeCover, Odyssey, OnStage, Road Runner, and so on) that make them for various specific sizes and models or stretchy generic sizes (small, medium, and large).

If you or someone you know is handy, try home-sewn functional dust covers made from a nice fabric. All the keyboards in my home studio (and there are a lot!) have nice Hawaiian flower print covers thanks to my wife's skills.

Cleaning the keys and case

From time to time, dust and fingerprints show up on your instrument. The case, the keys, and especially a touch-display need to be cleaned periodically. As I note earlier in the chapter, water is a no-go, so what should you use?

Most manufacturers recommend a soft, dry cloth to begin with. I like to use those disposable feather dusters to remove light dust or dirt. I always start from the back of the key and wipe forward, so I'm bringing any dust/dirt particles forward to the edge of the key where I can remove them. If dust has gotten into the knobs or sliders, you can use compressed air to blow them clean. Look for products that were designed for computers, cameras, and electronics.

You can graduate to a slightly dampened cloth if needed as long as you wring out most of the liquid. For tough stains, you can use a mild, nonabrasive cleanser in the cloth. You should never use any form of benzene, thinner, alcohol, or solvent on the keys or case. These products can mar or disfigure the plastic.

A dry microfiber cloth, like you'd use for eyeglasses, is the best solution for touchscreens. Any good dry product for cleaning eyeglasses is going to be safe. Some of the well-known cleaning products companies make electronic wipes or electronic cleaning cloths that are safe for computer screens, keyboard displays, and the like.

Moving from place to place

If you plan to transport your keyboard often, you should invest in a case or padded carrying bag for it. These items protect the keyboard from scratches and worse while making it easier to lift and carry. A thickly padded bag is fine for most situations, but if you need to stack a lot of things in the car and want to put stuff on top of the keyboard, look for bags that offer a solid or reinforced wall design, or consider getting a hard shell case.

You may think there's no harm in just sitting your smaller portable on the backseat while you make the short trip to practice, but you never know when you may need to slam on the brakes. The jerk who cut you off probably won't care that your keyboard just went crashing onto the floor, but you will. Better to put it safely in the trunk for the trip

For heavy keyboards, look into rolling bags or cases, which have sturdy wheels on one end so you don't have to carry the instrument when going along flat surfaces. If you need to carry more gear than just the keyboard, consider getting a folding rolling cart or convertible hand truck.

Whatever you choose, don't be afraid to ask someone for help when lifting a larger keyboard onto a stand, taking it down again, carrying a case, and taking it out/putting it into your car.

Here's a little upkeep tip for you yourself on moving the keyboard: Always lift heavy things with your legs, not with a bent back.

Solving Technical Problems

As with any electronic device, sometimes things go wrong with a keyboard. It may show funny symbols in its display, lock up or freeze, or simply not make sound. Perhaps you're just not sure how to do something or whether your keyboard can even do what you're thinking of. Here are a few tips to help you figure out what's wrong and what to do:

✔ If you hear anything funny or the unit freezes, the first action you take should be to turn it off, wait a few moments, and then turn it back on again. (Don't forget to turn the volume down on all your speakers and such). Sometimes the device just needs a fresh reboot.

✔ If restarting doesn't resolve the issue, look to your manual. Most owner's manuals include a basic troubleshooting section toward the back that goes over the most common scenarios users face. It may show you how to *reinitialize* the instrument, which resets it to from-the-factory status.

✔ If you've spilled any liquid in your keyboard or think something (dust, dirt, bugs, small candy, or whatever) has gotten inside the case, *never* try to open the unit yourself to look inside. Even with the unit off and the power cable removed from the wall, the insides of any electronic device aren't a safe place. You can get shocked or hurt worse by touching the wrong thing. Not to mention that you'll instantly void your warranty coverage. Leave this type of work to the professionals!

✔ Go online to the manufacturer's website and look in the support section for any frequently asked questions (FAQs) related to your product. As the name implies, these queries come up all the time, so the company writes a good explanation to keep from answering the same questions over and over.

✔ Search the entire web for your problem with your favorite search engine. Make sure the most pertinent keywords are in your search text, including the brand name, model name and number, and main issue terms.

Many brands have growing online communities, often not run by or directly affiliated with the company itself. These outlets can be great places to not only find answers to your problems but also meet other owners and share the fun of your product and music in general. Be sure to search these sites for answers before asking a question; often, the issue has come up before and has already been addressed. You may also want to try searching the web for general keywords such as "digital piano," "synthesizer," or "arrangers."

✔ If you still can't find your answer, try contacting the manufacturer's product support or customer service department. These departments often post their hours of operation and methods of contact on the company website. You may be able to e-mail the company or fill out an online form, which can save you a lot of hold time waiting on the phone. Unless you like hearing on-hold music and pitches for the other gear the company makes!

Know that these replies can often come hours, if not days, after you submit them, so if you absolutely need to get help right away, call and stay on the line. Be patient; expect that it's going to take some time to reach someone, so don't get frustrated right away.

See Chapter 18 for a list of popular and helpful sites for electronic keyboards in general.

Part II
Dipping Your ~~Toes~~ Fingers into Music Basics

Illustration by Lisa Reed

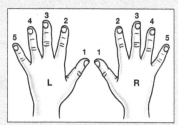

Illustration by Lisa Reed

Illustration by Jerry Kovarsky

web extras Find out about more-advanced chords with a free article at www.dummies.com/extras/keyboard.

In this part . . .

✔ Discover the elements of written music notation, including the staff, key signatures, note names, rhythmic divisions, and much more.

✔ Get your hands onto the keys — in the right way. Practicing good form and fingering is an essential part of playing the keyboard.

✔ Make beautiful music with basic chords and inversions.

Chapter 5

Musical Notation: Decoding the Musical Language

Can you imagine getting through your life without being able to read? "Sorry, officer, I didn't understand that little sign back there." "Just sign my name here? Okay!" Reading is easy to take for granted because it's so helpful in so many aspects of everyday life; you can't imagine not using it as a resource.

As a musician, there comes a time when being able to read the musical language can really help you. Sure, you can sometimes get away with playing by ear and just memorizing songs. Someone can show you how to play a song, and you hope you remember it. Plenty of famous musicians in lots of genres work(ed) this way. But if you read music, you can learn a new song from some sheet music, you can follow along in a lesson book without a teacher present, and you can tackle longer, more complex pieces of music.

Don't worry if those lines and figures and little dots don't make sense to you. In this chapter, I break it all down into easy-to-understand elements and decode the mysteries of the musical language so you can quickly see the basic structures of written music.

This chapter is only a brief tour of some of the main elements of musical notation. I strongly recommend you seek out further resources and instruction in this area. *Piano For Dummies* by Blake Neely (Wiley) is a great place to start. So is a real live teacher! Taking some lessons, seeking out a music school or store or community college course, or even watching some YouTube videos can really help you. Reading about playing can only do so much; seeing and hearing concepts discussed and played in real time can do a lot to make them clearer.

Getting Acquainted with Notes on the Keyboard

One of the beautiful things about keyboards is that they all share the same input mechanism: That familiar stretch of black and white keys is the same, regardless of whether you're playing a piano, an organ, a synth, or a MIDI controller keyboard. Take a look at your keyboard right now and notice that the shorter black keys are laid out in a repeating pattern — a group of two black keys always followed by a group of three black keys, as shown in Figure 5-1. This repeating pattern is your key to finding the various notes on the keyboard. You actually only need to remember 12 different notes (the sum of the white and black keys within that pattern), and they keep repeating all up and down the keyboard and up and down the musical staff (which I introduce later in the chapter).

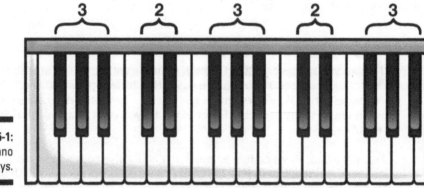

Figure 5-1:
The piano keys.

Illustration by Lisa Reed

Scoring a C-note: Finding C on the keyboard

Look at the black key groupings and find a group of two. The white key just below/to the left of the first black key in the group is the note C. Play it. Sounds nice, right? Now go to every one of those white keys just below the group of two black keys and play them (see Figure 5-2). They all sound nice and seem to be related to each other. You can play any of them together and they sound good. That's because they're all different versions of the same note, C. Some are higher sounding, and some are lower, but they're all the note C.

Figure 5-2:
Locating C
on the
keyboard.

Illustration by Lisa Reed

On the full 88-key piano keyboard, the C note in the middle of the range is called (wait for it) *middle C*. A lot of keyboard instruction books use middle C as a starting place, and so do I. If you have a piano or 88-note keyboard, you can count the C notes starting at the bottom; this note is the fourth C you come to. That's why another name for middle C is C4. This name comes in handy when you start using MIDI (see Chapter 13) and when you have a keyboard with fewer than 88 keys.

Each grouping of notes starting with the C is called an *octave*. So the groups of two and then three black keys (plus the seven white notes) are an octave. That's what the numbering system refers to: octave 1, octave 2, and so on. A full piano keyboard (88 notes) has seven octaves plus a few extra notes on the bottom. Most other keyboards have even groupings of octaves (ranging from C to C): A 25-key controller has 2 octaves, 37 keys means 3 octaves, 49 keys has 4 octaves, 61 keys equals 5 octaves, and 73 keys means 6 octaves. You sometimes see 32-key and 76-key keyboards; they have a few extra notes on the top or bottom of their ranges.

Exploring the white keys

With C as your anchor or home base, you can identify the rest of the notes. The basic musical language works like the beginning of the alphabet: A, B, C, D, E, F, and G. For music, things stop there and then start to repeat. You've got to admit, that's a lot easier than learning 26 different names, right?

I know what you're thinking. "If it's like the alphabet, shouldn't I start with A, not C?" That strategy seems to make sense at first blush, but as you learn the sound of the notes and the layout of the keyboard as it relates to scales and key signatures (which I cover later in the chapter), it just doesn't work that way.

Starting with middle C, you can go up the white notes on the keyboard (as shown in Figure 5-3) to C, D, E, F, and finally G, and then the alphabet starts over with A. Repeat and repeat as needed.

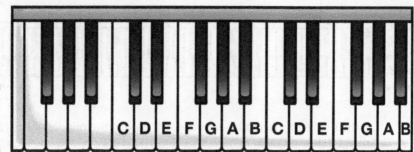

Figure 5-3:
The white
note names.

Illustration by Lisa Reed

Playing these notes in order may sound familiar to you musically. That's because those notes form what is called the *C major scale*. Have you ever heard or sung the song "Doe, a Deer" (actually called "Do-Re-Mi") from *The Sound of Music?* Do, re, mi, fa, sol, la, ti, do. The white notes all form this scale, making it the easiest one to pick up on the keyboard. That's another reason C is a good home base; that key and scale don't require the use of any of the black notes.

Just as you can use the group of two black keys to help find C, you can use the group of three black keys to always find F, which is located just below them. You may also start to remember that B is located just above the three black keys, and then your groupings start again.

Stepping up or down with the black keys

If the lettered note names are all associated with only the white keys (as explained in the preceding section), what's the deal with the black keys? They have names as well, but they're a little more complicated to explain. The black keys are commonly called the *sharp* and/or *flat* keys. (Yes, they can be both sharp and flat depending on what key you're in; you can read more about this topic in the later section "Weighing in on major scales.") For now, think of them this way:

✔ If you're moving upward (to the right) without missing any keys, you can call the black key by the name of the previous note and add the word *sharp* to it. So from C, you move up to the adjacent black note and call it C sharp (commonly notated with what looks like the pound sign: C♯). The black key above the F would be called F♯, and so on. Remember it this way: Something sharp has a raised edge, so you raise the note.

✔ If you're moving down from (to the left of) a note without missing any keys, you can call the lower black note the previous note name and add the word *flat* to it. So from G you move down to the adjacent black note and call it G flat (commonly notated as ♭: G♭). Something that's flattened is lower than it was.

Figure 5-4 labels all the sharp notes, moving up from C. Figure 5-5 goes the opposite direction, labeling all the flat notes moving down from C.

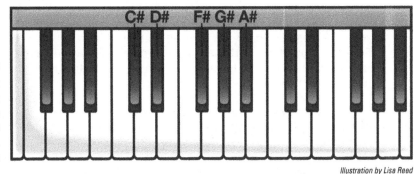

Figure 5-4:
The black notes labeled as sharps.

Illustration by Lisa Reed

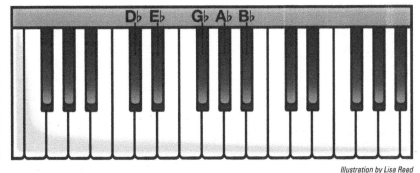

Figure 5-5:
The black notes labeled as flats.

Illustration by Lisa Reed

Making Sense of Music Notation

When you know the basic layout of the notes on the keyboard and their names, you've got a good foundation for understanding how the written musical language is communicated on the written page. (For details on these foundational elements, head to the earlier section "Getting Acquainted with Notes on the Keyboard.")

Music notation conveys a number of things, including what note to play. In the following sections, I break down each aspect of notation so you understand each element individually.

Sizing up the staff: Treble and bass clef

Long ago, the early music scholars came up with a system of lines and spaces called a *staff* or *stave* to represent notes or pitches. This setup worked fine for most instruments, but was too limited to represent the complicated nature of piano music. After all, you've got up to 88 keys/notes to cover and parts for 2 hands; communicating all that on a single line is pretty difficult. So they grouped two of these staves together so one could cover the higher notes and the other the lower ones. As a keyboardist, you need to know about both of them.

Each staff is a grouping of five lines and four spaces. The *clef* — either treble or bass — tells you what names to give those lines and spaces. The following sections delve into each of these clefs.

Starting with the treble clef (your right hand)

Simplistically, you can think of the upper staff, called the *treble clef,* as the right hand part. Figure 5-6 illustrates this clef with each part labeled.

Treble clef

Figure 5-6:
The treble
clef staff of
music.

Illustration by Jerry Kovarsky

From the bottom up, the lines are E, G, B, D, and F. Students traditionally use easy-to-remember phrases (called *mnemonic devices*) to memorize these notes, such as "Every Good Boy Does Fine" or "Elephants Get Big Dirty Feet." Some consider the first option sexist in today's politically correct society, and perhaps others feel the second is disparaging to elephants, who are nice creatures. So feel free to make up your own!

The lines skip a note each time; those notes — F, A, C, and E from bottom to top — are located in the spaces in between. "FACE" is an easy enough mnemonic to remember them, but you can make up a phrase if that helps you. So the treble staff represents the E above middle C to the F an octave above middle C.

If you need to go above or below the staff, you just add one or more small extra lines to each individual note to represent how much farther up or down it is. So going down from the low E on the staff, you have the D in space below, and then a note head with a short line through it to represent the next line note, middle C. Figure 5-7 shows some examples of notes above and below the staff of the treble clef.

Figure 5-7:
Notes
outside of
the treble
clef staff.

Illustration by Jerry Kovarsky

In the beginning of your reading studies, you should identify notes by counting the names up (or down) from the last line of the staff. So for the fourth note in Figure 5-7, you count from the high F line up past G (space), A (the first additional line), and B (the space above the added line) to come to the high C, which is on the second additional line. Over time, you'll come to instantly recognize the notes within two lines above and below the staff, and then you'll only have to count up (or down) from those.

Meeting the bass clef (your left hand)

The lower staff of full piano music is called the *bass clef.* It uses the same concepts as the treble clef in the preceding section, but the names of the lines and spaces are different. Looking at Figure 5-8 from the bottom upward, you can see the lines are G, B, D, F, and A. Common mnemonics to memorize include "Good Boys Do Fine Always" and "Great Big Dogs Fight Animals." Or make up your own; I'm partial to "Grizzly Bears Don't Fly Airplanes."

The spaces are A, C, E, and G from bottom to top. "All Cows Eat Grass" is an easy enough mnemonic to remember them, but as always, you can make up another phrase if you'd prefer.

Bass clef

Figure 5-8:
The bass
clef staff of
music.

Illustration by Jerry Kovarsky

The notes above and below the bass clef staff are represented by the same method as I outline in the preceding section. Figure 5-9 has some examples.

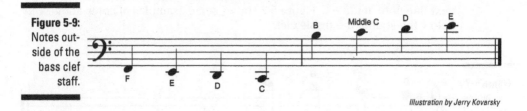

Figure 5-9: Notes outside of the bass clef staff.

Illustration by Jerry Kovarsky

Recognizing sharps and flats

If you read and play the notes of the lines and spaces, you play all white keys on the piano. You can easily find the A, B, C pattern and see how it repeats as you climb up either clef. To represent the black key notes, a symbol (commonly called an *accidental*) is placed before the note head, so you see the symbol before you play the note. Think of the accidental as a modifier for the note that follows. You may recognize these symbols from the earlier section "Stepping up or down with the black keys;" here, you're simply attaching them to the physical note rather than the written-out note name. Check out Figure 5-10 for some examples of these symbols placed before notes.

Figure 5-10: Sharps and flats are placed before notes.

Illustration by Jerry Kovarsky

In that earlier section, I classify flats and sharps as black keys adjacent to white keys as a general guideline, but that isn't strictly the case. The real rule involves what's called a half step. The *half step* is the smallest distance you can move on the keyboard, meaning there are no notes in between. So a sharp sign tells you to play the note a half step above the displayed note, and a flat tells you to play the note a half step below.

Looking at the keyboard in Figure 5-11, you can see two places where you don't have an adjacent black key to use: between the B and the C and between the E and the F.

Figure 5-11: No black keys appear between B and C and between E and F.

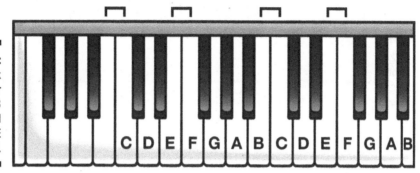

Illustration by Lisa Reed

These four notes are the exceptions to the "adjacent black key" guideline. The very next note above B on the keyboard is C. So to play a B♯, you actually play the white key C. To play a C♭, you play the white note B. To play an F♭, you play the next note lower from F, which is the white key E. And to play an E♯, you play the white note F.

Weighing in on major scales

A *scale* is basically a set series of adjacent notes. Earlier in the chapter, I mention the C major scale, but it's just one of many major scales. The sound of the major scale is defined by the size of the steps between each note; it is comprised of two whole steps, a half step, three more whole steps, and a final half step. Start on any note and follow that rule, and you'll hear a major scale (do, re, mi, fa, sol, la, ti, and do). So if you analyze the C to (shining) C white note scale — the C major scale — you get Figure 5-12.

The major scale isn't the only type of scale. The most common other scales are the minor scales, the chromatic scale, the blues scale, pentatonic scales, and groupings called modes (used in jazz and rock improvisation). They each differ in the groupings of whole and half steps used between the notes and in the number of notes that make up the full scale.

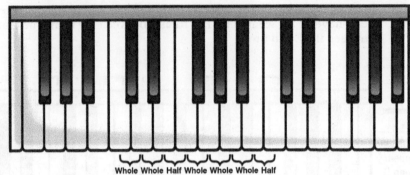

Figure 5-12:
The C major
scale.

Whole Whole Half Whole Whole Whole Half

Illustration by Lisa Reed

Major scales (and all such *diatonic* scales, actually) follow one other rule: You must always use the name of the next note in order without skipping a note name or repeating one twice in a row. So C always follows B, and A always follows G, for example. These restrictions affect how you use sharps or flats to represent the notes in a given scale.

Reading key signatures

Another part of the staff is called the *key signature;* it's shown in Figure 5-13. A song's *key* indicates what scale the song is based on. If a song is always going to need certain accidentals based on the key, the key signature tells you that upfront so that every single affected note doesn't require an accidental. This shortcut keeps printed music from getting cluttered with redundant instructions that keep telling you to always play an F♯, for example. Because the key signature takes care of global sharps and flats, you need accidentals for only notes that are different from that set of instructions.

Figure 5-13:
The key sig-
nature tells
you any flats
or sharps to
always use
for a given
song.

The key signature   The key signature

Key of G major   Key of A major   Key of Bb major   Key of F major   Key of D major   Key of Eb major

Illustration by Jerry Kovarsky

Another rule in music is that if an accidental is shown in a measure, it remains in effect until you cross the bar line. You don't need to put it in front of every affected note within the measure. In Figure 5-14, every F after the first one is played as an F♯ until the beginning of measure 2, when it automatically goes back to the regular F. (Measure and bar line relate to the organization of written music, which I cover in the later section "I've Got The Beat: Discovering How to Count.") So the bar line magically undoes any accidental.

Figure 5-14:
An acciden-
tal remains
in effect
until you
cross a bar
line.

Also an F#   Back to regular Fs

Illustration by Jerry Kovarsky

Say you need to undo an accidental within a measure. Enter the *natural sign* (♮) shown in Figure 5-15. It tells you to now ignore the previous sharp or flat and play the natural note. It doesn't just control accidentals placed within a measure; it can also tell you to not use one of the sharps or flats present in the key signature.

Figure 5-15:
The natural
sign, which
removes
the effect of
a sharp or
flat.

Natural sign   Natural sign

Sharp sign   Sharp sign

Illustration by Jerry Kovarsky

Putting both clefs together: The grand staff

When you understand the basic elements of the clefs, lines, spaces, key signatures, and accidentals in the preceding sections, you can put the two staves together and see the full system used by the piano and keyboards. This *grand staff* is two lines of music joined together, as shown in Figure 5-16. Each line uses different names for the lines and spaces, so seeing both at the same time takes some getting used to.

Figure 5-16: The grand staff joins together the treble and bass clef.

Illustration by Jerry Kovarsky

Beginners don't start reading the grand staff right away; it's better to start with one staff/one hand at a time. But whenever you see these two staves joined as they are in Figure 5-16, you know that it's piano music.

I've Got the Beat: Discovering How to Count

Music notation doesn't just tell you what notes to play; it also has to represent the timing of those notes: when to play them, how long to hold them, when to let go of a note, and such. This timing information is called *rhythm*. In the following sections, I break down how written music conveys rhythm.

Getting to know time signatures

The *time signature* is actually a piece of the staffs in the earlier section "Making Sense of Music Notation." It looks like a fraction (see Figure 5-17), and each number tells you something about how you count the music.

The top number tells you how many beats to count in the music before repeating the numbers. The most common top number is 4, meaning you count 1, 2, 3, 4 and then start again with 1. Some signatures start with a 3, meaning you count 1, 2, 3, 1, 2, 3, and so on. You can hear this signature in waltzes and popular songs such as Billy Joel's "Piano Man," Norah Jones's "Come Away With Me," and Jim Croce's "Time In a Bottle."

Figure 5-17:
The time signature tells you how to count the music.

Time signature

One Two Three Four One Two Three Four One Two Three Four

Illustration by Jerry Kovarsky

The bottom number tells you which type of note gets each beat. So 4 on the bottom stands for a quarter note, just like the fraction 1/4. (I introduce quarter notes in the later section "Understanding quarter notes, half notes, and whole notes.")

4/4 is such a common time signature that it's called *common time* and even has a special symbol to represent it (shown in Figure 5-18).

Feels like three

Another time signature that's often confused with 3/4 is called 6/8. Because it has six beats to the measure, you can feel it as two groups of three and count it 1-2-3-4-5-6. To some people, this setup feels like two bars of 3/4. But the two groups of notes are actually the important part here; they create a feeling of two strong beats that are divided up into three subdivisions. So you really count the measure as **1**-2-3, **2**-2-3, with a strong accent on the bolded

one and two; check out the correct notation in the nearby figure. So popular songs like John Mayer's "Gravity" and Jay Z's "My First Song" are really 6/8 and not 3/4.

Another common time signature that feels like three to some people is 12/8, which has four strong downbeats, each divided up into three subdivisions. This signature is the familiar time feel for older doo-wop and '50s pop tunes.

Illustration by Jerry Kovarsky

Figure 5-18: The common time symbol represents 4/4 time.

Illustration by Jerry Kovarsky

Obeying the measure and bar line

Grouping notes into smaller chunks makes visualizing, reading, and counting the beats easier. The vertical *bar line* is the instruction that tells you to start your counting over again. The range of the staff between two bar lines is called a *measure*. Both are shown in Figure 5-19.

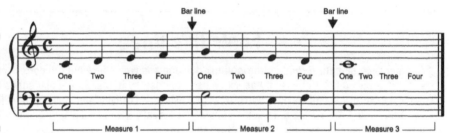

Figure 5-19: The bar line divides the staff into measures.

Illustration by Jerry Kovarsky

The measure contains only the number of beats indicated in the top number of the time signature. At the end of the measure, you know that as you cross the bar line you reset your counting back to 1.

Various types of bar lines tell you that a new section is coming up, that you need to repeat some measures over and over, that you're at the end of the song, and so on, but they're outside the scope of this book.

Understanding quarter notes, half notes, and whole notes

All notes aren't created equal. If they were, music would be very boring, with no rhythm or interest to get you tapping your toes and nodding your head — or whatever you do when the music moves you.

The most basic notes are held for full counts or beats. The first note in Figure 5-20 illustrates the *whole note,* which is held for four counts. (In common time — described in the preceding section — four beats is the full measure. Hence, the name whole note.) The second note in Figure 5-20 is called the *half note* and held for two counts — half a whole note. Notice it has a stem attached to it. This stem may be sticking up from the right side or down from the left side, depending on how far up the staff the note is.

The *quarter note* is the third note in Figure 5-20; it looks like a filled-in half note, with the same stem attached. You hold it for one full count, which is a quarter of a whole note. Now the design of the time signature makes full sense; in 4/4 time, the quarter note gets one full beat (the bottom of the fraction), and the measure has four beats (the top of the fraction) before reaching the bar line!

Figure 5-20:
Whole note, half note, and quarter note.

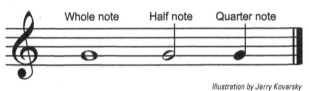

Illustration by Jerry Kovarsky

These three notes are the easiest to read and play because you hold them for full counts. Figure 5-21 shows a simple example of them used together, with the proper counting shown. You can play it with one finger on the keyboard or just clapping the rhythm while counting out loud.

Figure 5-21:
A simple rhythm/ counting exercise in 4/4 time.

Illustration by Jerry Kovarsky

When you're learning a new song, I recommend working on the rhythm this way — just clapping or playing a single note while reading the rhythm, not worrying about pitches at first.

Figure 5-22 shows the same rhythm applied to a melody with different pitches. You can try to play it by pecking at the keys with just your right hand index finger or by put your right hand thumb on middle C and trying to play the melody by using all five fingers. Just be sure to count the notes properly.

Figure 5-22: The 4/4 counting exercise with different pitches for the notes.

Illustration by Jerry Kovarsky

You may wonder, "Why aren't any of the notes held for three beats?" Wonder no more! If you add a dot after the note head, as shown in Figure 5-23, you add half of the note value to the base note. So a dotted half note is held for two counts plus one more count (half of two), for a total of three beats.

Figure 5-23: The dotted half note, which is held for three counts.

Illustration by Jerry Kovarsky

Figure 5-24 applies the same concepts to the time signature of 3/4. Here you have three beats per measure, and the quarter note still gets one beat. You don't use the whole note in 3/4 because you only count to three before the bar line/end of the measure. So the dotted half note becomes the full measure note.

Figure 5-24:
A simple rhythm/ counting exercise in 3/4 time.

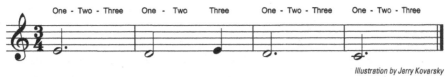

Illustration by Jerry Kovarsky

Playing eighth notes and more

You can play a lot of music by using the whole, half, and quarter notes in the preceding section. But the rhythm gets even more interesting when you have some notes that play faster than the main beat and when they occur in between the beats. In the following sections, I show you how to count the beat differently to fit in smaller note divisions and then introduce the notes themselves.

Dividing the beat

To get the hang of playing in between full-beat notes, you need to be able to count the beat in a divided fashion. Try this:

1. **Start counting a 4/4 pulse, saying "1, 2, 3, 4" over and over in time.**

2. **When you're comfortable, try saying "and" between each number: "1 and 2 and 3 and 4 and . . . ."**

   The 1, 2, 3, 4 are still in the same place, with the *and* occurring quickly in between (see Figure 5-25 for a visual representation of the concept).

Figure 5-25:
Dividing the beat into two equal parts.

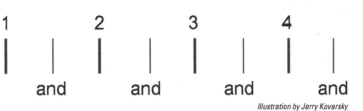

Illustration by Jerry Kovarsky

Listen to Track 22 to hear this divided counting exercise.

In this exercise, you divide the beat into two equal parts: the downbeat and the upbeat. The beat on which you say the number is the *downbeat,* the primary pulse in your counting. You say the *and* on the in-between beat, called the *upbeat.*

Applying the divided beat to eighth and sixteenth notes

When you divide the quarter note into two equal halves, they're represented by the note shown in Figure 5-26, called the *eighth note.* It's filled in like the quarter note but has a curly flag design on the stem. When you have more than one eighth note in a row, you connect the stems with a beam also shown in Figure 5-26.

Figure 5-26:
The eighth note divides the beat into two equal parts.

Eighth note   One   and   Two   and   Three   and   Four   and

Illustration by Jerry Kovarsky

The eighth note gets half of a beat, so when you're counting music that has eighth notes you should use the *and* between the numbers. As you get comfortable, you can learn to play two notes per beat without counting each one.

You can further divide the eighth note in half; the resulting note is called the *sixteenth note.* It looks like an eighth note with a double flag or double beam attached (see Figure 5-27). It divides the main pulse or beat into four equal parts. You count that this way: "1-ee-and-ah, 2-ee-and-ah, 3-ee-and-ah, 4-ee-and-ah," and so on.

Figure 5-27:
The sixteenth note divides the beat into four equal parts.

One - ee - and - ah   Two - ee - and - ah   Three-ee-and-ah   Four-ee-and-ah

Sixteenth note

Illustration by Jerry Kovarsky

Try keeping a steady beat (clapping or tapping your foot) and practice counting a few bars of quarter notes (1, 2, 3, 4 . . .). Then move to eighth notes, which are twice as fast (1 and, 2 and, 3 and, 4 and . . .). Move next to sixteenth notes, which are twice as fast as the eighth notes (1-ee-and-ah, 2-ee-and-ah, 3-ee-and-ah, 4-ee-and-ah . . .). Go back to the quarter notes and then try sixteenth notes again; now they're four times as fast. Be sure your clapping/tapping of the pulse stays the same (on the numbers); only your speaking of the rhythm is changing speed.

Track 23 demonstrates this alternating counting exercise.

Feeling confident? Try it the other way around! Keep counting only 1, 2, 3, 4; try clapping quarter notes (one clap for each number spoken) and then move to clapping eighth notes (two even claps for each number spoken). Don't change your counting; don't say "and" in between. Just clap twice for each number spoken. When you can go back and forth between clapping quarter and eighth notes, try going to sixteenth notes (four even claps per number spoken). It will be twice as fast as the eighth notes or four times as fast as your counting. Be sure to keep your counting perfectly steady at all times.

Listen to Track 24 to hear this alternating counting exercise.

Holding notes longer than a measure: Ties

When you want a note to hold across the bar line or for a different number of beats than any of the note types will allow, you use a symbol called a *tie*. This curved line (shown in Figure 5-28) connects two notes of the same pitch; when you see it, you don't restrike the second note; you just keep counting through the second held note.

Figure 5-28:
The tie symbol is used to add additional time to a sustaining note.

Illustration by Jerry Kovarsky

Depending on the rhythm, you also see ties used to add some additional time to a note within a single measure when a common note type could've been used. The purpose is to show the middle of the bar or the strong downbeats clearly, making the music easier to read.

Knowing when not to play: Rests

Written music isn't all constant notes; sometimes it includes spaces or even long stretches of silence. The symbols used to tell you to not play any notes for some period of time are called *rests,* and they follow the same rules for counting. Each duration of note I outline in the preceding sections — including dotted notes — has a corresponding rest (see Figure 5-29).

Figure 5-29:
The various
rest
symbols.

Illustration by Jerry Kovarsky

The rests are pretty easy to visualize, though some people get confused at first between the whole rest and half rest. Just remember that the whole rest hangs down from a line into the top of the space, and the half rest sits on a line on the bottom of the space.

Figure 5-30 shows a simple exercise involving notes and rests, with no dividing of the beat. Try practicing it first with a single note on the keyboard (index finger on middle C), not worrying about changing pitches. Be sure to lift your finger from the key for each rest; don't leave the note ringing out while you count the rest. Then try it with your thumb on middle C and use the other fingers.

Figure 5-30:
A simple
exercise
with whole
beat notes
and rests.

Illustration by Jerry Kovarsky

Check out Track 25 to hear the whole note/whole rest exercise.

The exercise in Figure 5-31 starts using eighth notes and eighth note rests. First work on just the rhythm without changing pitches; try the pitches when you're comfortable.

Figure 5-31:
A simple exercise including eighth notes and rests.

Illustration by Jerry Kovarsky

Track 26 demonstrates the eighth note/eighth rest exercise.

Using a metronome to help your timing

A *metronome* is a device that clicks in steady rhythm to help you practice your rhythm and time-keeping. Older versions were a vertical wooden case with a metal wand that swung back and forth. You had to wind them up to go. How quaint!

Nowadays, you can buy electric/electronic metronomes, or even metronome apps, that have lots of advanced features. Actually, you likely have a metronome already built into your keyboard. It may be labeled clearly, or it may simply be a click function that's part of your onboard MIDI recorder. (Check out Chapter 13 for info on MIDI recording.)

For many musicians, a metronome is a way of checking what tempo or speed a piece of music is supposed to be played at. The beginning of the music is marked in some fashion, often "♩ = XX," where XX is whatever tempo the composer wants. This designation means the main pulse or beat happens XX times per minute. You set that number on the metronome, and then the device clicks away at that speed to give you a reference.

I recommend that, as a student, you use a metronome to provide you with a steady pulse to play against. The tempo can be very slow; you're using it to help you practice steady counting.

Here's a sample experiment for practicing with a metronome:

1. **Set a slow tempo on the metronome to represent the quarter note and try any or all of the counting examples in this chapter with the metronome as an aid.**

2. **Stop the metronome and try counting for yourself.**

   The idea is to develop a steady internal clock for keeping time so that you don't use the metronome as a crutch.

3. **Set the metronome twice as fast and think of the click as the eighth note rather than the quarter.**

   You'll play the same, but it takes some getting used to not to be sped up by the extra clicks.

4. **Repeat Steps 1 through 3, moving the tempo to various settings and getting a feel for how they sound largely the same, only faster or slower.**

As you get more confident with the preceding exercise, set the metronome to a slow tempo and let that represent the half note, so it only clicks twice per measure. As it first clicks, say "1, 3, 1, 3 . . . ," one word with each click. Then fill in between the clicks with the 2 and the 4 until you can comfortably count all four beats against the two clicks. When that counting gets comfortable, try playing one of the examples in this chapter against the half-note click. Not as easy as it may seem! This test will really show whether you're rushing ahead of the beat or falling behind.

Listen to Track 27 to hear this metronome counting exercise.

Chapter 6

Developing Your Fingering and Basic Technique

Knowing what notes to play seems like the important part of playing a song. But it's how you actually play the notes that make a performance smooth and professional or clumsy and even painful. As a child, my first two influences were Bugs Bunny (yes, the cartoon rabbit) and Chico Marx. Unfortunately I later learned that their methods of playing weren't the best approach (and seem almost physically impossible — look them up online to see for yourself)!

You should concentrate on two main areas as you first develop your keyboard technique:

✔ **The physical shape and position of your hand and fingers:** Using a good hand shape and finger position lets you easily move from note to note, reach notes that may be a bit farther away, and prepare yourself for developing better and better technique, where you can play faster and move across the whole range of the keyboard easily.

✔ **Good fingering:** *Fingering* refers to choosing which finger to use to play each note and when (and how) you move your whole hand position to reach notes outside of your hand's natural reach. No single way of doing this is "right," but some choices are smarter than others.

In this chapter, I discuss the basics of these two principles and show you how to connect your notes, both by finger technique alone and then by using the sustain or damper pedal. You gain good insight into how to make your practice time as productive as possible and how to methodically master difficult passages of music in a short time.

This chapter refers to a lot of the fundamental music reading concepts in Chapter 5. If you're unfamiliar with reading music and haven't checked out that chapter, I recommend you head there now.

Getting in Playing Position

Playing a keyboard involves your whole body. Just wiggling your fingers about isn't enough; you need to consider your sitting/standing position, your neck and shoulders, your arms and wrists, and even your legs and feet. Good position and posture helps you to play better and to avoid any pain that can arise from developing bad habits, as I discuss in the following sections.

Assuming the position: Proper playing posture

First things first: Playing a keyboard should never hurt, cramp, or fatigue your hands, wrists, arms, or shoulders. Good playing posture is an important part of your technique and very important to avoid pain and fatigue; here are some guidelines for getting in the right position:

- ✔ **Relax your hands.** You don't need to keep them tense or to use undue pressure to hold the note down. After you've played a key, any further movements don't affect how the note sounds.
- ✔ **Be sure your back is straight and you aren't lifting your shoulders.**
- ✔ **If you're feeling any strain or pain, stop right away and reconsider your physical position.**

When you sit at the keyboard, your arms should hang relaxed from the shoulder. Bend your elbows so your arm forms a straight line from the elbow across the wrists to the fingers, as shown in Figure 6-1. If you're sitting too high or too low, this straight line may not happen; you should either adjust the height of your chair/bench or the stand the keyboard is on. I discuss stand adjustment more in Chapter 4.

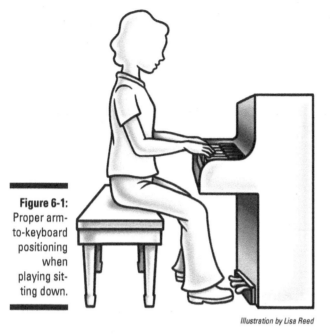

Figure 6-1:
Proper arm-
to-keyboard
positioning
when
playing sit-
ting down.

Illustration by Lisa Reed

If you're standing while playing, you still want the same level arm position, at least for your main piano-type keyboard. If you're using multiple keyboards stacked vertically on the same stand, the upper keyboard can't be at the perfect position, but try not to position it too high; your arms and shoulders will fatigue quickly when reaching up to play it.

Shaping your hand and fingers

How you hold your hand and shape your fingers enables you to use them as little hammers to easily play notes and move your hand position around the keyboard. Here's a simple trick to form the perfect bent finger position:

1. **Lay your hand flat on a table/surface, as shown in Figure 6-2.**

2. **Keeping the heel of your palm on the surface, slowly pull your fingers in so they curl inward.**

    The back of your hand (at the knuckles) will rise up a bit as you do this step. When your fingertips are on the surface, you're in good position; refer to Figure 6-3.

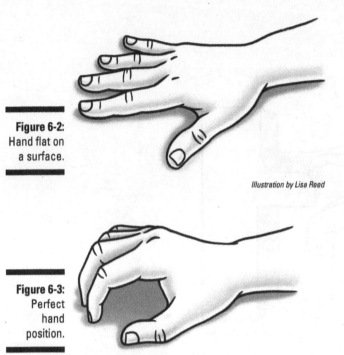

Figure 6-2:
Hand flat on
a surface.

Illustration by Lisa Reed

Figure 6-3:
Perfect
hand
position.

Illustration by Lisa Reed

TIP

Some teachers describe this position as looking like you could cup a small tennis ball in your hand. You can try that as well. The result is that your fingers are arched nicely, the tips of your fingers are ready to touch the keys, and your thumb forms a straight line back to your wrist and across your forearm.

Putting Your Hands in Place

When you've got hand shaping down (see the preceding section), you're ready to place your well-shaped hands onto the keys. The following sections help you get the hang of setting and changing the position of your fingers as you play keyboard.

Numbering your fingers

The easiest way to communicate what finger to use is to assign numbers to them. The common approach is to call the thumb 1 and continue across the hand in order, ending up with the pinkie as 5 as Figure 6-4 illustrates.

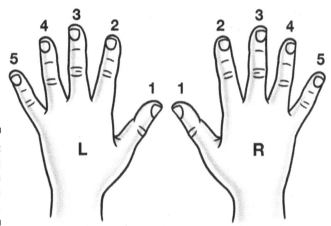

Figure 6-4: Numbering the fingers of each hand.

Illustration by Lisa Reed

Most lesson books and piano music use this numbering system to suggest the best fingering to use for each piece. I recommend you start by using the fingerings marked on the page, but you can eventually make changes if you find a better option for your hand size.

Trying out some basic placement exercises

Ready to actually play your keyboard? Place your right hand with your thumb (1) on middle C. Let your other fingers each cover the successive white keys (D through G). Keep your hand arched and be sure the tips of your fingers — not the soft, flat pads — are on the keys. Refer to Figure 6-5 for a good example.

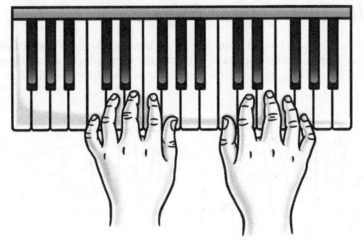

Figure 6-5:
The right hand in position on middle C.

Illustration by Lisa Reed

Now play the following music example (Figure 6-6), using the fingers as marked and holding each note for a full two-beat count. At a slow tempo, play the right hand alone first and then the left hand alone. Increase the speed as you get comfortable. When you feel confident, try both hands together.

Figure 6-6:
Playing two-beat counts with each hand.

Illustration by Jerry Kovarsky

Because your hands are built opposite, each hand uses different fingers to play the same note. Don't let this setup confuse you!

As you play, make sure that one note connects cleanly to the next. While your first note is sounding, you start to press down the next finger; at the moment that finger reaches the bottom (and sounds), you release the first note. This way, you have no space between the two notes but also no overlap. (In cases where the music actually calls for you not to connect the notes, you see specific symbols called *rests* that I discuss in Chapter 5.)

Listen to Track 28 to hear this example played.

Next, try the exercise in Figure 6-7, which mixes up the order of the fingers a little bit and holds each note for only one beat. Do it one hand at a time, slowly, and then try putting them together.

Figure 6-7:
Playing one-
beat counts
with each
hand.

Illustration by Jerry Kovarsky

Track 29 demonstrates this example.

These are some examples of simple patterns to develop your fingering and facility. Plenty of piano exercise books are available to further develop your chops. I used a book called *Preparatory Exercises, Opus 16 for The Piano* by Aloys Schmitt (Alfred Music) when I was teaching. You can also check out David Pearl's *Piano Exercises For Dummies* (Wiley).

Playing in one position

Not many songs let you play keeping your hands in the same place, covering the same five notes for the whole song. But I want to give you a chance to try something where each hand is playing a different part while staying in the same position. So here's a simple version of Beethoven's "Ode To Joy" from his Ninth Symphony (see Figure 6-8).

Practice each hand separately at first, slowly and then faster as you get comfortable. When you try putting the hands together, do it slowly, counting carefully. Note the dotted quarter note, which gets a count and a half (1 and 2), followed by an eighth note, which gets the last half of beat 2 (and).

Check out Track 30 to hear this example played with hands separately and then together.

Ode To Joy

Figure 6-8:
Hand independence ("Ode To Joy").

Moving to another position

The example in Figure 6-8 in the preceding section is in the key of C major, which uses only the white keys. You can also play the same piece in other positions; the next easiest is in G major. Place your right hand thumb on G and your left hand pinkie on G, as shown in Figure 6-9.

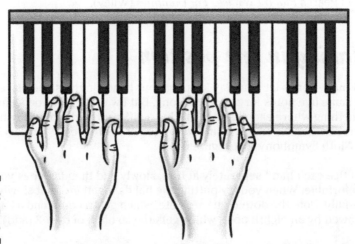

Figure 6-9:
Hands in the G position.

Now you can play the same example, just following the fingering instructions from Figure 6-8. Or you can read it correctly notated in the key of G major in Figure 6-10.

Ode To Joy

Figure 6-10: "Ode To Joy" in G major.

Illustration by Jerry Kovarsky

Try one more key, shown in Figure 6-11. Place your right hand thumb on D, and move your third finger onto the black key F♯. You're setting up the key of D major, which uses two sharp keys to form its major scale (you don't need the C♯ for this song). Your left hand pinkie goes on D and your third finger goes onto the F♯ black key.

Ode To Joy

Figure 6-11: "Ode To Joy" in D major.

Illustration by Jerry Kovarsky

Listen to Track 31 to hear Figures 6-10 and 6-11 played.

Stretching farther than five notes — and coming back

To play songs that require more than five notes, you need to move your hand position around. The simplest technique is to stretch a bit farther than the close five-note grouping and to then move the fingers to a new position. Figure 6-12 uses a well-known J.S. Bach melody to show how this approach can work. Pay attention to the key signature, which tells you to use F♯ in bar 3 (this example is in the key of G major).

Minuet

Figure 6-12: Stretching beyond five notes.

Illustration by Jerry Kovarsky

For the first note in bar 3, you need to stretch your third finger up pretty far to reach the E. Start to stretch up to the note while playing the two Gs at the end of bar 2. This way, you're ready for the note before it's time to play it. When you play the E, you bring your thumb back up quickly to the C, and your hand shape is back in the comfortable five-finger position. Then at bar 4, you bring your thumb back down to the lower G to finish the phrase. For that last bar, your hand is now covering a full octave, from G to G. This position is another important hand shape, which you use when playing chords. (That, however, is a discussion for Chapter 7.)

Track 32 plays this example.

Making Smooth Crossings

Stretching works well for medium moves in hand position, but often you need to move across more than five notes all occurring in a row. The two techniques in the following sections will cover all these instances.

Crossing a finger over

When you've played from the pinkie to the thumb and need to continue, you have to bring a finger — the second, third, or fourth finger — over the thumb. The easiest instance is where you just need the one extra note and then can return to your usual five-finger shape, as shown in Figure 6-13.

Figure 6-13: Crossing over a finger to momentarily play an extra note.

Illustration by Jerry Kovarsky

This phrase (also from the J.S. Bach Minuet in G Major) requires you to play the F♯ in bar 3 by crossing your second finger over the thumb and then bring it right back into position.

Listen to Track 33 to hear the Minuet example played.

Crossing a finger over can also be used as a transition to a new hand position. Play the example in Figure 6-14, the well-known Christmas carol "Joy To The World." Notice how crossing over the third finger in bar 3 allows you to move your hand to a second position to finish the phrase.

Figure 6-14: Crossing over a finger to move to a new hand shape.

Illustration by Jerry Kovarsky

You can hear this example in Track 34.

Because the hands are built opposite of each other, the right hand uses this crossing over technique when moving down in pitch. The left hand uses it when moving up in pitch.

Passing the thumb under

When you play a phrase from the thumb toward the pinkie and need to keep going, you must pass your thumb under your hand to transition to the new hand shape. You usually do so after playing the third finger and sometimes the fourth, but almost never the fifth (the pinkie); that's just too far to reach. Try playing the simple exercise in Figure 6-15. When you bring your thumb under, be sure you don't drop your wrist down, or you'll end up *accenting* the new thumb note (making it sound louder than the others).

Figure 6-15: Passing the thumb under.

Cross under

Illustration by Jerry Kovarsky

Listen to Track 35 to hear this simple exercise played.

Because the hands are built opposite of each other, the right hand uses this passing under technique when moving up in pitch. The left hand uses it when moving down in pitch.

Practicing crossings with a few easy scales

Scales and scale-based runs are some of the most common examples that use these crossing over and under techniques. Figure 6-16 illustrates a few different scales with their proper fingerings. Each ranges two octaves and is written for both hands. Play through each scale one hand at a time to get comfortable with the required fingering techniques.

If you're having trouble reading the notes above and below the staff, remember to count up (or down) from that last line in order (F, G, A, and so on). If necessary, you can write the name of the note in pencil.

Figure 6-16:
A few major scales to practice crossing over and under.

Illustration by Jerry Kovarsky

PLAY THIS!

Track 36 plays these scales.

Using a Pedal to Connect Notes and Sound Fuller

Playing connected notes is an important part of good keyboard musicianship. Your hands should do the work whenever possible, but sometimes you can't physically connect notes because of the distance your hand has to jump to reach the new note. Luckily, keyboard makers provide a *damper pedal* (the pedal on the right of an acoustic/digital piano, also called a sustain pedal) or a *footswitch* (the simple flat pedal that can be plugged into an electronic keyboard) to help you out with that very issue; see Figure 6-17.

Figure 6-17:
A flat switch pedal versus a damper-style design.

Pressing down on this pedal makes all the notes you're currently holding keep ringing after you release your fingers from the keys. They'll ring on until you let go of the pedal, which means you can hold your first note(s) while you move your hand to a new position to reach the next notes.

Look at the first part of Figure 6-18. The *Ped.* marking below the note tells you to press the pedal down right after playing the first note; and the bracket tells you to keep it down until you start to play the new note. Release it too soon, and the notes won't be connected; release it too late, and both notes will be ringing together. This timing takes some getting used to. You can make up other exercises by playing any note and then practicing connecting it to any other note; the timing of the pedaling is the thing to concentrate on, not writing a good melody!

Figure 6-18:
Practice connecting notes with the damper/ sustain pedal.

The second part of Figure 6-16 shows how to notate a series of notes, each connected by the pedal. Here, you connect the first two notes, but you lift up and then immediately press down the pedal again to grab the second note, and then repeat this movement for each new note. (*Note:* If you play additional notes while the pedal is down, they too will continue ringing. This approach produces a rich, ambient sound not unlike reverb — refer to Chapter 9. So in addition to connecting notes you can't reach, pedaling becomes an effect to make your playing sound richer.)

Listen to Track 37 to hear how using the damper/sustain pedal can add richness to your playing.

The number-one mistake pianists and electronic keyboardists make is overusing the damper pedal. Used sparingly, it adds richness to your playing. But held for too long, it makes the music muddy, unclear, and sloppy-sounding. It's not a magical solution to make everything sound better!

Don't use any pedal when first working on a new melody or song. Let your hands learn how to play it. When adding the pedal, use it judiciously and repedal often to clear (end) the sustaining sound.

Practicing Productively

Practice isn't just playing. It's a time to address something that needs to be worked on or improved. Sometimes you want to sit at your keyboard and just have fun, let off some steam, and wipe away the frustrations of the day. Great; do it! But when it comes time to learn how to play a new song, work on your technique, or master a piece of music, you need to be focused and have a game plan.

Practicing for a short but focused amount of time is better than sitting and noodling, not paying attention, or just going through the motions. If you want to see real progress in your efforts (or your child's efforts), you need to take the time seriously.

Let me share some advice and best practices from my years of experience:

- ✔ **Take breaks in between your periods of practice.** Doing so helps you regain the focus that's so important when you're practicing.

- ✔ **Break the music up into smaller sections or phrases and work on them over and over.**

✔ **Work one hand at a time so you can focus fully on what it's doing.**

✔ **Always start out slowly — much slower than a piece needs to be.**

✔ **Watch your posture and hand position.** Sitting for too long with a bent back or poor hand position will hurt, and you'll develop bad habits. I explain good posture and hand positioning in the earlier section "Getting in Playing Position."

✔ **Really listen to yourself; don't just think mechanically.** If you can record yourself, do it. (Chapter 13 has details on recording your playing.) You'll be surprised how different it sounds on playback when you're not busy playing it. You may notice small timing discrepancies or slightly accented notes that you didn't hear before. Or your performance may sound better than you thought because you were focusing on something technical that was troubling you and didn't pay attention to the fact that you got it!

✔ **If you're a parent guiding your child, make games out of exercises.** "Can you play it at this speed [clap a tempo]?" "How about moving up this octave?" "Can you just play the left hand part for me?"

Chapter 7

Going Chord Crazy

In This Chapter

▷ Discovering several chord types

▷ Seeing how chords and key signatures are connected

▷ Inverting chords for smoother playing

*O*ne of the beautiful things about a keyboard is its ability to play such a wide range of notes, many at the same time. Put a few of them together, and you have what's called a *chord*. I love playing chords and figuring out the chords from songs on recordings. When I write a song, I usually start by finding a few chords that I think go together well. Yes, I admit it: I've gone chord crazy over the years, and I'm inviting you to join me in my harmonic madness!

In this chapter, I present the basic structure and sound of the main chord types and how they relate to a given key center. You discover how to go from chord to chord smoothly and how to play them in simple shapes and then as a two-handed pianist. Smoothly playing chords with your left hand is essential if you play a keyboard that has auto-accompaniment (which I cover in Chapter 11). I also show you some of the most common song forms, called chord progressions, and how to play them using all these smooth chording techniques.

You can read about two other types of chords — 6th and 7th chords — in a free online article at www.dummies.com/keyboard/extras.

Getting to Know the Five Basic Chord Types

Most music uses some basic rules and structures; you can't just play any group of notes, call it a chord, and sound good. Chords are built on specific note relationships called *intervals*. As I explain in Chapter 5, the smallest distance between two keys is called a *half step* (also called a *minor second* interval). Two half steps are called a *whole step* (also called a *major second*).

Any further than a whole step and you stop calling them steps and only call them intervals. Figure 7-1 shows the main intervals within the span of an octave.

Figure 7-1: The intervals within an octave.

Illustration by Jerry Kovarsky

Listen to Track 38 to hear the intervals identified in Figure 7-1.

When an interval is called *major,* it corresponds to the notes from the major scale of the lower, or root, tone. When it's called *minor,* it's lowered by a half step from the major interval. The term *flat* or *flatted* is also used to mean lowered by a half step (flat 5 is commonly used), and *sharp/raised* indicates the interval moved up a half step (raised or sharp 5 is common). The term *perfect* is used for the most open-sounding intervals — ones that sound very pure and at rest.

All basic chords are built on three notes: the *root* (the name of the chord), the third, and the fifth. These names come from the note's step location in the scale of the same name (the third note of the scale, the fifth note of the scale, and so on). I discuss this chord-to-scale relationship more in the later section "Relating Chords to a Scale or Key Signature." You can also think of these terms as the interval relationship between the root and the other chord tone. The third is a third higher than the root, the fifth is a fifth higher than the root.

The different chord structures are referred to as *chord qualities.* This terminology means that for any given note, various chord types can be built on that root tone, and each has a different sound.

The major chord

The most common chord used in music is the *major triad.* (*Triad* just means three-note chord.) Shown in Figure 7-2, the major triad has a root, a second tone that's a major third higher (four half steps), and then another tone that's a perfect fifth higher (seven half steps) than the root. Another way to look at it is as a major third interval (four half steps) with another minor third interval (three half steps) stacked on top of it.

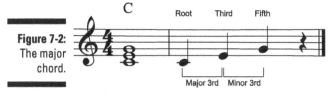

Figure 7-2:
The major
chord.

Illustration by Jerry Kovarsky

Track 39 plays the major chord.

Chords are often shown on music notation as symbols above the staff. The major chord is commonly written as just the root note letter (such as C) but may also be written as CM, CMaj, or Cmaj.

Play the chord in Figure 7-2 and listen to how it sounds. Many people say it sounds happy. Full. Proud. Majestic. Now play the three chords shown in Figure 7-3. Armed with those three major chords you're ready to start your own garage rock band; many a famous song was written with just those three chords!

Figure 7-3:
The basis
for many a
rock hit!

Illustration by Jerry Kovarsky

You can hear the chords from Figure 7-3 in Track 40.

The minor chord

If you take a major chord (see the preceding section) and lower the middle note by a half step, you get a *minor chord*. A minor chord has a root tone, a second tone a minor third higher, and a third tone a fifth higher from the root. In other words, it's a root, a minor third interval (three half steps), and a major third interval (four half steps). You can see a minor chord in Figure 7-4; if you play this chord, it sounds sad, moody, and mournful.

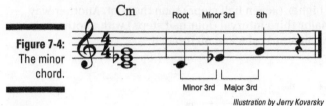

Figure 7-4: The minor chord.

Illustration by Jerry Kovarsky

Listen to Track 41 to hear the minor chord.

You typically write the minor chord as the root note's letter with a small *m* after it (Cm), but you can also write it as C– (this second notation mostly appears in jazz charts and books).

The diminished chord

A *diminished chord* (shown in Figure 7-5) is a major chord whose middle and top notes are each a half step lower. It has a root tone, a second tone a minor third higher, and a third tone a flatted fifth higher from the root. You can also think of it as a root, a minor third interval (three half steps), and another minor third interval (three half steps).

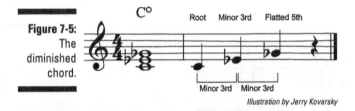

Figure 7-5: The diminished chord.

Illustration by Jerry Kovarsky

You can write the diminished chord as the root note letter with a small circle after it (C°) or as Cdim.

Play the chord in Figure 7-5; it sounds suspenseful. Dramatic. Unsettled, even. That's why it's a chord film scores often use to indicate that something bad is about to happen.

Track 42 demonstrates the diminished chord.

The augmented chord

If you raise the top note of a major chord by a half step, you get an *augmented chord* (also called a *sharp five chord;* see Figure 7-6). It has a root tone, a second tone a major third higher, and a third tone a raised fifth higher from the root. That's a root, a major third interval (four half steps), and another major third interval (four half steps) on top of it.

Figure 7-6:
The
augmented
chord.

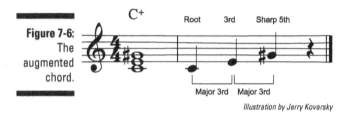

Illustration by Jerry Kovarsky

The augmented chord is written as C+ (because the fifth is raised by a half step) or Caug.

The chord in Figure 7-6 sounds suspenseful and somewhat exotic. It often serves as an intro chord before a singer comes in on a song. Play it for yourself to check it out (singing optional).

Listen to Track 43 to hear the augmented chord.

The suspended chords: Sus2 and sus4

The four chord types in the preceding sections are the main chords taught in usual classical harmony. But another chord has become so popular in music today that I want to share it with you. The *sus chord* or *suspended chord* means that the third of the major triad is suspended or delayed for a bit. Figure 7-7 shows the two common types of sus chord — sus4 and sus2 — and how they both move back to a major triad by moving the fourth back to the third (called *resolving*).

Figure 7-7:
The sus
chords.

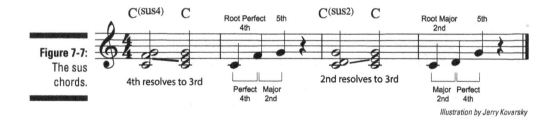

Illustration by Jerry Kovarsky

The *sus4 chord* is more common. It has a root tone, a second tone a perfect fourth higher, and a third tone a fifth higher from the root. That's a root, a perfect fourth interval (five half steps), and a major second interval (two half steps).

The more-modern *sus2 chord* has a root tone, a second tone a whole step (major second) higher, and a third tone a fifth higher from the root. In other words, it's a root, a major second interval (two half steps), and a perfect fourth interval (five half steps) stacked on top of it.

The sus chord is commonly written as the root note letter followed by sus4 or sus2, with or without parentheses. If music just shows the note and sus (as in Csus), it means the sus4 version.

Play the examples in Figure 7-7 to hear how they sound and resolve. These chords have a very open, floating character; many musicians use sus chords for their nice colorful quality.

You can listen to the sus chords from Figure 7-7 in Track 44.

Relating Chords to a Scale or Key Signature

Chords didn't just pop up one day when some early musician tripped and fell over his lute, accidentally strumming the strings as he hit the ground. They have a logical relationship to scales and therefore to the concept of playing in a given key signature. (Head to Chapter 5 for details on the key signature.) By understanding this relationship and memorizing it in all 12 keys, you give yourself a head start for anticipating what chords a song uses based on what key it's in.

The use and study of note relationships and chords is called *harmony*. A specific series of chords is referred to as a *harmonic progression* or *chord progression*. You can find many great books (such as *Music Theory For Dummies* by Michael Pilhofer and Holly Day [Wiley]) as well as videos, teachers, and schools to study more about these relationships; look for the general term *music theory*.

Recognizing the major scale chord tones

If you build triads from a major scale, using only the scale tones, you get Figure 7-8. (A *major scale* is comprised of two whole steps, a half step, three more whole steps, and a final half step. You can read more about these scales in Chapter 5.)

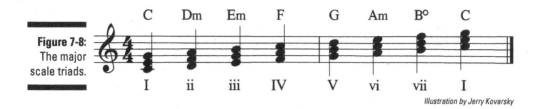

Figure 7-8:
The major scale triads.

Illustration by Jerry Kovarsky

You can see that there are major triads for the C, F, and G notes in this example. Minor chords occur on the D, E, and A notes, and the B is a diminished chord. Music theory uses Roman numerals to indicate the numbers — capital numerals for major chords and lowercase for minor. The chords are usually referred to by their number in the scale, so the first chord is the I (1) chord, the second is the ii (2) chord, and so on.

So the I (1), IV (4), and V (5) chords are major. The ii (2), iii (3), and vi (6) chords are minor, and the vii (7) chord is diminished. Figure 7-9 shows the scale tone chords for a few other keys.

Listen to Track 45 to hear the scale tone triads played in a few keys.

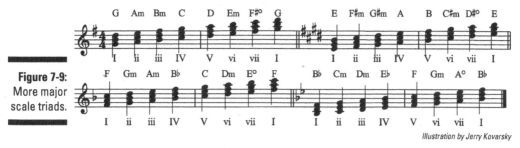

Figure 7-9:
More major scale triads.

Illustration by Jerry Kovarsky

Trying a few common chord progressions

Some very common chord progressions have been used for countless hit songs over the years. The basic blues progression in Figure 7-10 has been used not only for blues songs but also for most of the '50s and '60s rock-and-roll songs. Think Chuck Berry, Elvis Presley, and B.B. King. It uses the I, IV, and V chords from a given key, played in the order pictured. You can find many fancier variations of this setup, but this progression is the basis of the blues and early rock and roll.

Check out Track 46 to hear the blues progression chords.

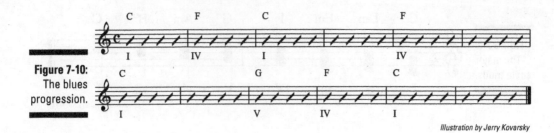

Figure 7-10:
The blues
progression.

Illustration by Jerry Kovarsky

TIP

The vertical slashes on the staff in Figure 7-10 are commonly used when writing a chord chart. They show you how many beats to play each chord and leave you free to play the chords however you want. I use this method here so you think of the chords and can try to play these progressions in more than one key. Good luck!

Countless pop songs from the '40s, '50s, and '60s, as well as the whole style of doo-wop vocal songs, are based on the four-chord sequence in Figure 7-11.

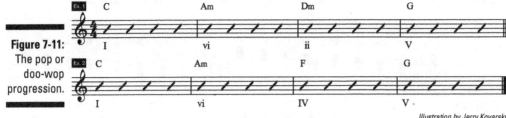

Figure 7-11:
The pop or
doo-wop
progression.

Illustration by Jerry Kovarsky

The first example uses I, vi, ii, V; the second uses the common variation I, vi, IV, V.

PLAY THIS!

Listen to Track 47 to hear both the doo-wop chord progressions.

Rearranging the Order of the Notes: Chord Inversions

Always playing chords with the root at the bottom means you have to jump your hand around the keyboard, which results in difficult, choppy-sounding playing. By simply rearranging the order of the notes of a given chord, you can make much smoother transitions. These different groupings of the notes are called *inversions;* you can read about them in the following sections. (*Remember:* Rearranging the order of the notes doesn't affect whether a chord sounds major or minor.)

The three triad inversions

You can play any three-note chord from three positions (shown in Figure 7-12):

- ✔ **The root position:** The traditional note grouping (root, third, and fifth)
- ✔ **The first inversion:** The root note moved to the top of the chord (third, fifth, and then root)
- ✔ **The second inversion:** The third moved up on top of the root (fifth, root, and then third)

As you play the three inversions, you can hear that the chord quality sounds the same.

Figure 7-12:
The three possible inversions of each type of chord triad.

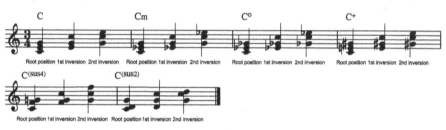

Illustration by Jerry Kovarsky

Listen to Track 48 to hear the chords and inversions shown in Figure 7-12.

Figure 7-13 shows you how to play the blues progression by always moving to the closest note to form the needed chord. Moving to the nearest note is called *voice leading* in music theory, where each note in the chord is considered a *voice*. Pay attention to the marked fingerings to play them as smoothly as possible.

Figure 7-13:
Using inversions to create smooth voice leading for the blues.

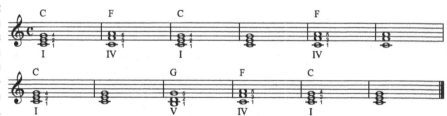

Illustration by Jerry Kovarsky

Listen to Track 49 to hear the blues progression played using chord inversions.

You can apply the same concept to make the pop/doo-wop progression sound smoother as well, as shown in Figure 7-14; Ex. 1 uses the ii chord, or the Dm, and Ex. 2 uses the IV chord, the F major. Now it sounds like what you hear on recordings, right?

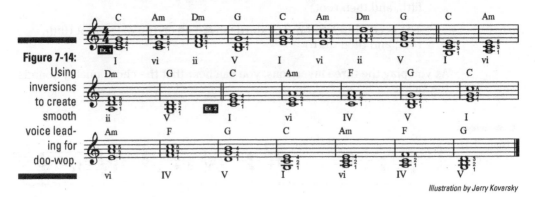

Figure 7-14: Using inversions to create smooth voice leading for doo-wop.

Illustration by Jerry Kovarsky

You can hear the doo-wop progression played using chord inversions in Track 50.

Three-note chords in your left hand

If you play an arranger keyboard or play in an ensemble with a bass player, you can use these types of inversions in your left hand for a smoother sound. Because the arranger style or the bass player always provides the root tone, you're free to use these close inversions. Figure 7-15 shows some possible ways to play the three-chord rock sound with some rhythm added. Each example starts on a different chord inversion and uses different rhythm patterns. If you have onboard drums, pick a simple rock pattern and play along with it. (Chapter 10 has the lowdown on playing with onboard drums.) Repeat each two bar phrase over and over.

Figure 7-15: Smooth left hand examples for I, IV, and V.

Illustration by Jerry Kovarsky

You can do the same thing for the doo-wop chords in Figure 7-16. I give you two variations for each starting chord inversion: one always using the straight repeated rhythm with good use of close chord movement and the other varying the rhythm a bit more. Repeat each two bar phrase over and over.

Figure 7-16 employs a time signature, 12/8, that you may not be familiar with. Each measure has 12 beats, and each group of three eighth notes forms a strong pulse. So it feels like each measure actually has four beats, with each beat getting three subdivided pulses: **1**-2-3, **2**-2-3, **3**-2-3, **4**-2-3.

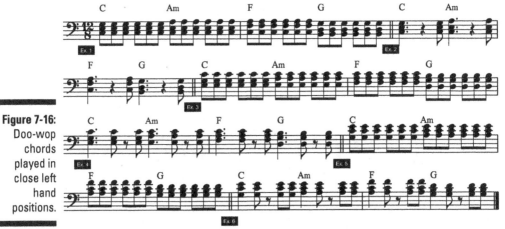

Figure 7-16:
Doo-wop
chords
played in
close left
hand
positions.

Illustration by Jerry Kovarsky

Listen to Tracks 51 and 52 to hear the blues and doo-wop progressions played using left hand chord inversions (shown in Figures 7-15 and 7-16).

Two-handed chords in a pianistic style

When you're playing chords on an acoustic piano or an electric piano, you use the closest inversion chords possible in your right hand and play the root note in your left hand — either a single note or two notes an octave apart for more power (best on acoustic piano). Figures 7-17 and 7-18 show the basic voicings and fingerings, and then examples with rhythm added to each hand.

Figure 7-17:
I, IV, and
V chords
played in
a pianistic
style.

Illustration by Jerry Kovarsky

Check out Track 53 to hear the blues progression played in a two-handed, pianistic fashion.

Figure 7-18:
Doo-wop
chords
played in
a pianistic
style.

Illustration by Jerry Kovarsky

Listen to Track 54 to hear the doo-wop progression played in a two-handed, pianistic fashion.

Part III
Using Common Keyboard Features

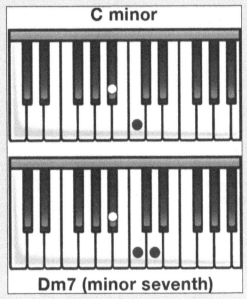

Illustration by Lisa Reed

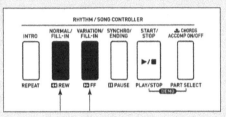

Illustration courtesy of Casio America, Inc.

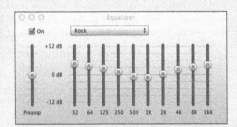

Apple iTunes screenshot courtesy of Jerry Kovarsky

In this part . . .

✔ Recognize the various names for the term *sound* among differ-ent keyboards. Explore the different methods used for selecting sounds and making them sound good while you play them.

✔ See and hear what adding effects to your sounds can do. You can tailor which effects you use to the sound you're going for.

✔ Work with your keyboard's onboard drummer to lay down deep grooves without sounding canned.

✔ Use auto-accompaniment to lead your virtual band through the songs you want to play.

✔ Discover what an arpeggiator is and how to use it within your music.

Chapter 8

Selecting and Playing Sounds

. . . .

. . . .

A likely reason you've chosen to play an electronic keyboard is that it offers more than one sound. As much as I love mashed potatoes, I can't eat them every day. So it is with a keyboard; having a variety of sound keeps you interested in playing longer. Can you imagine hearing Mozart played by Jimi Hendrix? Chuck Berry played with a flute? Nirvana played on a harpsichord? Okay, maybe that first one is a cool idea, but you get my point: Having the right sounds for the type of music you like to play is essential. And that's why a keyboardist is the luckiest musician of all. Your keyboard can transform into any instrument you want at the push of a button. No other player has that power, so use it wisely!

In this chapter, I clear up the confusing array of names manufacturers use to describe the sound you hear when you play a key, and I cover how to select the sound you want to use. I also give you tips on how to play each sound to be most convincing and to combine sounds in layers and splits.

First Things First: Understanding Some Important Terminology

One of the most confusing things about shopping for keyboards, talking about them with your friends, or just using them is the crazy array of names used to describe the choice of sounds available. I've already been using the term *sound,* and it sure makes sense to me, but it's never that simple. Is it the re-creation of a single known instrument such as the piano or a pipe organ? The combination of multiple instruments being played at the same time such as a whole orchestra or a big-band sax section? Two instruments being played together such as a guitar and a flute or an electric piano and a bass guitar?

All these things are possible, but this variety means you need a name for the individual "thing" a keyboard can reproduce, the combination of multiple "things," and so on. To make matters worse, each company has its own name for each of these "things," which is why I have to write this section in the first place. I can't promise to fix the world, but I can help you make sense of this small issue.

In the following sections, I clear up this confusion and introduce you to a few concepts about the Musical Instrument Digital Interface (MIDI for short), which I cover in even greater detail in Chapter 13.

A sound by any other name: Recognizing the various terms

To keep things simple and clear, I always refer to single "things" as *sounds*, and the combinations of "things" as *multipart sounds*. If only real life were so simple. Each manufacturer uses its own terms for these things, which creates a world of confusion. Take a look at the following tables, and you can see what I mean.

Table 8-1 shows a list of brand names and the name(s) they use for single sounds in their various keyboards.

Table 8-1	Brand Names and Individual-Sound Terminology
Brand Name	*Terms for Individual Sounds*
Casio	Tone (all)
Hammond/Suzuki	Voice (all)
Kawai	Internal Sound, Voice (all)
Korg	Program (synth, workstation), Sound (digital piano, arranger)
Kurzweil	Preset, Voice Preset (synth, stage piano), Preset Program, Sound Program (digital piano)
Moog	Preset, Patch (synth)
Nord	Program (all)
Roland	Patch (synth, workstation), Tone (digital piano, arranger), Registration (combo organ)
Yamaha	Voice, Sweet! Voice, Cool! Voice, Live! Voice, Mega Voice, Super Articulation Voice (all)

What a crazy and confusing list of terms all meaning the same thing. Can't we all just get along?

If that wasn't confusing enough, some of these words have other meanings in music tech terms. *Tone* can also mean the brightness or bassy quality of a sound. Many home stereos, guitar amplifiers, and other audio devices have a control for Tone that doesn't change to another instrument sound; it affects the EQ (brightness and bass amount) of the device. *Voice* is sometimes used when describing how many notes you can play at the same time, which is called *polyphony* (which means "many voices"). A guitar is six-note polyphonic (it has six strings), and an acoustic piano is 88-note polyphonic. As a side note, there are many instruments that can only play one note at a time (woodwinds, brass, the human voice, some analog synthesizers), and they're called *monophonic*. So a spec sheet for a keyboard may use the term 100-voice polyphony, meaning it can produce 100 notes at the same time. *Preset* can also mean a memory location that can't be changed or overwritten. Products that use this term list a number of Preset and User locations to describe what can't and can be changed.

Moving on to the multipart sounds, Table 8-2 shows how different brands refer to them in their keyboards.

Table 8-2	Brand Names and Multiple-Sound Terminology
Brand Name	*Terms for Multiple Sounds*
Casio	Tone (all)
Kawai	User Setup (stage piano), Registration (digital pianos)
Korg	Combination (synth, workstation), Performance (arranger)
Kurzweil	MIDI Setup (synth, digital piano)
Roland	Performance (arranger, stage piano), Live Set (synth, workstation)
Yamaha	Performance (all)

Note: When I present a tutorial for a specific brand of product, I use its terms, of course, to match the front panel and menu labels, but for general purposes I'm sticking with my terms. You can refer to these tables to translate my terms to your product's language.

Makes you wish you had a scorecard to follow, doesn't it? (Note to editor: That's a great idea! Editor: Just keep writing, Jerry.)

Defining GM/GM2

As you look at web pages, literature, keyboard manuals, and keyboard front panels and displays, you're going to come across General MIDI logos. *General*

MIDI (GM) is a standard that defined a set of sounds, instrumental effects, and numerous standard features so MIDI-based music could be shared among various devices (keyboards, computers, web pages, and even cellphones) and always sound the same. GM defines a set of 128 sounds that cover the most basic and universal group of instruments. So when you select a sound in the GM bank or group of sounds, it will sound similar to that same sound in any other brand or type of keyboard you have.

MIDI stands for *Musical Instrument Digital Interface,* a technology standard developed in 1983 by a number of keyboard companies to allow keyboards to "talk" to each other — to trigger sounds from one keyboard (the *master*) and have other keyboards (the *slave*) sound at the same time. This setup enabled layering of sounds between different keyboards and brands for a fuller sound. It has evolved into a universally supported and wonderful capability not only to play keyboards connected together but also to connect keyboards to computers for recording, sound editing, musical notation, and other activities. (I cover MIDI in more detail in Chapter 13.)

General MIDI 2 (GM2) is an expanded set of sounds that adds more diversity and variety to the library, but the concept remains the same: guaranteed sound conformity so that songs and arrangements can be reproduced with consistency and accuracy no matter what the playback device.

These logos indicate that the product includes the complete General MIDI sound set and responds properly to sound selection commands via MIDI. Figure 8-1 shows an example of these logos.

Figure 8-1:
The General
MIDI (GM)
logos.

The General MIDI Logos are trademarks of MIDI Manufacturers Association (MMA) and used with permission

Two other GM-like standards are brand specific. *GS* is a Roland standard that's similar to GM2, and *XG* is a Yamaha standard that goes even farther than GM2. But the idea is the same (as far as sounds are concerned) — a pre-specified listing of sounds that are always the same in products bearing the logo.

Head to www.dummies.com/extras/keyboard for links to the GM and GM2 soundsets. These sounds may be more basic or plain-sounding than the featured or main versions in your product, so don't start with them when first evaluating the quality of a keyboard!

I Love a Piano! Focusing on Acoustic Piano

The acoustic piano is the lord and master of the keyboard domain. Other than the theatre or jazz organist and the synthesizer player, everyone starts with the mighty piano. It's the sound you expect to hear when you see the familiar 88 black and white keys. It conjures up images of everything from virtuosic classical pianists like Vladimir Horowitz and Arthur Rubinstein to keyboard-banging rock-and-roll legends from the '50s like Jerry Lee Lewis and Little Richard to jazz masters like Dave Brubeck and Keith Jarrett and sensitive singer/songwriters like Elton John, Carole King, John Legend, and Alicia Keys.

A vast repertoire of music sounds good on acoustic piano: "Chopsticks," Bach, pop songs, Broadway show tunes, jazz, progressive rock, ragtime, new age music, and so on. So getting your keyboard producing an acoustic piano sound is step one in your exploration of available sounds.

For most digital pianos, stage pianos, and other types of basic keyboards, the product likely already wakes up with a full-range piano sound when you turn it on. So if you walk up to a keyboard in a music store or a friend's home and it's not on a piano sound, you can just turn it off, wait a few moments, and then turn it on. Voilà!

Just playing piano

A number of manufacturers recognize that you often just want to play a piano sound, so they make setting up your keyboard to be a full-range piano very easy. Typically, it simply requires the push of one clearly-labeled button: Piano, Play Piano, Piano Play, Just Piano, or a similar term. Pressing this button guarantees you full-range piano performance. This feature is most often included on more feature-rich products that have complicated front panels. Take a moment to see whether your keyboard has this feature and try it.

Ensuring the whole key range is playing one sound

Because the acoustic piano has an 88-key range, you want your keyboard to be playing the same sound across its full range, especially if it has fewer than 88 keys. Here are some of the most common reasons your keyboard may *not* be producing a full-range sound, and ways to fix that:

- Many electronic keyboards have the ability to split the keyboard so you can have two sounds at the same time, perhaps a bass for your left hand and a piano for your right. Look for a button labeled Split and turn it off.

- If your keyboard has a dedicated multipart sound mode, you need to put it into single sound mode by using the proper button on the front panel. What may seem like a split function may also be a multipart sound mode, so if you can't find a Split button or it isn't fixing the situation, multipart sound mode may be the culprit. Products that have different modes of operation almost always have a clearly labeled section on the front panel called "mode."

- If your keyboard can produce *automatic accompaniment* (backing rhythms and parts), it will likely split the keyboard in half so the lower range triggers the accompaniment. Find and turn off that function or change from that mode to single sound mode.

- If your keyboard has an onboard recorder or sequencer (MIDI recorder), it may be in that mode. Put it into single sound mode by using the proper mode button on the front panel.

Selecting Various Sounds

There are various methods for selecting the sounds you want to play on a keyboard. These differences relate to design aspects of your keyboard, such as the following:

- **How many sounds does your keyboard offer?**

- **Does your keyboard have a display?**

- **Is the display for reading information only, or is it a touch-entry device?** This setup is most often found on high-end workstations, professional arrangers, and digital grand pianos.

- **Does your keyboard have dedicated buttons labeled for each single sound?** This feature is most often found on simple digital pianos.

✔ **Does your keyboard have accompaniment features?**

✔ **Does your keyboard have dedicated sections for types of sounds it makes?** Some combo stage pianos have dedicated piano, organ, synth, and other sections that can all be active at the same time.

You can look at most keyboard designs as fitting into two groups for how you select sounds: designs where you select from labeled names or categories of instruments and designs where you select from a bank or numeric location.

A simple analogy to help you visualize this division better is that direct sound selection is like entering a library and seeing all the books laid out on a table in one big room, sitting out in open view in front of you. The other methods of sound selection are like walking into a multiroom library. Each room has different books in it, and they're organized by different methods depending on the brand of library you're visiting.

Many keyboards fall neatly into one method or the other, but some offer both sound selection methods. The more sounds a keyboard offers, the more complex the task of finding a specific sound will be. But fear not; the concept of how to select a sound is simple, and after you get the hang of it, you'll be flying around in no time!

From labeled names or categories

With this method, you can easily see the name of the sound or family of sounds you want (for example, you can easily understand that you'll find a pipe organ by selecting a button labeled Organs). You may see the sound name itself or select from a category.

Picking specific sounds by name

With this design, you see buttons on the front panel with specific sound names like Grand Piano 1, Grand Piano 2, Electric Piano 1, Electric Piano 2, Combo Organ, Pipe Organ, and Strings. It's the most direct and friendly way to select sounds. To select and play sounds on this type of keyboard, try the following:

1. **Press the first Piano sound button.**

2. **Play some notes on the keyboard.**

3. **Press other sound name buttons and play some notes on the keyboard.**

Easy! As you explore your keyboard's options, you get a great feel for all the sounds it offers you. And try pressing the same sound button again; some keyboards offer sound variations that you can cycle through with repeated button presses.

Products that use this direct method often don't have a display to give you any information. The only visual feedback you may get is a small light in the button to show which sound is active, or multiple small lights next to the button to show which variation of that sound is currently being used. Products that use this method include simple digital pianos, simple stage pianos, and entry-level portable keyboards.

Choosing sounds from within categories

The process for selecting sounds from categories is the same as for selecting from names (refer to the preceding section), but in this design you see more-generalized labels such as Piano, Electric Piano, Organ, Other Keys, Strings, Brass, and Synth. Because many sounds are often grouped together in this method, continually pressing a button doesn't work. You'd be poking at the front panel way too much to scroll through all the choices offered.

Instead, products that employ a category design almost always have a display and some sort of buttons, a dial, or a slider to scroll up and down through the choices. This setup allows you to navigate quickly through the list and always see which sound you're currently on. To navigate the choices, follow these steps:

1. **Look for buttons labeled + and –.**

   Alternately, they may be labeled up and down, value up and value down, or just graphic symbols ∧ and ∨.

2. **Press the + button and then play the keyboard.**

   Your sound will change to another sound within the same family or type of instrument.

3. **Continue pressing the +/– buttons to select more sounds.**

   If your product has a display, look at it as you make changes to read each sound name as you select it. Don't forget to play the keyboard as you go to hear and get a feel for the sounds available!

A typical list of sounds you can cycle through within the category labeled Piano may look like this: Grand Piano, Ballad Grand, Rock Piano, Honky-Tonk Piano, Mellow Grand, Warm Grand, Bright Grand, Dark Grand, Dynamic Grand, Upright Piano, Toy Piano.

For organ, the list may include Jazz Organ, Perc Organ, Gospel Organ, Rock Organ, '60s Organ, Theatre Organ, Church Organ, Pipe Organ Principal, Pipe Organ Tutti, Pipe Organ Flute 1, Pipe Organ Flute 2, Hymnal.

From a bank or numeric locations

Keyboards that use banks or numeric groupings have less-friendly or more-technical front panels without any familiar instrument names to help you. The reason is that they offer so many more sounds, often hundreds, and having that many sounds requires some method of organizing them so you can find them all. And that's a good thing!

Luckily, the setup isn't completely different from that of the keyboards in the earlier section "From labeled names or categories." You still press a button to select a sound, and you may use up and down controls to scroll through more selections. The following sections take you through how to use numbered buttons and categories or banks to select sounds.

Using a numeric keypad or numbered buttons to select a sound location

This approach lets you go directly to a location instead of pressing up or down repeatedly to span long ranges of numbers.

When in sound selection mode, you use a numeric keypad to choose a sound. You're actually choosing a sound location; depending on how many locations your keyboard offers you many need to enter two digits (00 to 99 being most common) or three digits (000 to 127 being most common). Type a number, play a sound; it's that easy!

Some products require you to press an enter button before the sound changes. You can use this feature during a performance to pick your next sound during a small break in the music and keep it ready and waiting without actually playing it. Then when you need the sound, you simply press enter. Some keyboards with an enter button don't require you to input all the digits, so you can just type 2 and hit enter instead of typing 02 or 002.

Choosing which bank or group of sounds you want to select from

If your keyboard has multiple banks, try the following:

1. **Make sure you're in single sound mode.**

2. **Type a number with the numeric keypad (or numeric entry method your keyboard offers).**

Remember, the number may be two or three digits and may require you to press enter.

3. **Play the keys to hear the new sound.**

4. **Locate and press one of the bank buttons to select another group of sounds, and play the keyboard.**

You have a new sound that uses the same location number as before, but from this new bank.

5. **Enter another number to select a new sound from this bank, and so on.**

Alternatively, you can use the up/down navigation buttons to move back and forth through the sounds within the current bank. This option is nice when you just want to go exploring and have no specific sound in mind. It's great for your first in-store demo.

The bank buttons may be labeled with letters, numbers, or a combination of both and may even have names like Preset, User, and so on. Some products use bank buttons plus dedicated 0 through 9 or 1 through 16 location buttons rather than numeric entry. Read the front panel layout section of your specific model's owner's manual for more information.

From the display screen

If your keyboard has a large display, all the methods in the preceding sections may be done from the display and perhaps some buttons surrounding it. So rather than bank buttons, numeric keypads, and so on, you may make your selection from the display itself. Some keyboards even have touchscreens that allow you to touch names or graphics on the screen itself to make a selection.

Common ways of presenting sounds by using large displays include

✔ Multiple columns of sounds that you can scroll through

✔ Multiple sounds on screen at the same time with dedicated buttons on the sides of the display to select one of the currently displayed sounds

✔ The choice of viewing (and selecting) sounds either by location or by category

Making Sure Your Selected Sounds Sound Right

After you've selected a sound, you're ready to consider a few concepts to help you sound like you know what you're doing. In the following sections, I help you make each instrument sound its best through playing in the right range of the keyboard and knowing whether to play more than one note at a time. I conclude by suggesting what sounds to use for the style of music you want to play. No rule needs to be a rigid order, but these tips can help you sound like a pro in no time!

Playing in the right note range

Your keyboard may have anything from 49 keys to 88 keys, like a real acoustic piano. The longer the keyboard, the more you need to consider what range of notes to play within to make your selected sound come across as natural and realistic.

One general rule you can follow is that only pianos, electric pianos, and other keyboard sounds will likely sound good across the full range of the keyboard. This guideline also holds true for many non-real synthesizer sounds. But even in these cases, the very far extremes of the keyboard (both low and high) may not sound great. Only the acoustic piano will sound good across every key on your 88-note keyboard.

So for every other sound, you need to consider what range that instrument can actually produce in real life. The beauty of an electronic keyboard is that it can do things that the real instruments may not be able to, or at least enables you to easily do what would take a real instrument player many years of study and technique development to do. A beginner student may only be able to play within a small range of notes at first; only through years of practice can she develop the ability to play very high (and low) notes on her given instrument. You can do that with your keyboard on day one without breaking a sweat — lucky you!

Here are some general guidelines of which sounds work the best for each range of the keyboard:

 ✔ **The lower end:** Anything that says "bass" (guitar, synth, and so on), string sections, contrabass, bari sax, tuba, trombone, pipe organ, tonewheel organ, tympani, and bass drum. Most full drumkit sounds start at the low end of the keyboard.

✔ **The middle:** Most brass and woodwind sounds (but be careful not to go too low for flute, piccolo, and soprano sax), solo strings, voices, all plucked strings (acoustic and electric guitar, banjo, harp, ethnic stringed instruments such as sitar, and so on), all keyboard instruments, and most bell and mallet sounds. Also consider that female voices can go higher than male voices, while males can go lower.

✔ **The upper end:** Most of the sounds listed for the previous two areas start to sound really bad as you get to the upper range of your keyboard. The last octave or two on an 88-key keyboard doesn't work well for anything besides real keyboard instruments, bells, perhaps piccolo, and full drumkits, which likely have a variety of percussion and sound effects at the top range of the keys.

You can explore this more yourself. Select a sound and try the various ranges of the keyboard. When an instrument is being played lower than its realistic range, it starts to have a darker and slower quality, losing its natural attack. Human voices/choirs start to sound like Darth Vader — deeper and full of breath. This effect can be fun to fool around with, but it doesn't sound real.

Listen to Track 55 to hear a few sounds being played far below their natural ranges.

As you go too high, an instrument starts to sound shrill or too piercing. You may no longer be able to even recognize what instrument it is. And sounds may even start to have a noticeable ticking or noise quality that's unpleasant. Voices become chipmunklike. If it doesn't sound good, don't go there!

Track 56 features a few sounds being played far above their natural ranges.

Sounding one note, or more?

All sounds work well when you're playing only one note, so you can play a melody with anything as long as you don't veer too far from its best range. But certain sounds don't seem as real when played in a *chordal* fashion (three and four notes at the same time). Here's some general advice for determining how many notes to play:

✔ **The only sounds that work well when you're playing two-handed are keyboard sounds, synth sounds, string/orchestral sections and blends, and non-distorted guitars.** So when you aren't using accompaniment features or don't have the keyboard split into two sound sections, don't choose other types of sound for two-handed playing.

- ✔ **If the sound is a wind instrument (you blow into it), it will sound better as a single-note melody.** Keyboards offer sax section sounds and brass ensemble sounds, but if you've selected a single woodwind or brass sound, play it one note at a time.

- ✔ **Bass instruments generally sound best with one note.**

- ✔ **Guitars have six strings, so they can certainly play chords.** But they don't use simple three-note chords like a piano/keyboard would. If you want to sound good playing these instruments on keyboard, spread your chords across two hands, using four to six notes to emulate a guitar more effectively. You can read more about chords and basic voicings in Chapter 7.

  Check out Track 57 to hear an acoustic guitar sound played poorly, like a piano, and then spread across both hands to sound more natural.

- ✔ **Distortion guitar sounds good with two or three notes but never in simple triads.** Playing a melody with a note a fourth below (five half steps) sounds great, as do root-fifth-octave "power chords." I discuss intervals such as these in Chapter 7.

Listen to Track 58 to hear a distortion guitar sound played poorly, like a piano, and then played with various two and three note intervals that sound more realistic.

Understanding the common styles of music for various sounds

Though I'm the first person to say rules are meant to be broken, I can suggest some common practices for matching the right type of sound to play melodies to a style of music:

- ✔ **Acoustic and electric pianos:** Work well for pretty much everything except heavy metal, punk rock, grunge rock, and polka (you gotta have an accordion for that!).

- ✔ **Combo/tonewheel organ:** Works well for pretty much everything and is the only keyboard sound likely to be accepted in heavy metal, punk rock, and grunge rock. Just use a more aggressive sound, not your jazz or skating sound.

- ✔ **Pipe or church organ:** Works best for classical and liturgical/church music but can also be used sometimes in rock, progressive rock, and heavy metal music.

- ✔ **Solo brass and woodwinds:** Work well for pop music, Broadway show tunes, jazz and big-band music, soul and R & B, Latin, folk, and new-age music. It's also good for some classical and liturgical pieces.

- ✔ **Acoustic guitar:** Works well for pop, country, new-age, folk, Latin (especially bossa novas and sambas), and some softer rock music. It's also good for some classical and liturgical pieces.

- ✔ **Electric guitar:** Depending on how clean or distorted your sound is, works well for pop, rock, country, new-age, soul and R & B, and jazz. Heavy distorted guitar works well for harder rock, heavy metal, punk rock, grunge rock, and annoying your neighbors. Especially if they play guitar.

- ✔ **Strings and string section:** Works best for classical and liturgical music as well as Broadway show tunes. You can also use it for effective introductions to many styles of music before moving into a more keyboard-based sound.

- ✔ **Mallet sounds:** Works for various styles depending on instrument. You can use vibraphone (vibes) for jazz and Broadway/big-band songs, while marimba, xylophone, and steel drum work nicely for island-tinged pop and folk music, reggae, and Latin music.

- ✔ **Synth sounds:** Works well with a variety of styles. This category is pretty broad, but in general most dance music from the '70s to today sounds better with synth sounds playing the melody rather than acoustic instruments. Many classic rock and progressive rock music features synth solos as well. Classical music and holiday selections also adapt well to synthesizer sounds, be they keyboard-based pieces or orchestral adaptations. Think Wendy Carlos, Tomita, and Mannheim Steamroller.

Using More than One Sound at a Time

The ability to play more than one sound at a time is another great benefit of today's keyboards and provides a distinct advantage over their acoustic brethren. As I mention earlier in the chapter, some single sounds in your keyboard are already combined re-creations, like a big-band brass or horn section or a string quartet. They're presented as a single sound but are obviously reproducing the sound of multiple instruments being played at the same time.

But what if you want to create multipart sounds that aren't pregrouped, such as combining a pipe organ and a choir, or a bass sound below a piano? That's where splitting and layering come in. A *split* means you have one sound for part of the range of the keyboard, and it changes to another sound, with no overlap, for another range. A *layer* indicates that you have two or more sounds playing across the same range of notes, so they sound at the same time when you press a key.

Some keyboards offer a category of splits or layers to choose from within, and others present another mode of operation (Programs and Combinations, or Voices and Performances, for example) that you select from by using the same methods discussed in the earlier section "From a bank or numeric locations." Playing more than one sound simultaneously is such a common need during live performance that many pro keyboards offer this option right on the front panel. The following sections give you basic directions for splitting and layering.

Your keyboard likely has other adjustments you can make after you layer or split two sounds, such as balancing the volume between the two sounds or panning the sounds to come out of each side of your stereo speakers or headphones. Check your product's owner's manual for more information about making these adjustments.

Layering sounds

Layering or blending two sounds together creates a wonderful, rich sound. Think of the sound of acoustic piano blended with some warm strings; it's the perfect sound for playing a sensitive pop ballad. Combining a pipe organ with some vocal choir sounds gives you just the right blend for praise and worship music.

Some products call layering Dual Mode or Dual Voice Mode. It simply means you're playing more than one sound at a time.

If your keyboard has dedicated sound name buttons like Grand Piano 1, Electric Piano, Pipe Organ, Strings, and so on, you may be able to easily layer two of them together. Try this method commonly found on digital pianos and stage pianos:

1. **Press and hold a piano sound button.**

2. **Now press another sound button.**

3. **Release both buttons and play the keyboard.**

   If your keyboard has this feature, you'll hear both sounds layered together.

Another common approach is to have a dedicated Layer button. Look at the front panel of your keyboard; if you have this feature, try these steps:

1. **Select a sound you want to use as the foundation.**

2. **Press the Layer button.**

   Information then comes up on the display to guide you in choosing the second sound you want to layer with the first sound.

3. **Use your product's sound selection/navigation method to find a second desired sound.**

4. **Select it for the layered element.**

5. **Play the keyboard and enjoy.**

Finally, some keyboards have dedicated buttons for Parts, Zones, or Layers. These buttons are usually labeled Zone 1–4, Upper ½ / Lower ½, or Part 1–4. By turning on and off different combinations of these buttons, you can add layers to your keyboard setup. This feature is most commonly found in arranger keyboards and more-advanced stage pianos/controllers.

Track 59 contains examples of single sounds combined to form a layer.

Placing sounds side by side (splits)

A *keyboard split* means that you have one sound for part of the range of keys; at a predetermined place, that sound stops and a new sound starts. A very common use for this method is to have a bass sound on the lower range of the keyboard with a piano/keyboard sound on the upper. Now you can play with a drummer and you sound like a trio as you accompany a vocalist. Use your keyboard's built-in drum rhythms, and you alone are already the trio and can jam with a horn player, a guitar player, or accompany that vocalist to create a larger ensemble sound with fewer people.

Another common setup is to have a chordal sound for the lower range of the keyboard (perhaps an electric piano) and then a solo instrument such as a flute, horn, or lead synth sound for the upper part.

Look at the front panel of your keyboard to see whether you have a dedicated Split button. If you do, here's a way to try splitting:

1. **Select a sound you want to use for the upper range.**

2. **Press the Split button.**

Information then comes up on the display to guide you in choosing the second sound you want to use with the first sound. Some keyboards automatically choose a bass sound when you press Split because that's such a common use.

Note: The keyboard uses a default choice of where the split occurs. The screen that comes up will also offer a way to change that. Ignore that option for now.

3. **Use your product's sound selection/navigation method to find a bass sound, and select it for the lower range element.**

4. **Play the keyboard and enjoy.**

Listen to Track 60 to hear some examples of single sounds combined to form a split.

Chapter 9

Using Effects to Enhance Your Sound

*H*ave you ever watched a guitar player in concert press on some little box with his foot at different parts of the song? Or rock his foot forward and back on a pedal? He's using effects to enhance and change his sound, turning different ones on and off for each part of the song. You can do the same with a keyboard.

Effects add qualities to the sound that the basic tone production method doesn't include, so using them can change the character of any sound. Over time, well-established groups of effects have developed, and I explain those in this chapter.

Your keyboard already has some effects configured with each sound, and you may or may not have much control over them. Working with the effects may be as simple as flipping an on/off switch or go into greater detail. Developing the ability to hear and identify the various types of effect helps you recognize them being used in the music you listen to and reproduce those sounds for the songs you want to play. To help you with that, this chapter also discusses the most common use of effects for each type of sound.

Categorizing Common Keyboard Effects

Effects are used in electronic musical instruments, amplifiers, large sound systems in performance venues, and recording studios. Often, you don't think about them; they've become a natural part of the sound you associate with an instrument. Some are easy to identify because they add a signature color and quality to a sound, but others are seemingly invisible because they correct or enhance the basic tonal nature of a sound without adding anything noticeable.

Here are the most common groups of effects; I discuss specific effects in more detail in the following section:

- ✓ **Tonal correction:** This effect is commonly called EQ for equalizer or equalization. It's like the basic treble and bass controls of a stereo but can be much fancier and more detailed.

- ✓ **Volume control:** *Volume* is often called *gain* in audio terms, but it means just what you think: the level of the sound. Effects such as a compressor, a limiter, and a preamp fall into this category.

- ✓ **Modulation:** *Modulation* is the broadest category of effects and the most obvious to hear. These effects add motion and color to your sound and can be subtle or wildly psychedelic. Popular effects include chorus, phase shifting, flanging, tremolo, and rotary speaker.

- ✓ **Tonal coloration:** This category is somewhat related to modulation but doesn't add motion. It just colors, or changes, the sound. Common candidates are distortion, amp models, and speaker simulators.

- ✓ **Ambience:** These effects simulate the characteristics of an environment such as a room, a large hall, a cathedral, or a canyon. Common effects are delay (distinct echoes) and reverb (a more indistinct wash of sound reflections).

Knowing these groupings, you can listen to a sound or a recording and start to define what you're hearing. If an acoustic piano sound seems to be very far away and has some subtle echoes, you think reverb and perhaps some delay. When you hear a very "crunchy" Clavinet (clav) sound with a thick, aggressive quality, you may rightfully assume it's being run through some distortion or perhaps an amp simulator (or a real guitar amp).

Meeting the Main Types of Effects

This book is about keyboards, not guitars or a recording studio, so the following sections introduce you to only the most common effects you'll find and want to use in your instrument. Note that I'm assuming you're using only onboard effects; you can buy additional boxes to run your keyboard through, but I don't cover those here.

Reverb

Reverb adds space around your notes and can make your sound seem farther away, even dreamy. It's short for *reverberation,* which describes the continuation of sound in a particular space after the original sound is produced and stops or decays away (I'll spare you the scientific details). Reverb produces a kind of hazy or blurred type of echo that's very pleasing to the ear and gives a sense of the space you're playing in.

The character of a reverb is defined by several factors, including the following:

- ✔ The overall size of the space you produce the sound in
- ✔ The number of surfaces the sound can bounce off of (how enclosed is the room, how high is the ceiling, and so on)
- ✔ The material of the walls (wood, concrete, glass, or whatever), which affects how much sound they absorb and how distinct the repetitions/reflections are

Put simply, various types of reverbs can make it sound like you're playing in all kinds of different spaces.

Keyboards typically give you a limited set of parameters you can use to adjust reverb. The most common are

- ✔ **Mix or wet/dry mix:** *Mix* controls how much of your original, unaffected *(dry)* signal is passed on and how much of the reverberated *(wet)* signal is introduced. Often, just a little wet signal is good enough to produce a nice, not-too-sloppy sound. But sometimes a lot more of the wet signal is nice, giving your playing a spacious quality and majestic sound.

  The more notes you play or the faster the tempo, the less reverb you want to use. This way, all your playing can be clearly heard without blurring together.

- ✔ **Type:** *Type* is an overall selection that sets the size of the space and other associated parameters, or even the method of producing the reflections. Common choices are room, hall, stage, cathedral, and so on. You may sometimes see *plate* or *spring,* which is a form of artificial reflection where a sound is played into a box that contains a metal plate or large spring, which vibrates from the incoming sound waves.

- ✔ **Size:** The *size* control defines the overall size of your chosen simulated space. So a small room may seem like a tiny hallway or closet, and a large room may be 10 feet by 20 feet or 40 feet by 40 feet. The idea of a small cathedral or canyon may seem funny, but remember that the type of room is defined not only by its floor space but also by characteristics like ceiling height and the materials the walls are made of.

✔ **Reverb time:** This control simulates how long the sound reflections take to die away or stop sounding. It's casually described as a length — a short reverb, a long reverb — and the reflections are sometimes called the *reverb tail.*

On many simple keyboards and digital pianos, mix and type may be your only control choices. More advanced reverbs that offer deeper programmability include parameters such as:

✔ **EQ:** Shapes the tone of the sound a bit.

✔ **Damping:** Simulates how much of the sound is absorbed; higher values cause the reflections to come back darker or less bright.

✔ **Pre-delay:** Pushes back the whole reflective simulation, so your original dry sound can be heard before the reflections start. Adding some pre-delay (or raising its existing value) helps your sound be clearer and more distinct before being wrapped in the ambience of the effect.

Track 61 plays examples of various reverb types.

Delay

Delay (sometimes called *echo*) is an ambience effect, adding the impression of space around your notes. But it works differently from reverb in that the reflections are distinct, clear echoes or repeats of the incoming notes. You've probably seen a cartoon where the character yells into the Grand Canyon and his exact words come back a few moments later. That's delay! Used very subtly, it adds some ambience to your playing, brought up more in the mix it becomes a highly rhythmic counterpoint to play against.

The most common delay parameters your keyboard will let you adjust are

✔ **Mix or wet/dry mix:** This control determines how much of your dry signal is passed on and how much the distinct echoes *(wet sounds)* are introduced.

✔ **Delay time:** *Delay time* controls the timing of the repetitions — specifically, the interval of time between the original signal and each repeat. It's usually represented in milliseconds but can be set to note values or even rhythmic figures in more advanced instruments.

✔ **Feedback:** This parameter manipulates how many distinct repetitions will sound. At most settings, these repetitions decay in volume with each occurrence, so they seem to fade out.

Be careful when adjusting this parameter! High feedback values can cause the repetitions to get louder and keep generating endlessly. This result can get very loud quickly and even damage your speakers and/or hearing.

✔ **Damping:** *Damping* adjusts the brightness of each repetition to simulate the effect of sound absorption; each occurrence gets darker. Along with the level decay that may be built into feedback, damping helps keep your playing from sounding too cluttered.

Track 62 demonstrates delay.

Chorus/flanging/phase shifting

Chorus, flanging, and phase shifting are modulation effects that produce a warm, swirling sort of thickened sound. Each one sounds different, but they're all closely related in concept and use, so I discuss them together in the following sections.

Listen to Track 63 to hear flanging, chorus, and phase shifting demonstrated and compared.

Chorus

Chorus is produced by constantly varying the pitch of a slightly delayed copy of your sound. When this variation is mixed back with the original signal, it produces a pleasing, rich result. The chorus effect was first designed to sound like a choir of voices singing together, with the slight imperfections in tuning and timing that produced an ensemble sound.

Common chorus parameters to adjust on your keyboard include these:

✔ **Mix or wet/dry mix:** Mix controls how much of your dry signal is passed on and how much of the original-plus-varied *(wet)* signal is introduced. Unlike reverb, mix sounds better at higher, or wetter, values for chorus.

✔ **Depth:** This parameter indicates how much pitch variation is produced.

✔ **Rate/frequency:** This control adjusts the speed of the pitch variations. Very slow to medium sounds good; too fast, and your sound takes on a wobbly, underwater quality. But maybe that's what you wanted!

More advanced choruses may have some built-in EQ to shape the tone of the sound a bit. They may offer a delay time parameter to determine the general amount of time the signal is delayed. This parameter setting can be the critical difference between chorus and flanging (see the following section): Values between 1 and 15 milliseconds produce flanging, while chorus starts at 20 milliseconds.

Flanging

Flanging is less warm than chorus because flanging's closer delay time sounds more metallic and less like close copies of the original signal. Flanging adds one critical additional parameter to the list in the preceding section: feedback.

Feedback routes some of the output back to input, so the whole process starts again but on an already-affected sound. This addition accentuates the sweep and creates some resonant peaks in the harmonics, not unlike resonance or Q in a filter (which I discuss later in the chapter). At extreme feedback settings, flanging can produce a whoosh sort of sound resembling a jet takeoff.

Flanging was first created by running two tape players with the same audio on each, producing an artificial doubling of a track (a common practice for doubling vocals). Pressing a finger slightly against one of the reels slowed the playback speed for a moment, acting like a close delay, and voila, the flange effect was born. The name came from the part of the tape reel pressed to slow down the mechanism. (Some credit the Beatles' producer George Martin for coining the term *flanger* in a nonsensical discussion of the technique with John Lennon. This story may well be true regarding the term, but Martin didn't invent the effect/technique.)

Phase shifting

Phase shifting differs from chorus and flanging in that it doesn't use a delay-line shifted copy of the incoming signal that has all frequencies shifted by the same amount. Rather, it mixes a copy of the sound that has been shifted slightly out-of-phase by an all-pass filter, which shifts different frequencies by different amounts. (Check out the later section "Filter" for details on this control.) This method produces a very rich, warm sound with more tonal peaks than chorus, for example, because it has a feedback loop in its design like the flanger does. And it sounds less metallic than flanging because of the differing frequency shifts.

EQ

EQ allows you to boost or cut the level of various frequency ranges within your sound. If you're old enough, you may remember the simple tone controls that used to be on TVs and stereos — sometimes just a single knob that made the sound brighter or darker, or separate treble and bass controls that boosted or cut the higher, brighter tones and the lower, boomy tones, respectively.

Today, you can find EQ settings (with names like rock, jazz, concert hall, acoustic, dance, and so on) on your music players and electronics. They show multiple columns, each representing a frequency or pitch area. If the bar is tall, it's boosting that range; if it's low, it's cutting the range. Figure 9-1 shows a common representation of this setup.

Figure 9-1:
Visual representation
of EQ.

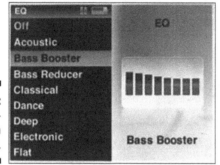

Apple iPod equalizer screenshot courtesy of Jerry Kovarsky

Your keyboard's EQ function gives you control over various frequencies that you can shape to change the tonal nature of your sound. The frequency ranges are represented as numbers in hertz (Hz) and kilohertz (kHz or k), such as 100 Hz or 2.5 kHz (2,500 hertz). Low frequencies are called *bass,* or *lows,* middle frequencies are called *mids* (naturally), and upper frequencies are called *highs.* EQs come in a couple of common types:

✔ A *graphic EQ* (see Figure 9-2) offers 5 to 31 frequencies, called *bands,* which are fixed values that can be cut or boosted.

Figure 9-2:
A graphic
EQ.

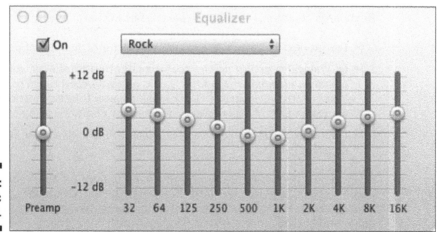

Apple iTunes equalizer screenshot courtesy of Jerry Kovarsky

✔ A *hi-shelf EQ* cuts or boosts frequencies above the value defined (like a brightness control).

✔ A *low-shelf EQ* cuts or boosts frequencies below a defined value (like a bass control).

✔ A *parametric EQ* offers some number of bands (usually between two and four); you can freely select their frequencies, so you can use them to flexibly shape the sound any way you want, as shown in Figure 9-3.

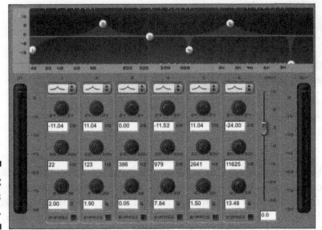

Figure 9-3: A parametric EQ.

Bias SuperFreq-6 EQ screenshot courtesy of Jerry Kovarsky

Some EQs combine these concepts, with a low-shelf band followed by one or two parametric bands and a hi-shelf band on top, for example. Or the outer bands can be changed from shelving to parametric as needed.

Keyboards commonly offer these parametric EQ parameters:

✔ **Frequency:** The pitch or frequency center for the band of EQ.

✔ **Q:** The width of frequencies that the cut or boost affects, sometimes called *bandwidth*. With a wide Q, you affect a broad range of your sound. You can use very narrow Q to reduce a harsh frequency or noise or add some extra emphasis to a specific noise or character of a sound.

✔ **Gain:** The amount that a band is boosted (a positive value) or cut (a negative value).

Many people think they need to boost a band to improve the sound, but cutting a band can often be more effective. Reducing a frequency that is already covered by another sound (cutting bass so you can hear the bass guitar and bass drum better) is a good approach.

You can hear demonstrations of shelving and parametric EQs in Track 64.

Distortion

Distortion adds a dirty, harsh quality to your sound. You're most familiar with this concept in rock guitar; the crunching rhythmic figures of classic riffs like "Smoke on the Water" by Deep Purple and "Satisfaction" by the Rolling Stones, the banshee wail of Jimi Hendrix, and the sound of grunge tunes by Nirvana and Pearl Jam are all well known examples. Varying levels of distortion may be called *overdrive, fuzz,* or *gain booster.*

Distortion is created by overloading the input to an amplifier, causing the circuitry to produce internal clipping or errors. Nowadays, electronics and software code can readily imitate it without the need for an actual guitar amp, which is why I'm talking about it in a book about keyboards!

Here are some common distortion controls you can adjust:

- ✔ **Mix or wet/dry mix:** This option controls how much of your dry signal is passed on, and how much of the distorted *(wet)* signal is introduced. Because distortion can be a very heavy effect, you get a better sound if you mix some of the dry signal into it for clarity, especially for keyboard sounds. For emulating rock guitar, you can never have too much distortion!

- ✔ **Type or model:** Many distortion effects are emulating other famous devices, be they classic guitar amplifiers, pedal effects (often called *stomp boxes*), or combinations thereof. The *type* control is where you decide which you want to use.

- ✔ **Input gain:** *Input gain* is the parameter that you turn up to produce the overloaded tone. Low values produce a slightly thicker, warmer sound, and higher values get crunchier up into full-out fuzz bliss.

- ✔ **Output level:** Because turning up the input increases the volume, you use this control to bring the overall level back down so you don't blow the roof off your home!

- ✔ **EQ:** Many distortion effects include some type of tone controls to help tame or shape the sound further. This setup can range from a single tone knob or parameter to multiband graphic and parametric equalizers. (The preceding section has info on these types of equalizers.)

Listen to Track 65 to hear various types of distortion demonstrated.

Rotary speaker

The *rotary speaker* effect emulates the famous spinning speaker cabinet (called a *Leslie*) invented for use with the Hammond organ. It was named after its creator, Donald Leslie, who wanted to make the organ sound more like a pipe organ, with its many rows of pipes spread out in a large space. What resulted is a strange yet wonderful-sounding contraption that has two spinning speakers inside: a small upper horn for the high frequencies and a larger speaker facing down into a rotating drum for the lows; see Chapter 2 for a visual. They spin at different speeds, producing a rich, moving quality to the sound. They can be switched to spin slowly or accelerate to a very fast speed, which is a dramatic effect that organists use to build excitement for various parts of a song.

The rotary speaker is an integral part of the tonewheel organ sound but has also been used by rock guitar players, on other electric keyboard sounds, and even on vocals (John Lennon famously sang through one on the song "Tomorrow Never Knows").

This speaker is a complex effect that may or may not have a wealth of parameters to adjust (you may only have the option to toggle the speed control from slow to fast). That said, common adjustable factors include the following:

- ✔ **Horn/rotor speed:** The upper horn can rotate at two different speeds, each of which may be adjusted. Similarly, the lower spinning drum (the rotor) has a two-speed control as well.

- ✔ **Horn/rotor acceleration and deceleration:** These items control the time the horn and rotor each take to transition from slow to fast and back again.

- ✔ **Mode:** *Mode* chooses whether the speaker is stopped or spinning. Completely stopping the speakers from spinning is called *brake,* and some designs allow all three states — brake, slow, fast — to be used. (Early Leslies had two settings: no spinning and spinning fast.)

- ✔ **Horn/rotor balance:** Microphones are usually placed by the rotary speaker to further amplify it in concert or to record it in the studio. This control positions the mic to be closer to the high horn (producing a brighter, thinner sound) or lower by the spinning drum (producing a bassier, heavier sound). More-advanced designs allow you to choose the position and distance for each microphone.

Listen to Track 66 to hear the rotary speaker effect.

Filter

A *filter* is a tone-modifying control that allows certain frequencies to pass through while blocking others. The point at which it gradually starts to remove the frequencies is called the *filter cutoff*. I discuss filters in greater detail in Chapter 14.

Common tone parameters you can adjust on your keyboard are

- **Type:** The most common filter type is called a *low-pass*, which allows all frequencies below the cutoff to pass through, gradually removing everything above it. A *high-pass* filter does the opposite, only allowing frequencies above the cutoff to pass through.

- **Cutoff:** The point at which the filter gradually starts to remove frequencies (by fading them out). Moving around this cutoff point (commonly called *sweeping* the cutoff) produces a very cool sound, most often associated with synthesizer sounds.

- **Resonance or Q:** This parameter emphasizes frequencies close to either side of the cutoff, like a sharp, narrow band of EQ boost. It produces a nasal, piercing quality at high settings and sounds great when combined with the sweeping of the cutoff. This control is a classic synth sound effect.

Check out Track 67 to hear demonstrations of various filters.

Wah-wah and auto-wah

The *wah-wah* is a filter placed into a rocking pedal to make it easy to sweep the cutoff with your foot while playing. Commonly used for guitar, it's also popular for keyboards, especially the clav.

The *auto-wah* (also called *envelope follow filter* or *envelope filter*) produces the sweep movement based on the incoming audio signal so you don't need to move your foot. Each note or chord played triggers the sweep, letting you easily play highly rhythmic parts without wearing out your ankle. Common auto-wah parameters your keyboard lets you adjust include the following:

- **Response/rate:** Controls the speed at which the filter opens up in reaction to the incoming signal.

- **Decay:** Sets the length of time the filter takes to close back down.

- **Range/manual/frequency:** Sets the frequency of the filter cutoff at the bottom and top of the sweep. This control is helpful to optimize the effect for the type of sound you're using it on (bass, type of keyboard sound, guitar). *Note:* This parameter is the only one that would be available for a wah-wah effect.

✔ **Sensitivity:** Adjusts the range of the sweep, based on the strength of the incoming signal. Low settings don't allow the range of the sweep to change much based on the incoming signal. At higher settings, soft levels produce very little sweep (a darker sound), and stronger signals produce a more full-range sweep.

Higher sensitivity helps produce the more expressive and dramatic auto-wah effect. But it needs to be adjusted to match your playing technique and how hard or soft your touch is. Adjust the setting up or down until it's easy to produce and control the range of sweep you like.

Track 68 plays examples of wah-wah and auto-wah.

Choosing Effects for Each Type of Sound

Certain instrument and effect combinations are matches made in rock-and-roll heaven! Some are commonly used based on musical genre (funk and wah-wah, for example), and others are associated with specific artists.

To help you get the sound you want for various songs, the following sections list the essential keyboard sounds and the effects commonly used and associated with them, often naming artists and songs as examples. ***Note:*** Reverb is used on pretty much everything, so I don't really highlight it here.

Piano-type and synth sounds

You can use keyboard effects with many common piano sounds:

✔ **Acoustic piano:** Sometimes a little EQ usage can help modify a piano for a specific song or style of music. Classical sounds good with a less bright, more mellow sound, and rock works with a much brighter piano to stand out when drums and guitars are playing. Some pop and rock music uses a little chorus on the piano (think of Journey's "Don't Stop Believin'"), and deeper chorus with more pitch variation (an increase of the depth parameter) helps make piano sound more honky-tonk.

✔ **Tine/Rhodes electric piano:** So many effects can work on this classic instrument:

• **Phase shifting:** Use subtle phaser settings to get that Billy Joel "Just the Way You Are" sound, Steely Dan/Donald Fagen tunes (check out "Green Flower Street"), late '80s Doobie Brothers ("Minute by Minute"), or the immortal sound of Richard Tee as featured on many Paul Simon, Grover Washington ("Just the Two of Us"), and Stuff recordings.

- **Chorus:** Using a chorus helps to get the sound of Jamiroquai as well as the whole L.A. '80s sound (think Al Jarreau, Toto, Quincy Jones, Chicago, and early Yellowjackets).

- **Distortion/wah-wah:** To sound like vintage/early '70s jazz, fusion, and rock artists, don't use any modulation effect. Do use EQ if needed to darken the sound a little bit. However, a little distortion (not too much) helps to get the aggressive solo sound of fusion players like Jan Hammer (Mahavishnu Orchestra's "Inner Mounting Flame"), Chick Corea (early *Return to Forever*), and George Duke (solo and with Frank Zappa), who often played through guitar amps. Many artists also used wah-wah, which is still a favorite way to "funk up" an electric piano (both tine and reed versions).

- **Delay:** You can use delay to get the spacey sound of early electric Herbie Hancock ("Mwandishi" and "Headhunters"), Brian Auger ("Live Oblivion"), Ramsey Lewis ("Sun Goddess"), and many reggae and dub recordings.

✔ **Reed/Wurlitzer electric piano:** This electric piano wasn't processed with effects as much, but the number-one application is putting a deep chorus on it to get that Supertramp sound ("Logical Song" and "Goodbye Stranger"). EQ and some distortion can help to get a stronger rock sound.

Though not as common, I (and many others) like the sound of both types of electric piano through a rotary speaker.

✔ **Clavinet:** Clavinet through a wah-wah or auto-wah is one of the classic sounds of funk music. Listen to songs like Stevie Wonder ("Higher Ground" and "Maybe Your Baby"), Billy Preston ("Outa-Space"), Rufus ("Tell Me Something Good"), Herbie Hancock ("Chameleon"), and the funkiest non-funk tune ever recorded, The Band's "Up on Cripple Creek". It was also prominently featured in reggae, like in Bob Marley/the Wailers "Burnin' and Lootin'" and "Get Up, Stand Up."

Distortion also sounds good on clav, which often was played through a guitar amp. You can hear this effect in varying degrees on the aforementioned Billy Preston songs, Stevie Wonder ("We Can Work It Out"), Led Zeppelin ("Trampled Under Foot"), Phish's "Tubes" and the always-amazing John Medeski (Medeski Martin & Wood).

✔ **Tonewheel organ:** A lot of famous organists have pretty specific and well-known sounds:

- As I note in the earlier section "Rotary speaker," tonewheel organ and the Leslie go hand in hand. Many jazz players are known for using only the brake and fast settings, whereas most rock, soul, and other players use the slow and fast speeds. Two prominent exceptions to that statement in rock/soul are Steve Winwood (solo and with Traffic and Blind Faith) and Booker T. (solo and with Booker T. & the MG's), who both favor the brake and fast settings.

- Progressive rocker Keith Emerson ran his organ through both Leslies and guitar amps to get more overdrive in his sound. He also used a distortion pedal effect on the smaller L-100 he'd abuse nightly to get feedback from it (find live versions of "Rondo" to hear/see this in action). Hard-rock organist Jon Lord (Deep Purple) stopped using a rotary speaker altogether, favoring using guitar amps to crank up his sound to match the rest of the band ("Machine Head" and "Made in Japan"). Jazz/rock organist Brian Auger is another famous non-Leslie user.

  - Tony Banks (Genesis) was known for running his tonewheel organ through a phase shifter and sometimes a chorus; listen to albums like *Wind and Wuthering, . . . And Then There Were Three . . .* , and *Duke.*

- ✔ **Synth sounds:** This group is a vast category, and basically, anything is possible. Have fun!

Guitar sounds

You really should add some effects to the guitar sounds coming out of your keyboard to make them more realistic and pleasing. Here are some ideas:

- ✔ **Guitar:** Guitar works well with a wide variety of effects. All the modulation effects can sound good, as do delay and reverb when you want to play more open, arpeggiated background parts. Andy Summers (The Police) and especially The Edge (U2) are famous for this approach. When you want to play stronger rock songs and take solos, distortion and amp models become an important part of your needed sound. Wah-wah works well for some rock songs and certainly for funky tunes, and auto-wah is perfect for funk.

- ✔ **Bass guitar:** Bass is the one sound that doesn't want much reverb, if any. Keeping it dry helps to anchor the feel and clarity of a song's groove. Sometimes subtle chorus or flanging can work, especially on fretless bass. For heavier rock and metal music, distortion is appropriate. Auto-wah can work for some funk.

Other sounds

What to do with more-orchestral instruments? Less is more:

- ✔ **Wind/brass instruments:** These instruments rarely require anything more than a little reverb to taste.

- ✔ **Strings:** All acoustic instruments sound good with reverb. String parts in songs sometimes come from real strings or from electronic string synthesizers and such. Slight chorus or phasing adds animation and movement to these instruments.

Chapter 10

Jamming with the Drummer: Playing Along to Rhythm Patterns

In This Chapter

▷ Manipulating basic drum patterns

▷ Stepping it up with variations, drum fills, intros, and endings

Drums and rhythm are the most primal aspect of music; all music fans have tapped on their legs/knees/steering wheels to their favorite songs. It's a natural reaction to a song with a good groove, and some people I know have taken this air drumming to a really high artistic art form.

If you don't know any drummers, onboard drum rhythms make a fine rhythmic partner for practicing and playing. Onboard drums are much more fun and inspiring rhythm-keepers than a metronome.

In this chapter, I take you through possibilities of using onboard drum machines and backing parts that feature drum and percussion rhythm. You discover how to use them as good practice and performance tools and how to vary the parts so things don't get boring. Chapter 11 expands on this idea for full-band auto-accompaniment, adding some controls that help the drummer and the rest of the band keep things interesting.

Getting Your Groove On: Working with Onboard Drum Rhythms

Playing in time is a fundamental part of a good performance. But keeping proper, even timing is only part of the process; the act of playing with a good feel is a more intangible but still critical element. Musicians use terms like *groove* and *in the pocket* to describe the act of playing with good feel. *Feel* relates to not only keeping steady time but also to subdividing the time with just the right nuance and perfectly in sync with the other musicians. You shouldn't *rush* (play slightly ahead of) or *drag* (play behind) the tempo too much or be generally unsteady (going back and forth between rushing and dragging).

Developing that sort of timing against a cold, impersonal metronome click is hard. But using preprogrammed drum rhythms can bring you much closer. Gone are the days of dinky little blips and beeps and canned auto-accompaniment patterns that sound like electronic appliances talking to each other. Nowadays, the onboard drum patterns in a keyboard were likely played by a real drummer and have highly nuanced and great feel. They can really groove!

So how do you know whether your keyboard has onboard drums? You can try reading the manual, but because you're reading my book, let me help you out a little:

✔ All arrangers and portable keyboards have onboard drums. Anything that has auto-accompaniment includes drums as part of its band.

✔ Many of the high-end home digital pianos include auto-accompaniment as well. They're like piano-centric arranger keyboards.

✔ Workstation keyboards all include drum programs, so you can write your own music with drums grooves. More and more, these instruments include preprogrammed drum patterns as well.

✔ Some stage pianos include preset, play-along drum grooves.

✔ Workstations, pro synths, and stage pianos with terms such as Rhythm, Rhythm Set, Drum Track, and Drum Pattern likely have this function.

Some keyboards (workstations and synths) use an arpeggiator to produce drum patterns, so look there for this function. I discuss arpeggiators in Chapter 12.

Selecting a drum pattern

An instrument with drums always has a beat ready to go; you don't have to dig through a bunch of menu options or anything special to hear them. Locate and press the Start/Stop or Play button, and something will start playing. If it doesn't, try playing a key on the keyboard, and then the drums will start with you. If what you get isn't the groove you want to play, check out the following sections to explore how various keyboards present their drum rhythms.

Portable keyboards

Simple portable keyboards don't always have full auto-accompaniment, but they often offer drum grooves. Casio calls them Rhythms, and Yamaha calls them Styles.

To select a different drum pattern (my generic term), do the following:

1. **Press the Style or Rhythm button.**

   Use the + and – buttons to move up or down to the next pattern or to scroll through the available patterns one at a time. Or use the *numeric keypad* (if available) to directly enter the number of a specific pattern you want.

   On these low-end models, the pattern names may appear on the front panel, as shown in Figure 10-1. On other models, the names are displayed on the screen.

2. **When you've selected the desired pattern, press Start/Stop.**

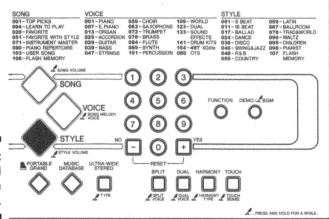

Figure 10-1:
Front panel
of a portable
keyboard.

Images courtesy of Yamaha Corporation of America

Note that you can usually scroll or select another pattern while the drums are playing, and it will start on the next downbeat.

Arranger keyboards and high-end digital pianos with full auto-accompaniment

Full accompaniment is more than you're looking for right now. You just want to have drums playing along with your keyboard playing, so find the button that turns off the rest of the accompaniment (see Figure 10-2). This button may be labeled Chords On/Off, Accompaniment On/Off, ACMP On/Off, Arranger Mode, and so on. On some Roland arrangers, you need to turn off all the Backing Type elements (Style, Song, and USB) until only drums remain. With the accompaniment/chords turned off, you can freely select drum patterns without calling up a full backing band.

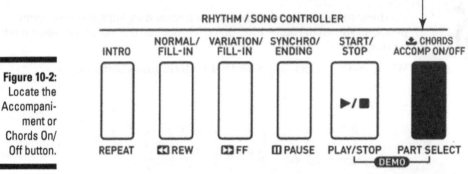

Figure 10-2: Locate the Accompaniment or Chords On/Off button.

Image courtesy of Casio America, Inc.

To select a different drum pattern, press the Style or Rhythm button. You can use the + and – buttons or value dial to move up or down to the next pattern or to scroll through the list of available patterns one at a time. If available, you can use the numeric keypad to directly enter the number of a specific pattern you want. Then press Play.

Higher-end models may present the Styles/Rhythms on multiple buttons, with each button representing a category of styles arranged by musical genre: Rock, Ballroom, Waltz, World, Jazz/Big-Band, and so on, as shown in Figure 10-3. Press the button for the category you like and select the specific drum pattern you want from the choices shown on the keyboard's display and then press Play. Note that you can usually scroll or select another pattern when the drums are playing, and it will start on the next *downbeat,* or start of a measure.

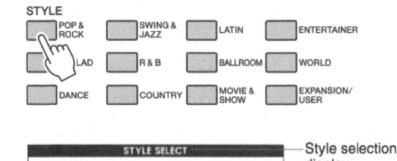

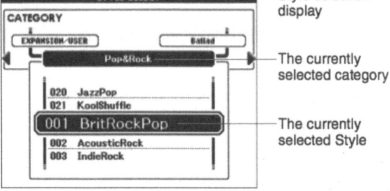

Figure 10-3:
Styles
organized
by category/
genre.

Style selection
display

The currently
selected category

The currently
selected Style

Images courtesy of Yamaha Corporation of America

Synths and workstations

Synths and workstations don't generally have full backing accompaniment but may have drum grooves set up behind their sounds. Depending on the product, the pattern is either created by a small phrase/pattern player or by an arpeggiator. Drums are usually incorporated in a multisound mode of some sort, be it a layer, a split, or a combination of both. (Check out Chapter 8 for details on splits and layers.) Korg calls these Combinations, Kurzweil calls them Setups, Roland calls them Live Sets, and Yamaha calls them Performances.

Some Korg models have a feature called a *drum track,* which is a drum groove set up behind their single sounds (called *programs*). They always have a dedicated front panel button for starting these drum patterns.

Selecting a different drum pattern is a little more complicated in these situations than for the instruments in the preceding sections.

1. **Go into Edit Mode for the multisound mode your product offers.**

   Note that some products have dedicated arpeggiator edit buttons or controls available right from the front panel, and you don't need to go into Edit Mode to adjust them.

2. **Find the page for the drum pattern (phrase) player or the arpeggiator.**

3. **Locate the Pattern/Arp number parameter; this number is the currently assigned drum groove for the sound.**

4. **Locate and select the pattern you want to use.**

   Use the + and – buttons, value dial, or data slider to move up or down to the next pattern or to scroll through the available patterns one at a time. Use the numeric keypad (if available) to directly enter the number of a specific drum/arp pattern you want.

5. **When you've selected the desired pattern press Start/Stop or Arp On/Off.**

Starting the pattern playing

Generally you press a Start/Stop or Play button and your drums start playing right away. That works out well if you want a few bars of drum groove before you come in with your playing. But if you want to start playing at the same time, pressing the button and getting your hand back to the keyboard in time for that first downbeat can be nearly impossible.

Workstations and pro synths that use an arpeggiator to create drum patterns start only when you touch a key on the keyboard. This setup is necessary because an arpeggiator rearranges notes you play to create more-complex patterns. So it needs some note trigger to do its thing even when it's used to create a background drum groove.

All keyboards with accompaniment offer a setting called *Synchro Start* or *Sync Start*. It waits for you to play the first note before it starts the drums or accompaniment. So pressing the Synchro Start button (see Figure 10-4) tells the drums to be ready to play but to wait for a key to be played to trigger the start of the groove. Perfect solution!

Figure 10-4:
Synchro Start waits for the first key to be played to start the drums.

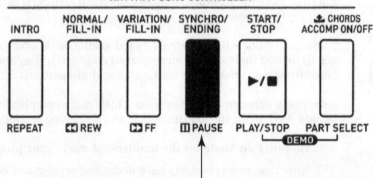

Image courtesy of Casio America, Inc.

Many higher-end keyboards offer the ability to set up a footswitch to perform the start/stop function, freeing up your hands to stay on the keyboard. That's a convenient way to do things, but it does involve buying the footswitch (they're always an option). The Synchro Start feature is a much easier approach.

Controlling the tempo

Every keyboard that offers rhythms, accompaniment, or arpeggiators has some type of tempo control on the front panel, whether that's up and down/+ and – buttons, a knob or dial, or a tempo parameter in the display.

If you're playing from print music, you can determine the tempo you need by checking to see how many *beats per minute* (BPM) a piece calls for. The music won't show the term BPM; as I discuss in Chapter 5, it will likely show "♩ = [a number]". That number is the BPM. So you use the controls to set the tempo to the right number.

Often, though, you don't have written music or don't have an indication of the required BPM. So you end up starting the drums, listening and adjusting the tempo, stopping the track, get set to play, and then starting the drums again. That procedure gets the job done, but it's not very professional; it makes you seem like you're not prepared. Thankfully, a better way exists!

Many keyboards offer a feature called *Tap Tempo,* which gives you the ability to tap on a button at the BPM you want and set the drum tempo to that input. Some keyboards have a dedicated button for this capability, but many use a combination of two buttons. In these situations, you hold one button down and tap on the second button. Look at the front panel of your keyboard to see whether it has this function.

When setting the tempo with Tap Tempo, you need to tap at least three times to give the keyboard a clear indication of the tempo you want. Watch the display; it will indicate when it has changed to the new tempo. I like to tap at least six to eight times to be sure I've settled into a steady groove.

To give yourself more choices for your pop song, ballad, or other mellow type of music, you can take many of the medium-to-fast grooves in your keyboard and play them at half speed. Cut the tempo in half by dividing the BPM by two or setting the tempo by ear. If available, you can use the Tap Tempo function; simply tap half notes rather than quarter notes to set your tempo, tapping on beats 1 and 3 rather than on 1, 2, 3, and 4. Count the quarter notes in your head (or out loud) and practice tapping on every other count; you'll get used to it quickly.

Adding Variety to Your Groove

When you start using onboard drum patterns, you'll notice something: The drummer never changes what she plays. No matter how you're playing, that drummer just plays the same beat over and over as you change from verse to chorus, during a solo, and from the intro to the ending. It gets a bit monotonous after a while. As good as the groove is, it quickly starts to sound like a machine.

That's because a real drummer would add some accents at choice spots in the tune. She'd play a small *drum fill* (a one-to-four-beat solo) to transition between sections and change up her groove as the song progressed to build up the excitement and add variety.

If you have a portable keyboard, an arranger, or a digital piano/arranger hybrid, you have some very wonderful options available to help improve your groove, as I discuss in the following sections.

Using pattern variations

Letting your instrument play the same pattern over and over is certainly the easiest way to go, but it can get pretty boring. Luckily, spicing up the groove a bit isn't all that difficult. The following sections show you how to utilize variation functions for both lower- and higher-end keyboards.

Basic options for simple keyboards

Inexpensive portable keyboards offer at least a basic variation for each of their drum grooves. Each drum pattern is actually two patterns in one. Figure 10-5 shows a typical button layout for this approach.

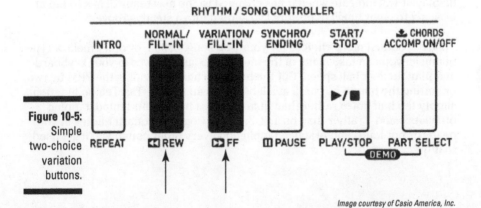

Figure 10-5: Simple two-choice variation buttons.

Image courtesy of Casio America, Inc.

This method actually has a nice way of giving you control over what plays. One button is labeled Normal and the other Variation; select whichever one you want when you need it. Couldn't be simpler, right? Here's how it works:

1. **Press Start/Stop and the Normal pattern plays.**

2. **Press Variation to switch patterns.**

   Note that the timing of when you press the button has an effect on what happens. The new pattern always waits and changes on the first beat of the next measure. So if you press the button earlier than that you won't hear the change until the downbeat comes around again. This delay allows you to preselect the variation change and get your hand back to the keyboard before it happens.

Track 69 presents various drum patterns and their variations from a Casio keyboard.

From a stopped state, you can press either button to start the drums, playing the selection you chose. You aren't forced to always start with the Normal pattern.

Figure 10-6 shows an approach Yamaha uses that requires fewer buttons but is less obvious to the eye.

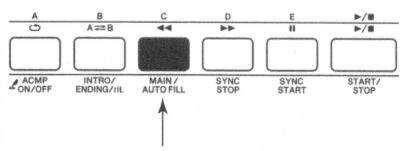

Figure 10-6: Using the same button to alternate variations.

Image courtesy of Yamaha Corporation of America

In this layout, each time you press the button labeled Main/Auto Fill, the drummer does a short drum fill and switches to the other variation pattern. The display usually shows you what is happening, so it identifies which variation is playing. Follow these steps:

1. **Press Start/Stop, and the Main A pattern plays.**

2. **Press Main/Auto Fill to switch patterns.**

This change always happens with a drum fill to lead into the new pattern. *Note:* From a stopped state, you can press the Main/Auto Fill button to pre-select Main A or Main B. Then you press Start/Stop to start the groove. So you don't always have to start with the Main A pattern. As always, the display shows you what is happening.

Listen to Track 70 to hear various drum patterns and their variations from a Yamaha keyboard.

More-advanced options on higher-end models

Higher-priced arranger keyboards offer more variations (three to four for each pattern). Figure 10-7 shows a typical button layout for a more advanced drum section; note the dedicated buttons for each of the variations.

Figure 10-7:
A more advanced arranger's drum controls.

Image courtesy of Yamaha Corporation of America

Variations always progress from simpler to busier or more complex. Perhaps the drums in the first variation are playing softly on the closed hi-hat cymbal, with a snare hitting on beats 2 and 4. In the next variation, the hi-hat part gets busier, and the snare adds some extra hits. Perhaps the most complex option has the drums really driving the groove harder, with more-complex snare and bass drum interaction and more crash cymbals. So the variations help to build the dynamic flow of a song in the same way that a real musician would.

To navigate multiple variations, just do the following:

1. **Press Start/Stop, and the first variation pattern plays.**

2. **Press any of the Variation buttons to switch patterns.**

From a stopped state, you can press any of the Variation buttons to preselect that pattern. Then press Start/Stop to start the groove you chose. The display and the lights built into each button show you what is happening.

You can hear various drum patterns and their multiple variations from a Korg keyboard in Track 71.

Digging into natural drum fills

Every arranger-type keyboard offers controls to select drum fills; some models have more than others. ***Note:*** Arrangers are specifically designed to offer these types of variations and fills to emulate the complete performance of a song. If you have a workstation, synth, or stage piano that has some drum grooves but no apparent fills, I'm sorry to tell you this is one of the differences in these types of instruments. Some of the drum patterns may have a fill preprogrammed at the end of the phrase, but you can't make it happen whenever you want, and you can't get rid of it.

Look at Figure 10-6 earlier in the chapter, and you can see that you always get a drum fill when pressing Main/Auto Fill to change to the variation. In all the other examples in the preceding sections, you can choose when to create a drum fill independent of changing variations.

Actually, you can get a drum fill to happen on the Figure 10-6 design without changing to the other variation. Just press the Main/Auto Fill button twice in a row. You "fool" the drummer into playing the fill and then returning to the current variation.

In Figure 10-5, pressing the button for the variation you're currently playing triggers a drum fill. After the fill plays, the pattern continues playing the same variation. If you want to use a drum fill to transition to the other variation, you need to press the new choice button twice (not too rapidly). The first press tells the drummer to switch to that pattern (Normal or Variation), which will happen at the next downbeat. The second press tells her to do a fill on her way there. So you need to do both buttons presses before the start of a new measure.

Check out Track 72 to hear drum fills added to various patterns from a Casio keyboard.

On a fancier arranger keyboard, the drum fill button is separate from the variations, giving you complete control over what happens. And you may have more than one drum fill to select from. Figure 10-8 shows a very complicated panel section (from the Korg Pa-3X) with some really cool controls over the drums.

Figure 10-8:
A feature-
rich drum
section
control.

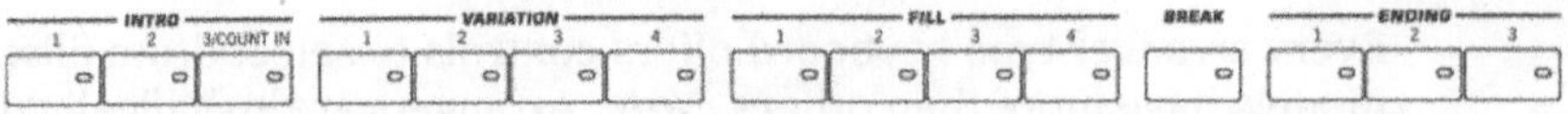

INTRO	VARIATION	FILL	BREAK	ENDING
1 2 3/COUNT IN	1 2 3 4	1 2 3 4		1 2 3

Image courtesy of Korg Italy

In this design you have four possible drum fills; each one gets progressively busier than the preceding one. Here's how to use them creatively:

1. **Choose a Style/Rhythm pattern you like, as well as the first of the four variations.**

2. **Make sure the chords and/or accompaniment is turned off so you have only drums.**

3. **Press Synchro Start so the drum will wait for you to touch a key on the keyboard.**

4. **Start to play, and the drums will begin.**

5. **At some point in your playing, before the end of a measure, press the first drum fill button.**

    The drums will do their thing and then return to the groove. Try each of the fill choices to hear how they differ and add to the performance.

Experiment with pressing the fill button at different times within a measure to hear how the drum fill differs. The earlier in a bar you press it, the more drum fill you get.

Listen to Track 73 to hear various drum fills added to patterns from a Korg keyboard.

If you press the fill button very close to the end of the bar, you may not hear a fill at all because the keyboard barely plays the fill before going back to the pattern. Press it too late, and you actually get a full measure (or more) of fill on the next bar.

Using fills to transition to a new variation is so common that most arrangers have a button called Auto-Fill that automatically adds a fill when you press a new Variation button. With that function turned on, you don't need to press as many buttons during performance.

Roland and Yamaha arrangers don't have dedicated fill-in buttons. Pressing the currently playing Variation button again produces a drum fill; pressing a different variation button produces a fill when the Auto-Fill button is turned on.

Some of the most advanced arrangers may have a button labeled Break, as shown in Figure 10-8. This feature is another type of fill, where the drums stop playing completely for a few beats and then come back in. This option can be a very dramatic way to pause for a moment in your playing, or you can use it so you can play a run, figure, or solo passage and have the drums get out of your way. Just remember that they're still keeping time and will come back in, so play in time!

Listen to Track 74 to hear a Break fill used within various drum patterns from a Korg keyboard.

Incorporating intros and endings

An *intro* is a beginning phrase that starts off a song and leads into the first section. With drums only, these patterns don't seem all that different from the main groove. They become important when you use the full accompaniment, providing some interesting parts for the chords you play.

I bring them up here because many arrangers offer a special type of intro called a *count-in.* This four-beat click sets up the tempo to give you a reference for what it sounds and feels like. This feature is similar to what happens in an actual band when the drummer counts off by clicking her sticks to give everyone something to follow. Look for it in your keyboard; it may appear on the panel or be a dedicated Intro variation. Read more about what you can do with intros and endings in Chapter 11.

Changing styles from section to section

This concept is more advanced, but it can be very musical, so I want to share it anyway. Many songs change their grooves significantly at some point in the tune. I'm thinking of songs where the bridge or a solo section changes somehow; common examples include

- ✔ The groove switches to a half-time feel. The tempo remains the same, but the drum plays as if the tempo were cut in half.

- ✔ The groove goes into a reggae feel.

- ✔ The song alternates between swing jazz and Latin feel.

The only way you're likely to re-create this switch is to change the drum pattern you're using by directly switching to another Rhythm or Style selection quickly. If your keyboard allows you to only step through patterns one at a time or requires you to type in a number, this shift is going to be impossible. If your model offers rhythm/style categories, you may get lucky and be able to alternate them easily enough.

If your keyboard offers some User locations for rhythms and styles, however, you're in luck. A *User location* is a place you can copy your own grooves to (or perhaps load new ones to, if your keyboard offers that capability). To achieve what I'm discussing here, you simply copy each of the needed patterns to adjacent User locations (see your keyboard's owner's manual for instructions on how to do this). Now you can easily toggle back and forth between the needed patterns by using the + and – buttons. Problem solved!

PlayThis! Listen to Track 75 to hear drum fills used to transition between different drum patterns on a Korg keyboard.

Chapter 11

Join The Band! Adding Accompaniment

In This Chapter

▶ Exploring auto-accompaniment basics

▶ Looking at chord playing methods

▶ Adding variety to your performance

▶ Working with mixing and cool extra features

. . . .

For some people, the concept of automatic accompaniment brings up images of hokey one-finger mall organ demos and corny '80s ads from the very companies I mention here. All too often, "serious" musicians looked down their noses at these products. And I myself am a rather snobby musician who likes serious music performed by equally serious and skilled musicians.

Well, I'm telling you that the sound realism and musical quality of the auto-accompaniment in today's keyboards are markedly improved and nothing to scoff at. They can provide a child, student, or casual player with tools that help him play better and enjoy his time making music, which is a wonderful thing. Across Europe, Asia, and the Middle East, accompaniment keyboards are *the* professional keyboard; very skilled players use them (in public!) with pride.

In this chapter, I help you get the most from your keyboard's auto-accompaniment features. I show you how to get them started and how you can feed them the chords they need to generate their full backing band parts. I take you under the hood a little to better understand the musical parts that make up their patterns and show you plenty of tips and tricks to keep the parts interesting and not canned sounding.

Playing with Accompaniment

The concept of using auto-accompaniment is simple: You play some notes on the lower range of your keyboard, and that tells the system to start playing some backing music in the key you gave it. You choose the style of music it plays from the choices presented on the front panel.

The result is the sound of a full band playing, giving you a professional backing track that you're in complete control over. You've moved up from being a solo pianist to being the leader of an ever-changing cast of musicians who can play any song in any style of music you need. All you need to do is pick the style of music and provide the band with some chords to follow.

Sound too good to be true? It's actually a marvel of technology; inside, your keyboard is doing some pretty amazing computational stuff, but as the player, your job couldn't be simpler. The following sections lay out what's really going on.

Understanding how auto-accompaniment works

Playing with accompaniment usually means you have a split keyboard, with the lower range (left hand) dedicated to playing notes/chords to trigger the accompaniment and the right hand having a live sound (or two) to play your melodies with. Some arrangers and digital pianos have a full-play mode, where you play acoustic piano with two hands and the keyboard uses your two-handed playing to determine the chords.

Accompaniment uses *styles* or *rhythms* — collections of MIDI-based music tracks that play various instrument sounds to produce the sound of a backing band. They've been played and recorded by skilled musicians to faithfully reproduce various musical styles. Some are written to sound generic so that you can play any song within that genre of music, and others are very specific re-creations of a famous song.

The unique thing about the accompaniment "engine" is that it can adapt these parts for any chord you give it, changing the notes within the pattern to fit the various root tones and chord qualities in music (major, minor, diminished, augmented, and so on; I discuss chords in Chapter 7). This adaptability is how auto-accompaniment differs from a prerecorded backing track, which rigidly plays back the exact notes you played to create the part. Accompaniment is interactive — able to change to any chord you play the instant you play it.

Starting a pattern playing

As I discuss in Chapter 10, the patterns that make up the accompaniment backing have various names: Casio and Roland call them *Rhythms*; Keytron, Korg, and Yamaha call them *Styles*.

Simple portable keyboards don't always have full auto-accompaniment, so look for a button labeled Chords, Accompaniment On/Off, ACMP On/Off, Arranger Mode, and so on. These options indicate that you have full accompaniment parts, not just drums.

To help understand what auto-accompaniment is and what makes it up, I want you to get the sound of it in your head (and ears). After you've heard a variety of selections, what I explain will make much more sense. Here's how to get a pattern playing:

1. **Press the Styles or Rhythm button.**

2. **Make sure the Chord/Accomp button is on.**

3. **Play a low C on the keyboard to start the pattern playing.**

   If you feel comfortable, try playing a C triad (C-E-G) instead. If the music doesn't start, press the Start/Stop or Play button while you play the note or chord.

   Accompaniment needs you to play a chord to tell the players what key and what chord type you want them to play (C major, F minor, and so on). So if you just press Start/Stop or Play, the drums will start without the rest of the band.

4. **With the music playing, select some other patterns and listen to how the music and parts change.**

   No need to play another chord for now; I just want you to hear how the parts sound for various selections. For simple models, you can use the + and – buttons to move up or down to the next pattern or to scroll through the available patterns one at a time. Or use the numeric keypad (if available) to directly enter the number of a specific pattern you want.

On low-end models, the pattern names may appear on the front panel, as shown in Figure 11-1. On other models, the names are displayed on the screen. Higher-end models present the Styles/Rhythms on multiple buttons, with each button representing a category of styles arranged by musical genre — Pop & Rock, Ballroom, World, Swing & Jazz, and so on — as shown in Figure 11-2. For models that present their Styles like in Figure 11-2, first press the button for the category you like. Now you can use the navigation method of your choosing to select the specific backing pattern you want from the choices shown on the keyboard's display.

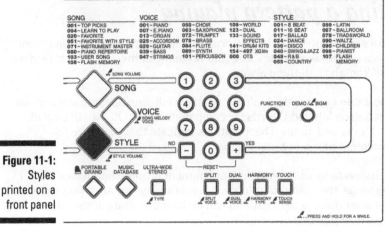

Figure 11-1:
Styles printed on a front panel

Image courtesy of Yamaha Corporation of America

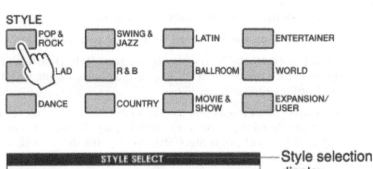

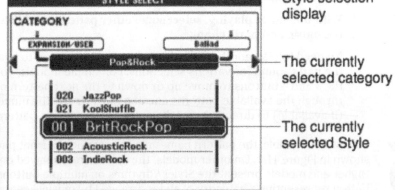

Figure 11-2:
Styles organized by category/genre.

Style selection display

The currently selected category

The currently selected Style

Images courtesy of Yamaha Corporation of America

PLAY THIS!

Listen to Track 76 to hear various styles being played using a simple C triad.

Appreciating what you hear: Breaking down an accompaniment pattern

An accompaniment pattern usually has the following elements:

- **Drums:** Drums include the traditional drumkit, with bass drum, snare, hi-hat, cymbals, and so on, playing a beat.

- **Percussion:** This element includes things such as tambourine, cowbell, shakers, congas/timbales/bongos, triangle, and other hand percussion, providing extra color to the rhythm.

- **Bass:** Bass presents the low notes that play some sort of rhythmic, moving series of notes. It may be an electric, acoustic (upright), or synth bass sound, depending on the style of music.

- **Chordal part(s):** *Chordal parts* are often a keyboard sound (acoustic or electric piano, organ, clav, and so on) and possibly some strummed guitar parts (acoustic or electric). Having a few tracks of this sort is common (just as a band may have multiple players).

- **Other sustained parts:** These options include string, vocal, and synth pad sounds — sustained chords for additional interest and sound variety.

- **Background melodic figures:** These elements can be string lines, brass and woodwind melodies, synth patterns and arpeggiations, and guitar licks.

Every part will not always be playing; parts may come in and out depending on a number of settings and factors, such as which variation you're using and the taste of the pattern programmer. (Chapter 10 has more on variations.) In general, an arranger keyboard uses up to 12 parts for these patterns, plus the live sounds that you can play on the keyboard along with the accompaniment.

Track 77 illustrates a style broken down into its separate elements or tracks.

Feeding the Band the Chord Changes: Chord Triggering

You have to play chords to tell the accompaniment engine what to do. All arrangers and portable keyboards offer a couple of ways of playing chords, some simpler than others, that I explore in the following sections.

Using the easy methods

Part of the fun of auto-accompaniment is how it can help fill out your musical performance when your skills aren't as well developed. Each brand offers an easy method of chord triggering, which doesn't require you to know what specific notes make up a particular chord. The following sections break down two methods for this process: Casio's and everyone else's.

These easy chord methods don't support the ability to play diminished, augmented, or suspended chords. You have to use a fingered mode instead; see the later section "Playing the chords yourself" for details.

Casio

Here's how to trigger easy chords for Casio keyboards:

1. **Press and hold the Chords/Accomp On/Off button until CHORDS:Fingered or F1 shows up in the display.**

2. **Use the + or – button to change the value to CHORDS:CC (meaning Casio Chord).**

   Now whenever you play a single note in the lower part of the keyboard, you'll produce a major triad.

4. **To change the kind of chord, press the root tone and one or more higher keys.**

   To play a minor triad, you press the root tone you want (C, for example) and any other note (white or black) above it. Check out Figure 11-3 for an example. To play a dominant seventh or minor seventh chord, press your desired root tone and any two or three notes, respectively, above it.

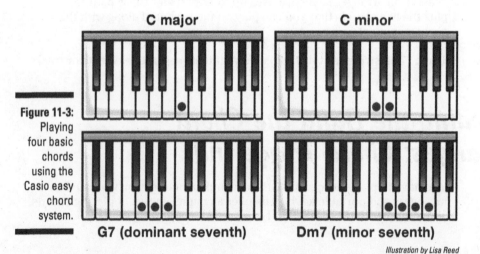

Figure 11-3: Playing four basic chords using the Casio easy chord system.

C major

C minor

G7 (dominant seventh)

Dm7 (minor seventh)

Illustration by Lisa Reed

Listen to Track 78 to hear these four chord qualities (major and minor triad, dominant and minor seventh) demonstrated.

Figure 11-4 shows how to play a simple chord progression by using the Casio chord method.

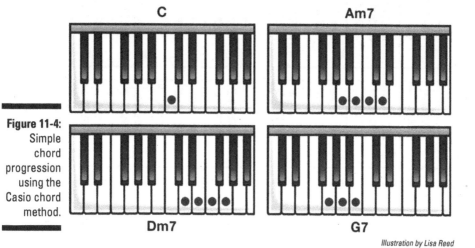

Figure 11-4:
Simple
chord
progression
using the
Casio chord
method.

Illustration by Lisa Reed

The other guys

Korg and Roland arrangers don't wake up with their easy chord method selected (Yamaha is ready to go!), so you need to turn that on before you continue. Here's how:

✔ Korg

   1. Press the Global mode button, followed by Mode Preferences.

   For most models, this sequence takes you where you need to go, but note that some models locate the easy chord function in the Style Play mode, Split Tab.

   2. Select the Style tab/page and choose the parameter Chord Recognition.

   3. Change the value to One Finger.

✔ Roland

   1. Press the Menu button, followed by Arranger Settings.

   2. Select the Type parameter.

   3. Change the value to Easy.

Now you're ready to trigger chords the easy way!

✔ **Major triad:** Play a single note in the lower part of the keyboard. Figure 11-5 shows an example.

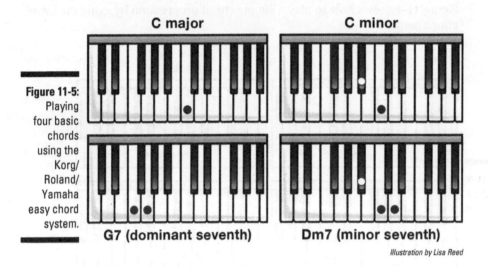

Figure 11-5: Playing four basic chords using the Korg/ Roland/ Yamaha easy chord system.

Illustration by Lisa Reed

✔ **Minor triad:** Press the root tone you want and any black note below it.

✔ **Dominant seventh chord:** Press the root tone you want and any white key below it.

✔ **Minor seventh chord:** Press the root tone you want and both a white and black key below it (three keys in total).

Figure 11-6 shows how to play the same chord progression from Figure 11-4 in the preceding section by using another brand's method.

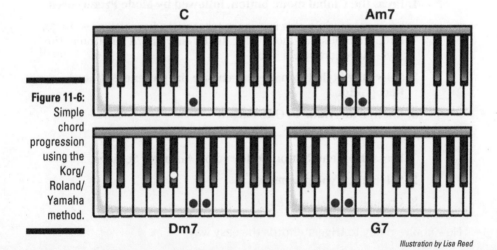

Figure 11-6: Simple chord progression using the Korg/ Roland/ Yamaha method.

Illustration by Lisa Reed

Listen to Track 79 to hear this simple chord progression played using a variety of styles.

Playing the chords yourself

The *fingered* method is self-explanatory: You play the full chords with your left hand and the system reads them and produces the backing parts. So you need to know how to play chords fairly well to use this method successfully. (I discuss chord playing in Chapter 7.) Depending on the manufacturer, this form of chord playing is referred to as Fingered (Casio and Korg), Multi Finger (Yamaha), and Standard (Roland) and is the default method for chord recognition for all keyboards when powered on.

If you've been working in the easy chord function I describe for Korg and Roland instruments in the preceding section, be sure to reset your keyboard to Fingered/Standard. The easiest way to do so is to simply turn the keyboard off and then back on, though you can also reverse the steps in the earlier section.

Here's a simple fingered-chord example to try if you don't read music yet. (But I strongly suggest you check out Chapter 5 to take full advantage of reading basic music notation.)

Figure 11-7 shows three basic chords to play: C major, F major, and G major, using chord inversions for the F and the G to make them easier to reach/play smoothly. Play these chords, using a variety of pattern choices. They sound good with most styles of music; you can hold each one for as long as you like at first and then try changing them at different timings as you get comfortable.

Play through the examples in Figures 7-15 and 7-16 in Chapter 7 to try this method out as well. Use a variety of styles and rhythms to hear how they work for different musical genres.

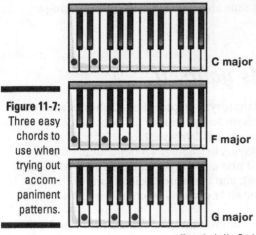

Figure 11-7: Three easy chords to use when trying out accompaniment patterns.

C major

F major

G major

Illustration by Lisa Reed

Listen to Tracks 80, 81, and 82 to hear some common chord progressions played with a variety of musical styles.

Spicing Up Your Performance

Good performances grow and develop in innumerable ways to keep things interesting. The band almost never just plays the same part over and over, only changing the chords it uses. Sometimes the players start out light and simple and get a little busier and more complex as the song develops, or they change the feel of the song for the bridge or a solo section. Maybe one person sits out at the beginning and only comes in for the chorus of the song.

Not changing any aspects of your performance is a dead giveaway that you're playing an auto-accompaniment keyboard (and not doing a very good job of hiding it)! In the following sections, I help you add all sorts of nice changes and variety to your playing.

Automatic drum grooves and full accompaniment share the same controls, so the following sections may seem familiar if you've read Chapter 10. But things are a bit more detailed with accompaniment because you're also dealing with chords and melodic figures, so I recommend you read this section too anyway.

Mixing things up with pattern variations

Lower-end keyboards usually offer one variation for each of their accompaniment patterns. Figure 11-8 shows how Casio presents this function.

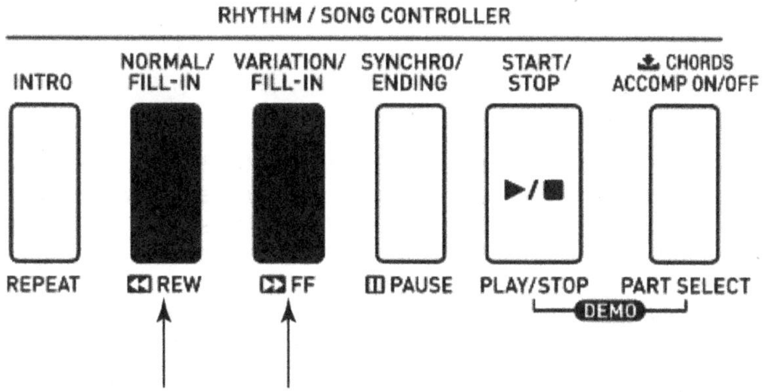

RHYTHM / SONG CONTROLLER

INTRO	NORMAL/ FILL-IN	VARIATION/ FILL-IN	SYNCHRO/ ENDING	START/ STOP	⬇ CHORDS ACCOMP ON/OFF
REPEAT	◀◀ REW	▶▶ FF	⏸ PAUSE	PLAY/STOP	PART SELECT

Figure 11-8: Simple two-choice variation buttons.

Image courtesy of Casio America, Inc.

The button labeled *Normal* is the more basic pattern, and the one labeled *Variation* is usually a bit fancier/busier. Switching between them is simple:

1. **Hold a chord and press Start/Stop; the Normal pattern plays.**

2. **Press Variation to switch to the busier pattern.**

   The pattern always waits to switch at the next downbeat, or new measure, so you can preselect it before the end of a measure and get your hand back to the keys in time for the new section if you want. Before you start the accompaniment you can select either button, so you can start with whichever version you like.

Listen to Track 83 to hear some patterns and their variations being demonstrated.

Yamaha approaches variations differently, using a single button to toggle between the choices as shown in Figure 11-9.

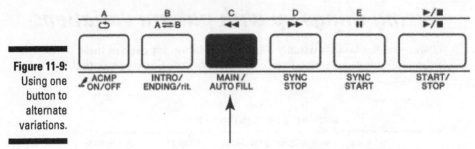

Figure 11-9:
Using one
button to
alternate
variations.

Image courtesy of Yamaha Corporation of America

When you press the button labeled Main/Auto Fill in this method, the drums do a short fill (see the following section) and then the variation pattern plays. Yamaha calls the patterns Main A and Main B; as usual, A is simpler, and B kicks things up a bit. Here's how the Yamaha process works.

1. **Hold a chord and press Start/Stop; the Main A pattern plays.**

2. **Press Main/Auto Fill to trigger the drum fill and switch to the Main B pattern.**

   Before you start the accompaniment you can toggle the button to choose either variation to start playing with; watch the display for feedback on what you're doing. During playback the display will always show you what is happening.

Listen to Track 84 to hear some variations preceded by drum fills being demonstrated.

As you pay more for an instrument, you get more features. Figure 11-10 shows the layout for a higher-priced model, with dedicated buttons for each variation. You typically get three or four variations for each pattern.

Figure 11-10:
A more
advanced
layout with
multiple
variation
buttons.

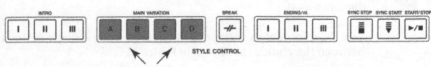

Image courtesy of Yamaha Corporation of America

Variations always progress from simpler to busier or more complex. You can hear this progression in the players, particularly the drummer, who usually start out simply and build with each variation. You'll notice additional players being added as you move up as well. So the variations help build the dynamic flow of a song in the same way that a real band would. To use the variations, follow these steps:

1. **Hold a chord and press Start/Stop; the first variation pattern plays.**

2. **Press a Variation button to change to another pattern.**

   Before starting a pattern you can preselect any of the available variations to start with that pattern. The display always shows you what is happening, along with the lights built into each button.

Listen to Track 85 to hear patterns with multiple variations demonstrated.

Including drum fills

Drummers commonly set up each change in a song structure with a few extra drum hits or a dramatic pause to make the transition between sections in a musical fashion. That small phrase is called a *drum fill*. The other band members may keep playing their parts during this break or play some accented hits along with him, as if they had rehearsed a cool break.

I cover the various ways to work with drum fills in Chapter 10. Refer to it and try the examples with accompaniment; just be sure you've triggered a chord to hear how the rest of the band behaves when the drummer takes his time to shine!

Trying intros and endings

An *intro* is a beginning phrase that starts off a song and leads into the first verse. It sets the tempo and the mood and establishes what key the song is in. Most arranger keyboards offer an intros feature, and it's a good option for players who aren't as familiar with playing intro for themselves. The intro plays through a couple of chords based on the chord you feed it. The phrase lasts between two and eight bars depending on the style you choose and the brand and model of your keyboard. Try it:

1. **Choose a style or rhythm pattern you like.**

2. **Make sure the Chords/Accompaniment button is on.**

3. **Press Synchro Start so the accompaniment will wait for you to touch a key on the keyboard.**

4. **Press the Intro button.**

5. **Play a chord on the lower part of the keyboard.**

   The intro will begin.

6. **Listen to the chord progression while watching the display.**

   The display counts down the measures of the intro and shows you when it goes into the regular pattern. You'll also know when the intro has ended because the chords will just stay on the one you first played.

Press a variation button before playing your chord to choose what pattern you want the accompaniment to start with when the intro is finished.

Fancier arrangers offer more than one intro pattern. The options vary in length and complexity; some may allow you to play the chords yourself throughout the intro, and some may just be a drum count-in (where the drummer just clicks the sticks). If your keyboard has multiple intro buttons, follow the earlier instructions, using each one to get familiar with what it does.

Track 86 demonstrates some intros.

Endings close out a song. Press the Ending button, and the keyboard plays a musical phrase of a few bars and then stops automatically. The chords it plays will match the key you started in, and the drummer will usually play a small fill to end things nicely. If your keyboard offers multiple endings, they may vary in length, and one may even allow you to determine the chords used for the final short phrase.

Try it for yourself:

1. **While playing an accompaniment pattern, press the Ending button.**

   If you have more than one, use the first one for now.

2. **Listen for how the band plays and then comes to a stop.**

   Notice how many bars it takes. This count tells you how much earlier in your song you need to press the button to match how you want the song to end.

3. **Repeat Steps 1 and 2 for each ending if your keyboard offers more than one.**

   The length and chord progression of the ending pattern may be different in each of the variations. Some will play their own chord choices, and others will let you make those decisions.

Pressing the Ending button two times will produce a tempo slowdown (called a *ritardando* or *ritard*) on some arrangers; I've found this true for some Roland and Yamaha units. A ritardando is a very musical way to end some songs. If the ending is multiple bars, you may be able to do the second press partway into the ending as a nice variation. Check to see whether your keyboard offers this cool function.

You can hear a variety of endings in Track 87.

One other cool way to start or end a song is by using a *fade-in* or *fade-out.* You've heard this effect in plenty of recordings where the music fades in and the band has already been playing or the band jams on and on and the volume slowly fades out, leaving you wondering just how long they played before stopping. Some arrangers have a button for this function; pressing it causes your music to automatically fade in or out, just like the pros.

Considering section-to-section style changes for full accompaniment

Lots of songs change significantly at some point. To re-create this shift, you need to change the backing pattern you're using, which means being able to directly switch to another rhythm or style quickly. I discuss how to do so in Chapter 10, but the process is slightly more complicated when you're using full accompaniment instead of just drums. The issue is that the new style or rhythm likely uses completely different instrument sounds for all the parts. You want to change the groove or feel, not the whole band. Flip to the later section "Changing who plays what part" for details on how you can change the sounds being used for parts of an accompaniment pattern. After you know how to do that (assuming your keyboard can do it!), you can modify the parts to all use the same drum, bass, keyboard, guitar sounds, and so on for the copies you saved into your User locations.

Track 88 demonstrates a style change within a performance, with the sounds already corrected to match between sections.

Mixing the Sound of the Band

Mixing a musical recording involves adjusting the volume balance of each of the instruments, deciding which speaker they come out of (called *panning*), and possibly adjusting or changing the effects that are being used. Mid- and higher-priced arrangers give you access to these functions in addition to letting you decide which sound is being used for each part. Taking control of these aspects of your backing band allows you to make the sound exactly the way you want it.

How do you know whether your keyboard has this capability? Look for a feature/parameter called the Mixer; it may be a dedicated button or a page within the Style/Rhythm Play mode (look in your manual, on the front panel, or within the menus). Figure 11-11 shows some example screens of mixers as presented in a few arrangers.

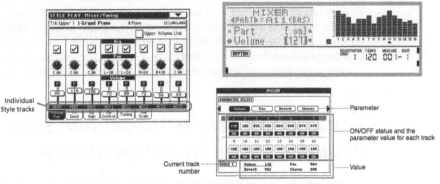

Figure 11-11: Example mixer screens for some arranger keyboards.

Individual Style tracks

Current track number

Parameter

ON/OFF status and the parameter value for each track

Value

Images courtesy of Korg Italy; Casio America, Inc; and Yamaha Corporation of America

Adjusting the volume of each section

A skilled musician/producer has already volume balanced all the styles and rhythms in your keyboard, so you probably don't need to make big changes. But I've encountered two common scenarios over the years that require a little adjustment here and there:

- ✔ **Slightly increasing or decreasing the volume of a backing instrument:** Perhaps you're having a little problem hearing the bass part clearly enough, or the string lines stand out a little too much for your taste. These fixes are small; you're not trying to redo the whole band mix.

- ✔ **Turning off a part:** This process is called *muting* a part or channel. For example, sometimes I really like a pattern except for one element I don't want to hear. No problem; fix it in the mix!

To change the volume of a part (it may be called a Part or a Track), you select it, use the interface controls to increase or decrease the volume parameter value, and then resave the style/rhythm.

Listen to Track 89 to hear the levels of parts being changed in an accompaniment pattern.

To turn off a part entirely, you may have two options. If your mixer design has a dedicated *Mute* parameter, you can use that parameter to turn off the part. If it doesn't have a Mute, simply turn the part volume all the way down to 00. Again, be sure to resave the Style/Rhythm.

Some parts play only during a specific variation in a style or rhythm. So be sure to check all the variations your keyboard offers to find and be able to hear them.

Some arrangers have front panel controls for turning sections of the backing pattern on and off. These may be organized in categories like rhythm, bass, chords, sustaining, melodic, and so on or may be set up to create a trio (drums and bass plus your live playing) or small band (drums, bass, and chords only). These options are great ways to drop down the size of the band for a section and then bring them all back in without having to remix or edit anything.

Varying the reverb effect

In mixing music, effects such as reverb are commonly used to add spaciousness to the sound and to help blend everything together. Other effects, including equalization (commonly called EQ), adjust the tonal color of a sound. (I discuss effects in more detail in Chapter 9). The most common and easily fixed issue I've found with effects settings in backing patterns involves the amount of reverb that was used. Many times the drums just have too much of it, for example. Or a background part sticks out a bit too much and sounds plain. Adding some reverb to it can help it better blend into the background.

Reverb is always presented as an overall effect, and you can route each part to use it to varying degrees or not at all. This parameter may be clearly labeled as Reverb or be one of several FX Send options. (Chorus is another effect commonly presented as an FX send.) Each part or track in your style/rhythm mixer has a setting for this option (shown in Figure 11-12). Decrease the number to lessen the amount of reverb; increase the number to add more.

Some keyboards label the FX sends alphabetically or numerically. You can raise each send's level, and your ears will tell you which one is the reverb easily enough.

In Track 90, you can hear various examples of reverb being adjusted within a style.

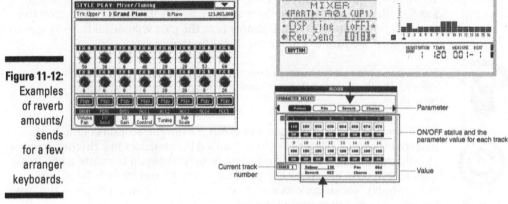

Figure 11-12: Examples of reverb amounts/ sends for a few arranger keyboards.

Images courtesy of Korg Italy; Casio America, Inc; and Yamaha Corporation of America

Changing who plays what part

For each category of sound, your keyboard offers a number of choices. For example, it has more than one acoustic piano sound; multiple electric pianos; different organs; various acoustic, electric, and synth basses; and so on. You can explore changing some of these choices around and extend the versatility of your instrument by making copies of your favorite styles and rhythms and reorchestrating the band.

This setting may be in a Style Play menu or in the Mixer itself (see Figure 11-13 for some example screens). On some arrangers, you must edit the style or rhythm itself to change the sound on a given part or track. After you've found the sound choice parameter (however you have to get there), you can try other choices, which I like to do when the pattern is playing. This way, I hear the new sound choices in context against the rest of the band.

Here are some suggestions of groups of sounds that you can exchange with each other to experiment:

- ✔ Pianos, electric pianos, clavs, organ, and mallet sounds (vibes, marimba).

- ✔ Acoustic guitar, electric guitar (not rock lead/distortion), 12-string guitar, clav, fast attack/fast decay synth, and harp.

- ✔ Most solo brass and woodwinds/reeds, although the octave may not always be right (trombone, tuba, baritone sax, and bass clarinet all play an octave lower). Some synth lead sounds may work well in exchange as well.

- ✔ Acoustic, electric, and synth bass/lead sounds. Sometimes you can use a strong acoustic piano sound in place of a bass for a nice sound.

- ✔ String ensembles, synth pads/chords, vocal ensembles, and organ, as long as the attack and release of the sounds are close enough. (Check out Chapter 14 for info on attack and release values.)

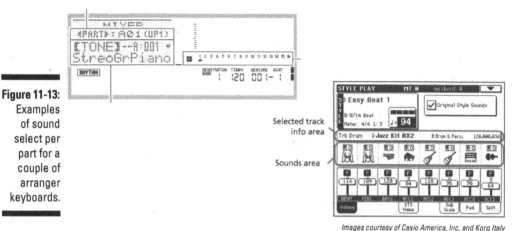

Figure 11-13:
Examples
of sound
select per
part for a
couple of
arranger
keyboards.

Images courtesy of Casio America, Inc, and Korg Italy

Listen to Track 91 to hear sounds being changed within a style.

When you use a second style/rhythm as another section of the same song (as described in the earlier section "Considering section-to-section style changes for full accompaniment"), write down the name/program number for each sound in the main style or rhythm so you can reference them to reorchestrate a second one. This way, you can have, say, a rock verse and a reggae bridge, all using the same sounds.

Letting the Keyboard Make the Choices for You

Arranger keyboards and high-end digital pianos are very advanced instruments; they're actually pretty complicated to even the average tech-minded electronic keyboardist. The front panel has so many buttons, and you seem to need an extra set of hands just to operate all the features. To counteract that, the instrument designers build in a variety of timesaving functions to automate these choices. They often set up a bunch of options for you so you can quickly make the sound and setting features you need, and they offer features that you can configure for yourself to do the same. The following sections give you some a few to check out.

Taking advantage of one-touch settings

Most mid- and upper-end arrangers offer three or four sounds for live playing on the keyboard. Most are for the right hand part of the key range, with maybe one to layer with the left hand while triggering the chords for the accompaniment. These sounds aren't always all active at the same time; you usually choose between them to vary your melody playing at different parts of the song. For example, you may switch sounds (like starting a melody with a flute and changing to trumpet at the bridge) or layer a second sound on top of the first (like adding strings behind your piano).

To extend these possibilities even farther, you can save and recall sets of these sounds as part of your accompaniment. Called Single Touch (Korg) or One Touch Settings (Roland and Yamaha), these buttons instantly recall all four sounds, with their volume, panning, effects, and key ranges all predecided, and some fancy extras thrown in. If your keyboard has this feature, try it out to see how easily it recalls a wide variety of sounds that have all been chosen to work with the current style or rhythm you're using.

Advanced models from Casio have an extended version of this function called a Registration. Along with saving the selection of live sounds, these one-touch settings can also recall the rhythm pattern, tempo, and some other cool extras. But they don't have to change any of the accompaniment parts when selecting a new rhythm; a Global Mode setting can disable that, so they only will recall the live part sounds and effects and so on just like the other brands offer.

Yamaha also has a Registration feature, which recall sounds and other settings. It differs from the One Touch settings in that it has nothing to do with the accompaniment memories. So you may end up choosing some sounds that don't go well with the style of music you're playing.

Diving into the music database

As you develop a large repertoire of songs you can play, remembering what style or rhythm, tempo, and other settings to use for each song becomes confusing. Plus, setting all those things up takes time; no keyboardist wants to leave the audience waiting while he pokes around the front panel of his keyboard.

The more-professional arrangers take care of this problem with yet another type of memory, called a SongBook (Korg), Music Assistant/Performance List (Roland), or Music Finder (Yamaha). This feature stores all the needed settings for a specific song (sounds, accompaniment, tempo, effects), along with text reminders such as the key you like to play the song in, lyrics, other text notes, and more. It's a database, so you can search for songs by title, artist, genre, and many other tags much like you can in your computer media player. The keyboard comes with many songs already defined, and you can add more of your own and download and share entries with other users around the world. Figure 11-14 shows some example screens for this feature.

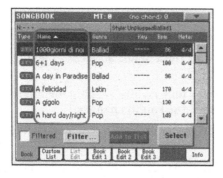

Figure 11-14:
The Korg
and Yamaha
music
database
main
screens.

Images courtesy of Yamaha Corporation of America and Korg Italy

Using Some Fancy Extras

But wait, there's more! Modern arrangers have a number of other cool features that help your playing sound fuller and fancier without any extra work on your part. I cover some of the more common ones in the sections that follow.

Adding harmony to your melodies

Block chords is a style of playing right hand melodies where the melody is harmonized with additional notes below it to form full chord voicings, using smooth voice-leading similar to what I discuss in Chapter 7 regarding chord inversions. Organ players often use this technique, as did jazz pianist George Shearing, and it's popular in jazz and dance big-band arranging within their sax section writing.

And you can too; it's just a button push away. Look on your front panel for a button labeled Ensemble (Korg), Harmony/Echo (Yamaha), or Melody Intelligence (Roland). Turn it on and then try the following:

1. **Set up your accompaniment to play.**

2. **Start the accompaniment with a simple C major chord.**

3. **Play a single note with your right hand; notice it's playing a whole chord.**

4. **Move around to some other notes while keeping the left hand chord the same and listen for how the sound changes.**

5. **Hold a C note with your right hand and change your left hand chord to an F major.**

   Notice how the melody (right hand) part changes; it's now adding harmony using notes that match an F chord.

6. **Change your left hand chord to an A minor and hear the change.**

7. **Stop doing what I tell you and experiment; have fun!**

Your keyboard may have different settings for the type of harmony it creates when using this feature. Read your owner's manual and explore all the possibilities.

Listen to Track 92 to hear examples of auto-harmony.

Hitting the chord pads

Some arrangers offer some buttons called *pads* or *multi pads* that you can use to tap out drum beats and trigger sound effects or even phrases of music. This setting is a fun way of adding more sounds and parts to your playing without having to worry about playing the right keys on the keyboard. These chord pads have various names and operate in a variety of ways:

- ✔ **Momentary/Hit:** Touch the pad and a sound triggers once. This option is good for playing a single drum sound or synth sound effect (such as a zap).

- ✔ **Once:** A musical phrase plays one time and then stops. You can use this method for something like a harp arpeggio or flamenco guitar strum flourish.

- ✔ **Looped:** A musical phrase or sound keeps playing endlessly (in time with your accompaniment parts) until you turn it off. This function can add an additional percussion groove or a cool synth arpeggiated phrase (or even trigger the sound of endless audience applause).

Each style and rhythm has its own saved settings for the pads, so take some time and explore them.

Track 93 demonstrates some chord pad applications.

Chapter 12

Exploring Arpeggiation

∙ ∙

In This Chapter

▶ Understanding how an arpeggiator works

▶ Walking through simple and more complex arps

▶ Introducing major arp features

▶ Choosing sounds that work best with arpeggiation

▶ Varying your arp performances

∙ ∙

*I*f you're a fan of late-'70s and '80s pop, synth-pop, and new wave music, or the club dance music since the turn of the 21st century (trance, electro, hardstyle, and so on), then you've heard an arpeggiator in action. Early synth artists and producers such as Jean Michel Jarre, Giorgio Moroder, Gary Numan, Thomas Dolby, Howard Jones, and Duran Duran used synths and arpeggiators in many of the pop and dance hits of their eras. Not sure what I'm talking about? Have you heard any of these songs?

✔ Donna Summer: "I Feel Love"

✔ Duran Duran: "Rio," "Save a Prayer," and "Hungry Like the Wolf"

✔ Eurythmics: "Here Comes the Rain Again"

✔ Talking Heads: "Once In a Lifetime" intro

✔ Irene Cara: "Flashdance (What a Feeling)"

✔ Cyndi Lauper: "All Through the Night"

✔ Alan Parsons Project: "Games People Play"

✔ Erasure: "Drama," "Chains of Love" intro

In each of these songs, you hear a repeated synth figure of some sort; up high in the background, for the bass line, or providing an outline of the chordal harmony. That's an arpeggiator (often abbreviated *arp*) in action, and for many people that type of sound is the definition of the sound of a synthesizer in popular music.

In this chapter, you discover the basics of arpeggiation and some of the most common settings to tweak. This information will open up the feature for you and help you explore it in your playing. I know that not all keyboards have this feature, but it's a cool tool to know about.

Tracing the Roots of Arpeggiation

The word *arpeggiate* means to play the notes of a chord in a broken fashion, one at a time. It comes from the Italian word *arpeggiare,* which means "to play on a harp," which was a common way of outlining the harmony or chords of a piece of music.

Practicing arpeggios is an essential part of serious piano study because it builds technique and the ability to cleanly go up and down the full range of the keyboard.

Listen to Track 94 to hear examples of arpeggiated chords played on the piano.

Not every person who ever wanted to play a keyboard develops that level of technique, though, so in the late '60s, organ manufacturers added a simple form of auto-accompaniment that took the held notes of a chord and played them one after another to produce arpeggios. Though your image of those big console home theater organs may be of hokey show tunes and cheesy Latin drum grooves, this feature is how Pete Townsend created the keyboard part for the Who song "Eminence Front" on a Yamaha E-70 home organ.

The first synthesizer to include an arpeggiator was the Roland Jupiter 4, released in 1978. Many others followed, and arpeggiators were quite popular in instruments through the mid-'80s. After falling out of favor for a period of time, they came back with a vengeance, with many new features and capabilities. Many of today's synths, workstations, and software synthesizers include arpeggiators, as do computer software sequencers and digital audio workstations (DAWs).

Looking At Some Arp Examples

In the most basic scenario, an arpeggiator takes the notes you hold on the keyboard and plays them one after the other, in a direction that you can choose (up, down, or up and down). Figure 12-1 shows a simple C major triad that produces various repeating patterns when held and driven by an arpeggiator. (Check out Chapter 7 for information on triads.)

Figure 12-1:
A basic arp pattern.

Illustration by Jerry Kovarsky

In this example, holding down a three-note chord can produce these various patterns based on the three most common settings for the note direction, or *order*.

Track 95 plays Figure 12-1 on a synth sound.

Which notes you play on the keyboard doesn't matter; the arpeggiator obediently plays them back for you over and over. A common use of this function in many of the songs I mention earlier in the chapter was to just hold a single note or an octave to produce a pulsating rhythm or alternating bass line without sounding like a full chordal arpeggio.

Moving to a more complex example, playing a two-handed chord like the one shown in Figure 12-2 gets you a more complex arp pattern. A cool aspect of such a *running arp* pattern is that it doesn't have to repeat at the bar line of your music, so using an odd number of notes produces a less regular-sounding repeating pattern than using an even number of notes. Holding down a five-note chord creates the pattern in Figure 12-2.

Figure 12-2:
A two-handed arp pattern.

Illustration by Jerry Kovarsky

Check out Track 96 to hear Figure 12-2 played on a simple synth sound.

Of course, you don't have to hold down the same chord all the time. By changing chords, you make the arp pattern sound more interesting and less repetitive.

Another technique you hear in a lot of music is the player pressing notes down to trigger the arp for a little bit, letting go to introduce space or rests, and then playing some notes again.

Listen to Track 97 to hear various examples of changing chords and using space to make simple up/down arpeggiated patterns more interesting.

Early modular synths, many analog synths, and some modern keyboards have a function called a *step sequencer,* which many people confuse with an arpeggiator. A step sequencer allows you to define the pitch for each step of a pattern and then always plays back that pitch. The only interaction with the keyboard may be to allow you to transpose the whole pattern to another note or key from the keyboard. But the step sequencer is a pre-programmed riff, or pattern; it's not changing chord qualities or the span of the note intervals based on what you play on the keyboard, so the riff doesn't really change. The result may sound the same to your ears, but the step sequencer isn't as interactive as the arpeggiator. To its advantage, it can produce more-complex patterns. A step sequencer was used for Pink Floyd's famous "On the Run" synth pattern, for example.

Exploring More Arpeggiator Features

If all an arpeggiator could do was play back the notes you hold on the keyboard, the effect would be cool but get boring and predictable pretty quickly. And other than using them on different sounds, all arpeggiated parts would sound much the same. Thankfully, arpeggiators have gained many new features over time and grown to be very complex and creative. In the following sections, I take you on a tour of the most common features of a modern arpeggiator; of course I can't be sure what specific keyboard you own (if any), but by listening to the audio examples, you can get a clear idea of what is going on.

Extending the range

In its most basic setting, an arpeggiator just repeats the exact notes you play, over and over again. A *range parameter* gives you a choice of how many octaves to repeat the pattern of notes, usually expressed as one, two, three, and sometimes even four octaves. By setting a range parameter, you can tell the arpeggiator to play the original notes and then to then play those same notes again up an octave, and yet again up another octave, and so on.

Track 98 presents various patterns being played first at one octave and then expanded to two, three, and four octaves. The examples have some effects and filter sweeps included to sound more interesting — as they'd be used in a song.

Changing the timing/speed

Of course, any arp pattern is being played in some rhythm, and they usually are very simple timings — perhaps eighth notes against the tempo. All arpeggiators give you some choices for this timing resolution. As you increase the *resolution,* or subdivision, of the beat, the arp pattern plays back faster and sounds busier. But it's always in time with your music. Common timing options can range from a whole note per step down to sixteenth notes, various triplet timings, and even 32nd notes. (Head to Chapter 5 for details on these note lengths.)

If all your sound is coming from one keyboard, this timing happens automatically. If you want to use multiple instruments or a hardware keyboard and sounds running from your computer, you need to connect them via MIDI and set the MIDI synchronization between the devices. One device will produce what is called the *Master Clock,* and all the other devices will be set to listen to this *external MIDI Clock.*

Check out Track 99 to hear a pattern being played along with a drum rhythm and then switched between various timing settings.

Getting into the swing of things

Swing is a way of playing a rhythm where the notes aren't equally timed; when you play two eighth notes, the first note is longer than the second, producing a pleasing, lopsided feel. I'm sure you've heard the term related to a style of jazz music played in the late '30s and '40s. In fact, the swing pulse of rhythm is a core component of jazz playing. But it's also used in boogie-woogie, country, blues and rock shuffles, and hip-hop music.

More-modern arpeggiators offer swing as an adjustable parameter (sometimes called *shuffle*), so your pattern can go from a very even, straight feel to this cooler, more lopsided feel. Swing may be presented as a percentage or a strength value, but increasing it makes the relationship between each group of two notes more irregular, with the first note getting longer and the second getting shorter to make up the difference.

In general, swing rhythms have a *triplet* feel, where the quarter note is divided into three parts. The first note holds for the first two triplets and the third is the last triplet, as shown in Figure 12-3. In print music, the rhythm is still written as straight eighth notes and then just marked as "swing feel" or something similar. Writing everything as triplets would make the music difficult to read.

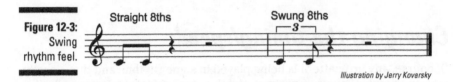

Figure 12-3:
Swing
rhythm feel.

Illustration by Jerry Kovarsky

Track 100 features a pattern being played straight along with a swung drum rhythm (which sounds bad) and then gradually swung to feel better against the groove.

Higher swing strengths on arpeggio patterns work best with swing/jazz, shuffle, 6/8, 12/8, and hip-hop/R & B drum grooves. (If those fractionlike numbers are foreign to you, read up on these time signatures in Chapter 5.)

Making the notes shorter/longer

Increasing and decreasing the duration of the notes being played is a very effective technique in making an arp pattern fit the music or vary as a part develops. This parameter may be called *length, duration,* or *gate time* in various arpeggiators. If you increase the duration to the maximum, the notes will play completely connected, or *legato.*

Listen to Track 101 to hear the duration/length of the notes in a pattern varied over time.

Hearing the notes being held along with the arp

Some arpeggiators can sound the notes being held down along with the generated notes from the pattern. This feature results in a kind of layered sound, where you can hear a chord sustaining while the arp bubbles up beneath it. It's a great sound and works well as long as your keyboard has enough *polyphony* (ability to generate enough new notes or voices) to keep the chord sound sustaining while all the other notes are generated. This parameter is called different things by different companies: Often, it's just *keyboard* or *kybd,* but Yamaha calls it *direct,* for example.

Track 102 lets you hear a sound sustaining while the arp plays beneath it.

Keeping the arp playing without holding the keys

If you want the arp pattern to keep repeating for a longer period of time, you don't always need to keep holding the keys. *Latch* (sometimes called *hold*) is a parameter that keeps the pattern playing based on the note(s) you played until you press another key or chord. So you can feed the arp a few notes, let go, and let it do its thing while you play another part of the keyboard range or another keyboard (or get your audience to clap along). To stop the pattern, you can either turn off the latch function or stop the arp.

Adding variety with different patterns

You don't have to use the same pattern for a whole song. Changing the pattern from section to section can be a great way to add variety to you music. If you're playing a song that has a more traditional form with verses, a chorus, a breakdown or solo section, and so on, you can try changing to a subtly different pattern for one of the sections and then returning to your original pattern later on. Or not. Feel free to experiment and find instances where adding some variety is just what you need to keep your music from getting too predictable.

Trying Out Some Different Sounds: Matching Sounds and Arp Patterns

No keyboard law defines what sounds you can and can't arpeggiate; feel free to experiment away! That said, I do have some tips and practical advice for matching sounds and arp patterns:

✔ **Sounds with a fast attack work well at any tempo.** If a sound has a slower attack and you're playing at a fast tempo or using a fast timing subdivision (sixteenth notes, for example; see Chapter 5), the results can be kind of sluggish and unclear. The sound just doesn't have enough time to speak before the next note is being triggered. In this case, you need to adjust the amp envelope attack to a faster value. I discuss this parameter in Chapter 14.

- ✔ **Sounds with long releases don't work as well.** You have to adjust the amp envelope release (also in Chapter 14) to a shorter value. Soft string ensembles, spacey vocal pads, and other atmospheric sounds typically need this type of edit to work.

- ✔ **Most synth sounds are great to use.** People associate arpeggiators with synths, so this pairing is a match made in synthesizer heaven. However, swirly sound effects and evolving imaginative synth sounds may not work that well, especially at faster tempos/timing.

- ✔ **Plucked and short decay sounds are good choices.** Consider guitars; other plucked string instruments (including ethnic sounds); mallets and tuned percussion; and keyboard sounds such as piano, electric piano, clav, and harpsichord.

- ✔ **Short noises and non-pitched percussion work well.** Not everything has to be about chords and harmony; sometimes a unique arpeggiated sound effect adds a nice texture to a part.

Be sure to match the arp range to the sound used. Some sounds don't sound good at their extreme ranges (either at the top or the bottom), so be sure to pick your trigger note range carefully and consider how many octaves to set the range to. Judge where the sweet spot is for a given sound or arp pattern.

Adding Fun Sound and Effects Tweaks

Sometimes just finding the right arp pattern, sound, and chord(s) is enough for a song. Mix it well, and you'll be happy. But often arpeggiated parts get to sound a bit static and predictable when you just leave them running on their own. So varying any or all the parameters discussed earlier in this chapter will help your music greatly.

But wait, there's more! Here are a few cool tips to further enhance your arp-ing adventures:

- ✔ **Sweep the filter as the pattern plays.** This move is a classic. Many musicians and producers use a sound that has a low frequency oscillator (LFO) slowly modulating the filter cutoff, so this effect happens automatically. I cover these parameters in Chapter 14.

- ✔ **Pan the sound back and forth as the pattern plays.** Arpeggiated parts sound great when they move back and forth between the speakers. I like the panning cycle to be different than the pattern length so it doesn't seem to repeat so regularly. A slow pan for a fast arp pattern sounds great, as does a faster pan on a slower part. Using an LFO to modulate amplifier pan position makes this task easy.

✔ **Put a delay effect on your sound.** Timed delays work wonderfully combined with an arp pattern. Slower arp patterns with shorter note durations leave space so you can hear the delays. Don't let the delay regenerate too many repeats because that can get in the way of your new notes. And be sure the delay is mixed back a little so it's supporting echoes, not just a sloppy wash of notes. Listen to The Edge, the guitarist from U2; he's a master of this effect, even though he (not an arpeggiator) is playing the parts.

✔ **Let go of your notes once in a while, especially when using delays.** Many arpeggiators have a latch or hold function, which keeps the notes playing even when you lift your hands off the keys. (See the earlier section "Keeping the arp playing without holding the keys.") Turn that off so you can be in control of introducing rests and space into the pattern as you want. Going manual also lets you use delays with more repeats or longer repetition times. Feed the keyboard a chord, let a few notes arpeggiate, and then let go and just listen to the stream of echoes that follows. Repeat and enjoy.

Listen to Tracks 103 through 106 to hear filter sweeps, panning, and delays in action.

Part IV

Moving into More-Advanced Keyboard Features

Courtesy of PreSonus Audio Electronics, Inc., © 2013

Examine keyboards' fun practice features in a free article at www.dummies.com/extras/keyboard.

In this part . . .

✔ Gain a fundamental understanding of the various forms of recording available today. Audio and MIDI recording offer some distinct options.

✔ Go under the hood of your sounds to explore how they're created and what simple tweaks you can make to vary and personalize them.

✔ Take a tour of the onboard learning systems that Casio and Yamaha offer in a number of their keyboards.

✔ Play along with your favorite recordings and figure out the songs while you're doing it. Playing by ear is a great skill for keyboard players to develop.

✔ Connect your keyboard to a computer or tablet. You can take advantage of all sorts of great music software to enrich your keyboard experience.

Chapter 13

Laying Down Tracks: Recording Your Playing

. . . .

In This Chapter

▶ Defining MIDI and audio recording

▶ Introducing one pass recording

▶ Examining multitrack MIDI recording and editing

▶ Transferring your music from keyboard to computer and beyond

. . . .

*M*ost of today's electronic keyboards offer some form of recording, so you can capture and then listen back to your playing, compose and create a complete musical production, and all steps in between. It's pretty amazing to realize that what used to take tens of thousands of dollars of complicated and specialized equipment, a room designed for recording, and a group of musicians with expensive instruments is something you can now achieve within the humble keyboard that sits in front of you. Okay, that's more than slightly exaggerated (I used to write marketing copy), but what you can do is still very exciting.

Look at your keyboard; you probably see the word(s) *recorder, sequencer, music recorder, song,* or something similar to indicate that it has some sort of recording function. Even easier: A button labeled Record or REC is a sure sign you have this capability.

In this chapter, you discover the basics of both audio and MIDI recording, how the techniques differ, and why you'd choose one form over the other. I give you a basic overview of how to do these types of recording, although I have to keep it in general terms because each keyboard differs in controls, interface, and other operational aspects. But I can give you enough information to help you greatly when it comes time to crack open the manual for your specific model. Plus, I show you how to get your music out of your keyboard and onto your computer and then how to share it with family, friends, and fans around the world.

Exploring the Two Basic Forms of Recording

As an electronic keyboardist, you have two forms of recording technology available: audio recording and MIDI recording. They're very different from one another, each with certain advantages, so I introduce both in the following sections.

Addressing audio recording

For most people, a recording is something you listen to — a record, a cassette (who remembers those?), a CD, or an MP3. These are all products of *audio recording*, the act of capturing the sound of singers, players, and instruments and storing them on a device capable of reproducing them whenever you want. Capturing the sound is the key distinction of audio recording; you're capturing the actual sound of what is happening as you hear it, frozen in time for all to hear and enjoy.

Audio recording comes in two flavors: analog and digital. Both use some type of device to convert the live sound waves produced by the player/instrument into a signal. The most common is a microphone (shown in Figure 13-1), though electronic instruments can hook up to the recorder directly, and a keyboard with recording capability can do its own recording. *Analog recording* gear converts the sound into a voltage or electrical signal that can be routed through various devices and then usually stored onto magnetic tape. (Figure 13-2 shows a common analog studio recorder.) Analog recording was the only form of recording for decades and is still used in professional recording studios that favor the warmth and tonal qualities of recording to tape.

For the vast majority of users, the development of digital technology and computers has paved the way for digital recording. In *digital recording*, the sound is converted into 1s and 0s (a kind of electronic code) and can be stored onto a hard drive, digital storage media such as an SD card (the same kind your camera and smartphone use), and such. The sound can be run through other devices before being converted into the digital format or be manipulated later in the digital format to produce the same results. Most of the stand-alone recorders, either small hand-held devices (see Figure 13-3), desktop-sized studios in a box, or larger systems employ digital recording, as do all computer-based recording packages (commonly called digital audio workstations; see Figure 13-4).

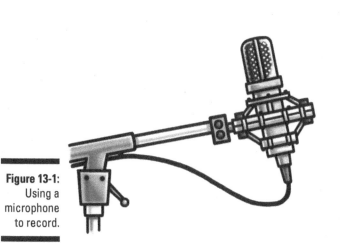

Figure 13-1:
Using a microphone to record.

Illustration by Lisa Reed

Figure 13-2:
A pro studio analog tape recorder.

Photograph courtesy of Roy Hendrickson

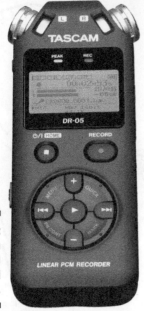

Figure 13-3:
A common
hand-held
digital
recorder.

Photograph courtesy of TASCAM

Figure 13-4:
Audio
recording
computer
software.

Image courtesy of PreSonus Audio Electronics, Inc., © 2013.

Digital recording has many functional advantages over analog recording, mostly in the ability to edit the recording. To rearrange a song, for example, tape has to be cut and joined back together, which is a difficult task to do accurately. Digital data can easily and freely be copied, pasted, and manipulated.

Making sense of MIDI recording

MIDI is a digital language that electronic instruments and devices use to speak to each other. It communicates information such as what key you've pressed on a keyboard, how hard you played it, how long you held it, and so on. Unlike audio recording, it captures only the gestures that produce the sound, not the sound itself. Therefore, you can't listen back to a MIDI performance without it being connected to and replaying a MIDI device live. That device may be a hardware instrument you can see or a software instrument running on your computer (or phone!), but it's being played in real time as you listen back.

The beauty of MIDI as a recording method is that it's infinitely editable. Figure 13-5 shows a screen shot of MIDI data in what's called an event edit list. You can select, edit, copy, or delete each MIDI event in this edit list as you want. Hit a bad note or don't like the sound you played? No problem; erase it or, better yet, change it to the right note/another sound! Didn't play with the best timing? You can fix that later. Can't play something fast enough? Record it slowly and then speed up the playback later; your recorder will now play the MIDI device at whatever tempo you set it to. These examples are just a few of the things you can do with MIDI editing.

MIDI sounds like the universal answer to all recording, right? Well, it's not. As I note earlier, it's a digital language. You can't capture your singing voice with MIDI, unless you're some sort of MIDI robot I don't know about. So a live person or an acoustic instrument isn't going to be able to be MIDI recorded. And eventually, you're going to want your MIDI recordings to be captured as audio so you can listen to them anywhere, away from your MIDI gear, and share them with your friends and the world.

Position				Status	Ch	Num	Val	Length/Info
1	1	1	1	Control	1	7	127	Volume
1	1	1	1	Note	1	G1	39	. 3 3 237
1	1	1	1	Note	1	A#2	46	. 1 2 39
1	1	1	1	Note	1	D3	72	. 1 2 8
1	1	1	1	Note	1	E3	62	. 1 2 17
1	1	1	1	Note	1	A3	62	. 1 1 208
1	1	4	190	Control	1	64	127	Sustain
1	2	4	61	Note	1	A2	61	. 1 3 128
1	3	2	1	Note	1	A#2	55	. 1 1 158
1	3	3	214	Control	1	64	0	Sustain
1	3	4	1	Note	1	G3	71	. 3 29
1	4	2	38	Control	1	64	127	Sustain
1	4	3	1	Note	1	D3	75	. 173
1	4	4	236	Control	1	64	0	Sustain
2	1	1	1	Note	1	D1	32	. 3 0 215
2	1	1	1	Note	1	D2	41	. 3 2 83
2	1	1	1	Note	1	A2	45	. 1 1 74
2	1	1	1	Note	1	A#2	49	. 1 1 88
2	1	1	1	Note	1	D3	76	. 1 1 77
2	1	1	1	Note	1	D#3	58	. 1 1 64
2	2	1	140	Control	1	64	127	Sustain
2	2	4	1	Note	1	A#2	58	. . . 72
2	2	4	1	Note	1	D#3	65	. . . 3
2	2	4	1	Note	1	A3	73	. . . 79
2	3	1	166	Control	1	64	0	Sustain
2	3	2	58	Control	1	64	127	Sustain
2	3	4	1	Note	1	D4	92	. 2 122
2	4	1	1	PitchBd	1	48	66	= 304
2	4	1	23	PitchBd	1	96	67	= 480
2	4	1	43	PitchBd	1	16	69	= 656
2	4	1	63	PitchBd	1	112	70	= 880
2	4	1	83	PitchBd	1	64	72	= 1088
2	4	1	103	PitchBd	1	112	74	= 1392
2	4	1	123	PitchBd	1	64	77	= 1728

Figure 13-5:
A MIDI
event edit
list.

Apple Logic Pro 9 screenshot courtesy of Jerry Kovarsky

Capturing What You Hear as It Happens: One Pass Recording

The most basic form of recording is to capture a performance as it happens. Whether it's one person playing solo on a single instrument, a small group, the playback of your electronic keyboard that has drums and accompaniment, or a symphony orchestra doesn't matter. You set up the recording system as needed, press *record,* and it all happens at the same time — in one pass. The following sections help you set up one pass recording for both the audio and MIDI approaches.

Tackling audio recording in one pass

The ability to record one complete audio performance from your keyboard is becoming a more common feature on many digital pianos, stage pianos, arrangers, and workstations. Basically, with this option anything that can be produced by the keyboard all at once can be recorded.

Typically, the keyboard has a USB port that you can connect a memory stick or drive to; that's what the keyboard records the digital audio onto. (Note that some workstations and arrangers have an internal hard drive that can be used as the recording medium.) The recording is made as a stereo *wave* file (abbreviated as WAV or .wav), which is the most common digital audio format for use on computers. Without getting too technical, the settings for this wave file will be at the right resolution to be able to listen to on any device, to burn a CD from, and to share with anyone you want.

Recording a one pass audio track is simple and doesn't require a complicated setup:

1. **Make sure your keyboard is in the right mode (single sound, multisound, accompaniment playback, or whatever).**

2. **Choose the audio recording feature.**

   This function may be a dedicated button, but you may have to select Record and then choose audio as the format. The method of choosing varies from product to product; read your keyboard's owner's manual for specific help.

3. **Select where to record to: internal hard drive, USB stick or drive, and so on.**

   Your owner's manual will tell you what to do.

4. **Press Record or Start and begin playing (or sit back while the keyboard plays).**

5. **Press Stop when you've recorded what you want.**

   Your wave file is now on your memory stick or hard drive, ready to be listened to, shared, or brought into your computer as I discuss later in the chapter.

 One pass audio recording is a great way to capture your practicing or playing so you can listen back to yourself. Hearing your recorded playing once in a while is a good idea because it lets you evaluate how you sound and how your practicing is progressing. You'll find that you hear yourself differently this way compared to when you're involved in the act of playing. Plus, it's a fun way to share your music with friends and family or share your child's progress with others.

Grabbing a one pass MIDI recording

Being able to record one pass of MIDI is even more common than audio recording on today's keyboards. You often don't even know your recording function is MIDI recording; many digital pianos and stage pianos just call it a music recorder and don't bother to explain the technology. On most keyboards, though, the MIDI recorder is called a *sequencer*.

Recording a one pass MIDI track is straightforward and simple for live playing. Your keyboard may have a simple Record button and a Start/Stop button, or it may have a more complete set of buttons called *transport controls* as shown in Figure 13-6. These controls are copied from the buttons that were used to operate tape recorders and digital recorders.

Figure 13-6:
Recorder
transport
controls.

Image courtesy of M-Audio

Here's how to make a one pass MIDI recording:

1. **Select the sound you want to use.**

2. **Choose the recording feature.**

   This capability may be a dedicated button, or you may have to select Record and then choose MIDI as the format. It varies from product to product, so check out your owner's manual.

3. **Press Record or Start.**

   Note: Some products don't start recording the moment you press Record. They go into a record-ready state and usually start a click sounding so you can listen to the current tempo to get ready to play. You typically must press Start or Play before it begins recording. (For some products, you start recording from this wait mode the moment you play a note.)

   In general, MIDI recorders default to playing a click when recording so that the recorded data can be matched up to bars and beats for later editing. So you should set the tempo of the click/recording before you start. You can easily do so during the record-ready time by pressing Record and using the front panel tempo controls to set the speed.

4. **When you're ready, press the Start or Play button, or just play away!**

5. **Press Stop when you're finished.**

6. **Relocate to the beginning of the recording.**

For some keyboards, you do so by pressing Stop twice. For others, you have to hold the Rewind button.

7. **Press Play to listen to your recording.**

   If you don't like what you played, you can just do it over by pressing Record (and perhaps Start or Play) and trying again. You can rerecord as many times as you want; each new recording erases the previous one.

Most workstations, higher-end portables, and mid-to-high-end arrangers have to be in Sequencer Mode to do any MIDI recording. For these products, you have to set up a sound on the first recording part or track and often have to copy it with its effects to sound like it did when you were just playing the sound. You may have a shortcut to do this job, or it may require a more complicated set of steps. You should look to your owner's manual for more info and read the following section.

Recording Multitrack MIDI

If you want to record more than one sound via MIDI (either at the same time or by building up parts one at a time), you need to use the full sequencer of your keyboard. Perhaps you want to record your keyboard playing along with an accompanying drum groove or to record all the backing parts from the auto-accompaniment features of your digital piano or arranger. You may want to add more parts to your solo piano performance to make a full production from it. All these situations require you to create different parts, one for each distinct sound or part that is playing.

The design/layout and capabilities of each product's onboard sequencer (and computer-based sequencers/DAWs) is somewhat different, but the following sections explain the concepts; you can then go to your product's owner's manual and support documentation and videos for more-specific help.

Setting up your session

The basic concept of any multitrack recorder/sequencer is that for each sound you want to record, you use a separate track. Think of each track as another instrument or player that's going to provide a part for your song. Each track is set to a different MIDI channel; this way, each instrument gets only the notes, controller information, and program change meant for it.

You choose a sound (such as piano, drums, bass, and so on) for each track and can adjust the volume and the *panning* for the track (which speaker it's coming out of). Note that you can adjust all these parameters again later, when you're ready to mix your song, as I discuss later in the chapter.

The most confusing part of setting up for recording in a sequencer has to do with assigning the effects used for each sound. When you play a sound by itself in single sound or multisound mode, that sound has already been programmed to use specific effects — certainly some reverb and quite possibly some coloration effect like chorus or phase shifting, with very specific settings for each effect. Guitars may have distortion and so on. (Chapter 9 has details on various kinds of effects.) When you first call up a sound on a track in a sequencer, however, it likely doesn't have any of these effects assigned, so it sounds very different and very plain. You must reassign, or reconfigure, the effects yourself with those exact settings to get the sound back to the way it is in the sound mode. To do so you need to understand the structure of your effects system for your specific keyboard. (Don't worry; I'm not going to have you take apart your instrument or anything.)

Some effects are commonly *global,* meaning every sound in the sequencer or song can share the same effect. These overarching effects are called *master effects* or *system effects;* they may be limited to certain choices (the two most common being some form of reverb and chorus), or you may be able to freely choose what effects go in these master locations. Each track or sound has a *send amount* parameter to run it into each master effect, so you can decide on a sound-by-sound basis how much effect to give. If your model always pre-assigns the master effects, the parameter may even say Reverb Amount and Chorus Amount.

Some systems will have a Chorus block for a master effect that can use any form of modulation effect (chorus, flanging, phase shifting, and perhaps even delay). Other systems allow you to change the Chorus block for a *digital signal processing (DSP) block,* which you can use to produce a wide variety of effect choices configured as a master effect, so all the tracks can share it.

Other effects are configured on a per-track or per-part basis. This design is called an *insert effect* or *insertion effect* because you place it in-line with a given track or part such that it's not available to all parts. This configuration usually applies to the more special, colorful types of effects such as deeper modulation effects, distortion, and rotary speaker. It doesn't have a send amount because you choose how much of the effect to hear with a wet/dry or mix parameter within the effect itself. (*Dry* is the unaffected sound; *wet* is the sound with effect added in.) ***Note:*** Each product is different, but keyboards usually have a limited number of these insert effects, so every track/sound can't have its own effect.

You don't always have to go to the hassle of figuring out what each sound's effects are and manually reprogramming them in the sequencer mode; many instruments have a Copy With Effects or Copy Effects From Sound menu command you can use when assigning a sound to a track. This may be a one-step process for all effects — master and insert — or you may have to do it separately for the master effects and the insert effects. Look for this type of helper to get your first sound/first track set up so it sounds the way it should.

Recording the first track

You've picked the sound you want to record first and you've copied back the effects it uses so it sounds good when you play the keyboard. (Check out the preceding section for more on how to complete those tasks.) Just follow these steps to record:

1. **Press Record or Rec.**

   For some keyboards, this function gives you a count-in of four clicks, and then you're recording. Play away! For other keyboards, you need to press Play or Start while in this record-ready mode to start actually recording.

   You're working with MIDI recording, so the tempo doesn't matter; you can always change it later. You may want to set it a little bit slower so you can concentrate and play cleanly for now.

2. **Press Stop when you're finished playing.**

3. **Relocate to the beginning of the recording.**

   I explain how to do so in the earlier section "Grabbing a one pass MIDI recording."

4. **Press Play to listen to your recording.**

   Repeat Steps 1 through 3 to record over it if you don't like what you hear.

Adding more tracks

Your first track/part sounds great; time to move on to the next. Here's how to record subsequent tracks:

1. **Look at the interface for your sequencer and find how to select track 2.**

You didn't have to think about track selection to record the first track, but now you need to change to a different track so you don't record over your first part and lose that perfect performance!

2. **Choose a sound for this second part.**

   Remember that it will probably sound dry at first. *Warning:* Don't use one of the copy commands related to effects at this time. If you do, you'll likely change the effects that your first track uses.

3. **Go to track 2's send parameters and dial in a little reverb and/or the other master effect to suit your needs.**

   Remember that you can always add to and improve this mix later. Just get the sound close enough so you feel comfortable playing it.

4. **If needed, reassign or copy the desired insert effect (which may be called Insert or DSP effect) for track 2.**

   If you want more than just the master effects, determine whether you can reassign an insert effect or copy only that effect from the program you selected to your second sound. Some products have up to five or six insert effects. Your sequencer likely has 16 tracks, but with multiple insert effects you can decide which tracks really need the extra sonic help and which can get by with only using the master effects.

   Play the keyboard; you'll hear this second sound and can judge whether you have the effects set up the way you want. As with the master effects, don't worry about getting the sound perfect at this stage. You'll be able to tweak these settings again later when you have all your parts recorded.

   With your sound parameters set, you can practice your new part before recording it by pressing Play and playing along with the previous track(s). You don't need to record until you're comfortable and ready to go.

5. **Repeat Steps 1 and 2 in the preceding section to record the part.**

6. **Relocate to the beginning and press Play to listen to your two parts playing together.**

   If you like what you hear, great. If you like your playing but not the sound you chose, keep the track and change the sound later through the wonders of MIDI. (You can read about how to do so in the later section "Refining Your MIDI Recordings.") If you hate the whole thing, rerecord the second part until you're happy.

Repeat the preceding steps, selecting a new track each time you want to record a new part. Pick your sound, adjust the effects as needed, and record away!

Recording multiple parts at the same time

If you want to record multiple parts at the same time, such as all the auto-accompaniment at once or your live playing plus some arpeggiated parts and drum grooves, you need to set up your product for multitrack recording. Some common approaches for this process are as follows:

✔ Many arranger or auto-accompaniment-based keyboards have a special mode (sometimes called a Backing Sequencer) for their recorder to do multitrack recording or have a special track called Style Track or Acc Track designated for all the accompaniment parts. (In reality, it's more than one track, but the manufacturers hide that from you for simplicity.) You need to enable the live keyboard part you're playing plus this special track to capture everything at once. All the sound choices, mixing levels, and effects are automatically chosen for you when you pick the special track that you want to use.

✔ Some workstation keyboards have a special command or menu selection for copying a multipart setup into their sequencers; this option takes care of all the track and channel assignments, configures the effects, and readies the recorder for recording all the parts at once. This command may be called One Touch Recording or Copy To Sequencer.

Refining Your MIDI Recordings

As I note throughout the chapter, MIDI recording captures only the gestures you made, not the resulting sounds. MIDI technology gives you the freedom both to make tweaks and changes here and there to smooth out imperfections and to completely change aspects of what you originally played. The following sections discuss several of the most common adjustments you want to know how to make.

Fixing small mistakes

Any keyboard that has a multipart MIDI sequencer is going to have an edit mode of some sort, and all recording software for computers has sophisticated edit modes. If you really don't like what you played, of course, you're better off to just try again with a new recording. But if your part is pretty good, with only a few small issues, editing the MIDI data is the way to go.

Adjusting the timing of your playing

If your rhythm was a little sloppy or you started to play ahead of or behind the beat, you can use an edit tool called *quantize* or *quantization*. This function lines up all your notes to the nearest subdivision of the beat that you select. Basically, any note in the track that doesn't play exactly on the subdivision you've selected gets moved forward or backward so it now appears in the right spot. The size of the subdivision (eighth note, sixteenth note, and so on) you should use depends on the type of part you're playing. Long, sustained chords can be quantized to half notes or whole notes, for example. I talk about rhythm and subdivisions in Chapter 5.

You can almost always undo edits of this sort to revert the track back to its original state, so you can experiment with different timing resolutions (levels of subdivision). I always try to use the finest or highest resolution (greatest level of subdivision) that still gives me a good result. I may start with 32nd notes or sixteenth notes to see whether that level fixes the problems without changing the feel of the majority of the track. If you choose a resolution that messes with a lot of the notes you played, moving them around in ways you don't like, just undo the command and try another setting. The coarser the resolution you use (perhaps eighth notes or quarter notes), the more likely it is to adversely affect your recorded performance.

If only a few notes of your performance are off, you don't have to quantize the whole track. If your sequencer allows you to view an event edit list, you can find the bad note and edit the timing location it starts at to move it to the right place. This approach is certainly more detailed editing, but it may be safer than changing the feel of your whole track with a quantize command. Figure 13-7 shows a MIDI event list with a bad note highlighted so you can change the start time to fix it. The highlighted note was played a little late; by changing the 6 to a 1, you can move it back on time with the rest of the chord that was played.

Some sequencers offer another type of view of your data to use while making edits. A *piano roll* view (shown in Figure 13-8) displays notes as small dots or rectangles along a grid where the vertical axis represents the notes of a keyboard and the horizontal axis represents the time in your recording. You can scroll from the beginning (far left) to the end (far right), selecting, copying, deleting, and dragging notes to change their timing (left to right) or their pitches (top to bottom). In Figure 13-8, the highlighted note was played a little late; by dragging it slightly to the left, you can move it back on time with the rest of the chord that was played.

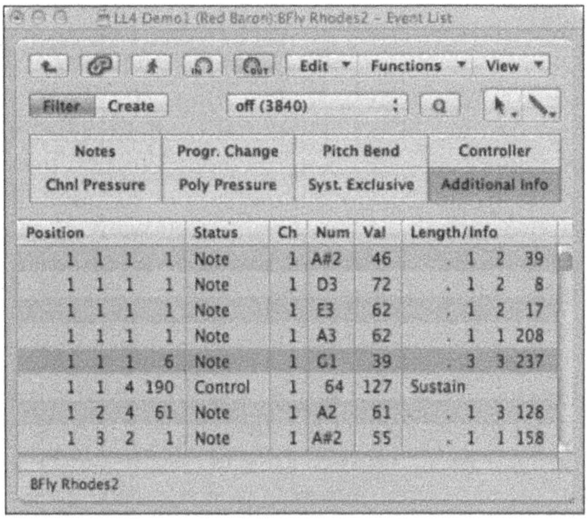

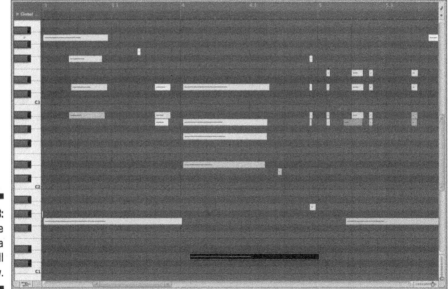

Apple Logic Pro 9 screenshot courtesy of Jerry Kovarsky

Figure 13-7:
Editing note
timing in a
MIDI event
list.

Figure 13-8:
Editing note
timing in a
piano roll
view.

Apple Logic Pro 9 screenshot courtesy of Jerry Kovarsky

Correcting wrong notes

Everyone makes mistakes at times, including playing bum notes. If you've played a lot of them, I recommend recording another pass. However, if your recording has only a few bad notes, go in and edit them in either event list or piano roll views. (I introduce these views in the preceding section.) Listen to the song, pay attention to the measure and beat where the mistake occurs, and isolate and change the note to any other note you want. ***Remember:*** The note will still be played in the same place, at the same level, and for the same duration. The only change will be to the pitch.

A common mistake for all keyboard players is hitting two notes together when you meant to play only one. Your finger may slightly graze the side of the intended key and grab the adjacent note along with it. These small mistakes are easy to find in editing modes. I prefer piano roll view if possible because you can easily see the two notes next to each other.

Here's a great pointer for finding those accidentally brushed notes: They'll always be much quieter than the main note (a characteristic easily seen in an event list) and will often be very short in duration (a characteristic easily seen in piano roll view). So when you see two notes occurring right next to each other at the exact same timing location, look for those two attributes. That will always be the bum note!

Changing the pitch of a note

You can also use the editing features of your sequencer to enhance your MIDI performance without losing that perfect take. If you're writing a song, for example, you can always go into edit mode and change a note or two in your melody to try out new melodic ideas. Here are a few other ways to use this capability:

- ✔ **Try alternate bass notes.** If you always played the root for each chord, you can make your part more interesting by changing some of the notes to the fifth or creating more of a walking bass line. (Flip to Chapter 7 for info on chords.)

- ✔ **Add more notes to your chords.** Playing large chords can be difficult. No problem: Take a given note in the chord, copy, it, and then change its pitch. This way, you make a three-note chord a four-note chord, adding a seventh or other fancier tone. If you find it hard to reach octaves while playing other notes in between, just build them up after the fact.

- ✔ **Change your left hand part.** If you played single notes, you can turn them into octaves by copying each note and then changing the pitch of the copied note to an octave higher or lower. You can also do the reverse to make octaves gentler: Delete each octave note, turning it into single notes in the left hand.

✔ **Try out different drum sounds.** The various drum sounds in a drum program are arranged across the keyboard so that you can easily play a normal drum part within a two-octave range (MIDI notes C2 through C4). That leaves a lot of other sounds that are assigned to rest of the key range. Many are percussion sounds such as congas, triangle, shakers, and the all-important cowbell, but you usually also find alternate bass and snare drums as well as different cymbals. For your recorded drum part, you can try out these variations by using the note shift/change function.

Say your snare drum is E2. Now locate another snare drum sound — perhaps A1. When you find a possible replacement, go into edit mode and select all the E2 notes (consult your owner's manual for specific instructions). After you've selected all the E2s, you can change them to the new note, A1.

I like to change some but not all of the snare hits to make the drum part more interesting. This strategy works best if you can find a second snare that sounds similar to but slightly different from the original to remain natural-sounding. Or change to a different snare drum for the bridge or solo section. Changing select crash or ride cymbal notes can also make a part sound more natural.

If you change all the notes, you put the song into another key. This process is called *transposing,* and it's commonly a separate function or edit choice. Common reasons for transposing include helping a singer be in a comfortable range for his or her voice — men and women rarely sing in the same keys — and letting guitar players use more open strings (which sounds good when strumming chords and playing strong, distorted parts) Piano players like to play in C major, for example, because it uses all the white notes. But guitars sound really good in E major because so many of the open strings work well for that key. No problem; transpose to the rescue!

Editing notes played too softly or too loudly

Sometimes as you play, a note's volume comes out a little too loud or soft relative to the other notes around it. You can easily fix this discrepancy by editing the velocity of the note. I prefer to make these changes in event edit view if at all possible because I can clearly see and highlight the MIDI velocity value that I want to change. Remember that you can always undo an edit and try again until you find the value that best matches the music.

Some sequencers let you *scale* the velocity of a given track or range of notes. You encounter two interpretations of this concept:

✔ **Scale to create crescendos or decrescendos:** This option takes the range of notes that you select and alters their velocity to *crescendo,* where each subsequent note is slightly louder than the one before it, or *decrescendo*, where each subsequent note is slightly softer than the one before it. You can usually set the start velocity and the end velocity to achieve the most natural gradation in *dynamics* (changes in volume).

✔ **Scale all the velocities relative to their current values:** This approach keeps all the relative dynamic values between notes the same but can increase or decrease them all by a chosen amount. Whether you think of it as adding or subtracting some value from each level or multiplying each level by some value, the result should be clear: Your whole part gets softer or louder but still sound the same dynamically.

You may be thinking, "Why not just use the mixer to change the level of the track?" Good question! As I note in Chapter 14, you can use touch to change a lot of aspects of a sound, such as switching multisample layers or the velocity routed to the filter. When you scale the velocity of the MIDI data, you interact with these settings in ways that changing the volume of the track doesn't. I often use this type of command on parts where the switching of velocity layers in a performance isn't feeling just right or where I simply didn't play a part as softly or loudly as I wanted.

Mixing your MIDI song

After you've recorded all the parts you want and are happy with the performances, it's time to mix your song. *Mixing* is the act of adjusting the blend of sounds and parts in a song to make them all sound good (volume, panning, and effects), blend together without clashing (EQ), and ensure each part can be heard without overpowering each other (volume). If you hear nothing but drums (or everything but drums) or your piano left hand, the guitar chords and bass guitar are creating a muddy mess. that's no good.

Your sequencer or recorder menu has a page that may be labeled something like Mixer or may just be the main track view page. It has controls for the level of each track, a pan knob, and perhaps some control over effects.

EQ (equalization) may be available as its own set of parameters or may be part of the effects. It's an important tool in the mixing process, so be sure to find out where it's available in your keyboard.

To first experiment with mixing, I suggest the following approach:

1. **Pick a single track and note its current volume level.**

   Good choices to start with are the drums or the bass if your song has these parts. (If it doesn't, try a supporting part behind your keyboard sound such as strings or a synth pad part.)

2. **Bring its level all the way down to 000 and notice how that change affects your perception of the whole song.**

3. **Bring the level up slowly and listen to the results.**

   Don't look at the value; use your ears.

4. **When it sounds good to you, look at what value you ended up at.**

   There are no wrong choices; it's just personal taste.

5. **Repeat Steps 1 through 4 with other parts, always taking note of the starting level.**

You can certainly bring all the volume sliders down to 000 and then try to build up the mix from scratch, but I suggest doing so only after you've gotten used to the sound of a good mix.

I can't give you one rule or magic formula for making a song sound good. Here are a few suggestions to help you achieve a good balance in your mix:

✔ **Don't allow the melody to get buried or lost within the other instruments.** No matter what type of music or instruments you use, the melody of your song is the most important thing.

✔ **If you're having trouble getting your melody loud enough, try lowering the levels of the other parts instead.**

✔ **Consider starting by getting the drums' and bass's balance right (if your music has those sounds).** Bring the drums up first and then add the bass, raising its level until it sounds strong and tightly connected to the drums — especially the bass drum. Then start adding other tracks without overpowering those first two sounds.

✔ **The main parts of your music (melody, drums, and bass) should be panned center.** Other parts can be panned slightly to the left or right to add aural interest to your music. Having everything come from the center or equally from both speakers sounds a little plain.

✔ **Don't overdo the reverb levels.** If you increase the reverb send for every part, your song will sound sloppy and become a wash of echoes. A safe starting point is to put only medium reverb at most on your drums, use no reverb for your bass, and then add reverb to other parts carefully as you go.

Here's a good basic concept: Adding reverb to a part makes it sound farther away. You want your important melodic parts to be close, so don't overdo their reverb. Want a part to move back in the mix? You can lower its volume, but you can also feed it more into a reverb to move it farther away.

✔ **If you find that parts are getting too thick or muddy sounding, you can use EQ to help make each track work in the combined mix.** Try cutting the levels of some frequencies to help parts sound distinct. Your bass drum and bass are the most important low frequency sounds, so try cutting the lows from other parts to let the bass part stand out clearly. (Do this cut on the other parts first, before just boosting the lows on the bass/bass drum.)

Too many high frequencies may fight with your melody, so try cutting them on some other parts if they're getting in the way. If you want a part to stand out a little bit more, boosting some higher EQ can really help. Pick your chosen parts carefully, though; you can't just boost the EQ on everything.

✔ **You can make some parts more colorful and interesting by adding some specialized effects treatment to them.** If you have any available insert effects left unused, experiment with them. (You can read about insert effects in the earlier section "Setting up your session.") You can also consider using the insert effects to put a different type of reverb on a part or two.

Note: I can't possibly do justice to the important subject of mixing music in this small chapter. If you're interested in discovering more about this topic, search out Jeff Strong's *Home Recording For Musicians For Dummies* (Wiley). It's a great book on the complete art of recording and mixing, and you can apply many of the concepts there to using a keyboard recorder or sequencer.

Getting Your Song out of the Keyboard and into the World

After your MIDI-based song is mixed, you need to capture the sound of it to allow others to hear it away from your keyboard. Translation: You need to make an audio recording of the song. If your keyboard can record both MIDI and audio, it will have some sort of command, often called Bouncing or Bouncing Down, to record the whole song to audio. Follow the instructions from your owner's manual.

If your keyboard can only do MIDI recording, you need an external audio recorder or computer software and audio interface for your computer to make the recording. You connect the main audio outputs of your keyboard to the audio inputs of the recorder or audio interface, and then you can capture/record the song.

When you use audio recording, however, you're already saving your work to some form of media as you record. And most products record in the industry standard wave file format, so moving your performance over and sharing it with others is simple.

If you've recorded to a memory drive or media card of some sort, you can just unplug it from your keyboard and plug it into your computer. (I cover the basics of audio recording in the earlier section "Addressing audio recording.") The drive then shows up on your desktop (though your computer may take a moment to read the drive). After the drive is visible, open it up and show its contents. You'll either see a file with the .wav extension at the end of the name or some folder structure (like a digital camera uses) that you need to navigate into until you come to the wave recorded files.

With the file you want visible, move or copy it to your hard drive. I recommend you make a folder somewhere on your computer for saving your personal recording files to. After the file is on your computer, you can play it, import it into your music library, and consider how to share it with your friends. Here are some common ways to share:

- **E-mail it.** Because you're using wave files, the file size may be too large. (Some e-mail systems can't accept files larger than 8 to 10 MB, for example.) First, you should compress the file (the most common form is .zip) and see how much smaller it gets. Compressing is a good first step because it doesn't degrade the quality of your music file; it just packs it smaller to send it. If it becomes small enough to send, great. When your recipient gets the file, he can unzip it, and it will be back to its full size and pristine audio quality.

- **Use a file transfer service.** If the file is still very large after compressing, you can consider using one of the many online options for sending bigger files. You upload your file to a service's website; the service stores it and sends your recipient a link so he can download the file privately through his web browser, avoiding the e-mail size limits. Many services offer free file transfers for files up to 2 GB and paid options for larger files.

- **Upload it to a music-sharing site.** Many sites allow you to share, stream, and offer your music for free or paid download. These sites often perform the file compression for you; you upload your wave file, and they take care of the rest. Popular sites include Soundcloud (https:// soundcloud.com), Reverb Nation (www.reverbnation.com), and YouTube (www.youtube.com — yes, you can share just audio files there). When the music is uploaded, you can post a link to your social media accounts to share it with your friends and family. And potentially anyone with an Internet connection; remember that these sites may be visible to the population at large (certainly the case for YouTube), so consider just how public you want to make your performance.

Retaining quality as file size goes down

If your compressed file is still too big to send, another choice is to convert your wave file to another audio format that makes it smaller. MP3 is the most widely used format and is fine for casual use, but note that it degrades the sound quality of your music to some degree. Your computer music player application (such as Apple iTunes or Windows Media Player) can probably perform this conversion. If you go this route, check the settings to be sure you're using the highest-quality conversion. Often, such programs are set to convert to 128 Kbps (kilobits per second) format, which is too low and compromises your audio quality. Use the highest setting, which is 320 Kbps.

Other formats for compressing music sound better, such as Apple's Apple Lossless Audio Codec or ALAC format, MP4 (shown as either .mp4 or .m4a) Ogg Vorbis (.ogg), and FLAC. I highly recommend them for your own use, but keep in mind that not all your recipients may know about or have the right playback applications for these file types, so check in advance before sending them. Depending on the size, you may now be able to e-mail it or stay within a file sharing service's free limits.

Chapter 14

Editing Sounds

In This Chapter

▶ Breaking down the various forms of synthesis

▶ Connecting sound's basic attributes to editing parameters

▶ Looking at common edit scenarios

*L*ocated inside your new keyboard is a wonderful world of sounds. Sure, their names are on the front panel, but inside your instrument is where the sound-making really happens. Most keyboards offer some ability to shape their sounds and even make new sounds of your own. Your keyboard may be called a digital piano or an arranger, but all electronic keyboards are actually a type of synthesizer at their roots. They generate tones called *waveforms*, which are molded and shaped to sound like the instruments you recognize (and some you don't!).

Some keyboards are preset synthesizers; they offer you no apparent control over the sounds they provide. Most others offer some degree of variability, from slight tweaks to make sounds brighter or darker to the ability to have the sound keep ringing when you take your finger off the key.

In this chapter, I open the door to how sounds are made and how you can modify the sounds to meet your taste and needs. If the thought of editing sounds conjures visions of some mad scientist plugging wires into a large panel of jacks or of a DJ surrounded by boxes with blinking lights, this chapter will show you that editing sounds can be much easier than you may think.

Meeting the Main Forms of Synthesis

As I first mention in Chapter 2, synthesizers/electronic keyboards generate their sounds by using a few different techniques. Some are better for realistic and imitative sounds, and others are extremely flexible to make those never-before-heard noises that have been swimming in your head. Understanding a little bit about these forms of synthesis helps you when you're ready to dive under the hood of your keyboard and make it sound and play the way you want, which I help you do later in this chapter!

Surveying sampled sounds

By far the most common method used in keyboards today is called *sample-playback*. When you see terms like *PCM playback* or *ROMpler* and see waveform memory listed in MB (megabytes) and GB (gigabytes), you know the instrument uses this form of sound production.

Sampling is a technique for digitally recording any sound and playing it back from the keys of your keyboard. A single recording of a sound is called a *sample;* because it's a recording of the actual thing, it sounds very realistic — until you assign it across multiple keys on a keyboard, where it plays slower and faster to produce lower and higher pitches, respectively. It quickly loses that authenticity the farther away from the original pitch you go, producing, for example, the Darth Vader and cartoon rodent voice effects from the natural human voice.

To avoid this unwanted effect for natural instrument sounds, the manufacturer records many different pitches from the source instrument, so notes are only stretched a few steps if at all. This approach is called *multisampling* and produces (you guessed it) *multisamples* — groups of samples assigned across the keys of a keyboard.

Editable sample-playback-based keyboards often provide a multisample list to show you the various waveforms you can use to make sounds.

Sampling has a lot of benefits and some drawbacks:

✔ **Pros:**

- **It's very realistic, especially for the attack/start of a note.**
  Sampling is still the way to go for re-creating the acoustic piano,
  for example. Getting the sound of many players at the same time (a
  string orchestra or a big band mixing saxes and trumpets) is best
  achieved with sampling.

- **It can reproduce any sound possible in a way that other forms of
  synthesis can't.** If it's recordable, it's usable. Want to play "Jingle
  Bells" with barking dogs? Sample playback is the answer.

- **It lets you create realistic imitative sounds much more easily.**
  Your job is mostly done for you already by the recording itself.

✔ **Cons:**

- **It's not very editable.** A recording can't be changed all that much.
  It's a captured moment in time, like a photograph. Some other
  forms of synthesis (such as modeling, which I cover later in the
  chapter) are more malleable and interactive.

- **It's more expensive (at least if done well.)** Samples require memory to be stored, which affects the cost of a keyboard. If a manufacturer allocates less memory to the recording of an instrument (to save cost), the sample isn't as realistic. Cheaper keyboards often stretch samples across more keys and use shorter recordings and other memory saving methods, which affects their sounds. The highest-quality sampled sounds come on higher-priced keyboards.

Flip to Chapter 3 for info on how memory-saving shortcuts can affect the sound of a piano.

Digging into digital synthesis

Digital synthesis is a general term that can encompass a lot of possible technologies. (I discuss one, frequency modulation [FM] in the nearby sidebar.) To keep things easily explainable here, I use the phrase *digital synthesis* to describe most technologies that don't use straight sample playback as their basic building block. Some sort of computer code (often called digital signal processing or DSP) generates the waveform. The sound isn't a recording of an existing instrument or object; it's produced entirely by digital processing. That's a key distinction between digital synthesis and the sampling in the preceding section.

Besides FM, other popular forms of digital synthesis include additive, wavetable look-up, resynthesis (using additive technology), phase distortion, phase vocoding (another form of resynthesis), granular, and waveshaping.

Getting into the science of frequency modulation

Frequency modulation (FM), as implemented by Yamaha in the '80s and '90s in its classic DX series of keyboards, is a good example of digital synthesis. In the original implementation, a digitally generated sine wave was modulated by another sine wave to produce timbral variations. (I explain sine waves in this chapter's "Oscillator" section.) Normally, a sine wave is very pure sounding and plain. But when one modulates another, some extra tonal qualities result (technically known as *sideband harmonics*). Based on the pitch and the level of the modulating sine wave, a variety of possible *timbres* (sound characteristics) can be produced. By adding more groups of these paired waveforms and cascading multiple steps of modulation, these FM-based synthesizers produced very interesting and unique sounds. FM is still being used in various products today, both hardware and software.

This big catch-all area has some general advantages and disadvantages:

✔ **Pros:**

- **It's highly interactive and able to be manipulated and modulated.** Sounds that are digitally produced can often be very expressive, and you can easily change their character in real time.

- **It can be very fresh and unique.** If you're looking for more-imaginative sounds for your music, explore non-sample-based technologies.

- **It doesn't require large amounts of costly memory to store data.**

✔ **Cons:**

- **It's less likely to be able to convincingly reproduce known, complex acoustic instrument sounds.** Sampling still wins in this regard.

- **It's usually more complex to program and edit.** Many forms of digital synthesis are complicated, and familiarity with one form doesn't always help you when you're faced with another.

- **It varies from synth to synth.** Many digital synthesis types are unique to a given manufacturer or even model. So fewer other musicians know how to use them, and less general-purpose information and instruction is available. With other, more-common forms of synthesis, you can find online info, books, videos, and other resources to help you.

Perusing physical modeling and virtual analog

Physical modeling and virtual analog are two separate synthesis methods, but they're related in concept. The following sections lay them out.

Physical modeling

Physical modeling creates the sound of a specific type of instrument by studying how it physically and mechanically produces its sound and then re-creating each piece or component of the original device by using DSP processing. With this approach, you vary parameters that replicate the instrument's material makeup and its reaction to how it's played.

Common instruments that keyboards reproduce using physical modeling include electric pianos (both the tine and reed versions), plucked strings, brass and woodwind instruments, melodic percussion (such as marimba), and the drum parts of a drumkit (cymbals are still commonly sampled).

Here are some of the pros and cons of physical modeling:

✔ **Pros:**

- **It's 100 percent focused on a specific type of sound, so all the processing power and technology is devoted to the singular task.** This expert approach can produce highly detailed and nuanced sounds.

- **Like digital synthesis, it's highly interactive, expressive, and changeable and doesn't require lots of memory.**

✔ **Cons:**

- **It's still relatively new and doesn't always sound completely natural to expert ears.** Some users talk about a "plastic" quality to the sound.

- **It can be more complex to program and edit.** It involves terms and concepts that may be unfamiliar (dispersion?), and it can produce strange results when varied too far. If you don't understand some of the science of the object being modeled, you can get frustrated when things don't work like you intended.

- **It's still evolving.** Because the technology is relatively new, today's model will likely be eclipsed quickly by newer, better models. Or cheaper models.

Virtual analog

Virtual analog synthesis is dedicated to re-creating the sound and approach of older analog synthesis. It's a form of modeling that re-creates electronic circuits and tone generators rather than physical, mechanical acoustic instruments. Each component in a given analog synth has a unique sound and behavior/response, and each design offers different routing and sound manipulation possibilities. Emulating and capturing the character of the many classic synth models has grown into a very popular category of instruments.

Virtual analog synths are rarely referred to as being "physically modeled," but that's often what they're doing. In software, you can find exact re-creations of older, classic instruments (such as the Minimoog, ARP 2600, and Prophet 5). In other software instruments and in all virtual analog hardware instruments, the approach is about creating new designs that offer more extensive features based on some of the classic components and building blocks.

Analog synthesis gave name to many of the parameters and tools of synthesis still used today. So when you hear about oscillators, filters, envelope generators, and so on (say, in later sections of this chapter), you're in analog/virtual analog synthesis territory.

Like all synthesis methods, virtual analog has its advantages and disadvantages:

- Pros:

  - **Like physical modeling (see the preceding section), it's focused on a specific type of sound production, which means it can produce truly accurate analog sounds.**

  - **It beats sampling for re-creating analog sounds.** The parameters can be manipulated and modulated exactly as their analog forbearers. If you want to get those classic synth sounds, virtual analog produces them far better than sampled versions of the older instruments.

  - **It's based on well-known technology and instruments, so a lot of resources for learning how to use and program it are available.**

- Cons:

  - **It can't produce the sound of acoustic instruments very well.** It certainly can't produce the core bread-and-butter keyboard sounds (pianos, organs, and so on) you may be looking to play.

  - **It often has limited polyphony.** *Polyphony* is the ability to play more than one note at a time. Be sure to check whether the virtual analog keyboard you're looking into can play enough notes to produce the chords you want or can create keyboard splits and layers.

Relating Sound Characteristics to Synthesis Parameters

Understanding some fundamental concepts about sound can help you get into adjusting or editing sounds in your keyboard. All musical sounds can be broken down into three basic aspects or qualities:

- **Pitch:** *Pitch* is the musical frequency of a note (commonly called by the note names I discuss in Chapter 5) or the perceived frequency of a nonmusical noise (because a thunderclap or a car horn doesn't have a single, distinct pitch). This aspect of a sound can slightly drift or change over time, especially from the initial attack of the tone until it settles in to a sustained state.

- **Volume:** *Volume* represents the loudness of a note and, most importantly, how that loudness changes over time (from the moment you initiate the sound through what happens when you release your finger from the key).

✔ **Timbre**: *Timbre* is the tonal quality of the sound. This aspect is the most complicated to explain without overloading you with scientific detail, but think of it as what makes a sound uniquely identifiable — the musical equivalent of *je ne sais quoi*. If you play the same note at the same volume on a flute and on a trumpet, you can easily tell which instrument is producing which sound. That's because of their timbral qualities. (If you're scientifically inclined, check out the nearby sidebar "Falling for timbre" for the nitty-gritty details.)

The following sections help you use these sound characteristics to classify sounds and then apply your knowledge to understanding synthesizer tools.

Describing sounds' qualities

If you take some time to think about the three aspects of sound, you can then describe sounds based on them. How would I describe a note played on the piano? Well . . .

✔ It has a sound that is very strong at the attack. It sounds the moment it's struck; its volume is at its loudest right away.

✔ It's rich in character. I can tell the fundamental pitch, of course, but it has a complexity to it (related to pitch and timbre) that seems to get plainer or hollower as it sustains; the timbre changes over time. *Remember:* The timbral quality at the start is often the most easily identifiable part of a sound; if you were only listening to the later, sustaining part of the sound, you probably wouldn't recognize it as a piano sound.

✔ It slowly dies away until it fades to silence; the volume changes over time.

One thing you may notice about my descriptions is that most of them are centered on volume and how it changes. The volume-over-time characteristic of a sound is the easiest to notice. Ask yourself these questions:

✔ **Does it start right away at full volume or gradually rise up to a level?** Struck and plucked instruments hit full volume right off the bat. Most wind and bowed instruments, on the other hand, take some time to reach full volume, as do softer choir sounds. This gradual volume change can also be a chosen technique for playing, such as in a slow, romantic string performance, where the player swells up a dramatic, sustained note.

✔ **Does it stay at full level for as long as you hold a note or decay quickly?** Organs do the former, as do most wind and bowed instruments. Most drums and struck percussive instruments decay quickly; they can't sustain their sound. They hit hard and then quickly fade away.

✔ **Does it decay slowly while a note is sustaining?** Pianos and guitars do (actually, most plucked strings do).

✔ **Does it continue to ring (even slightly) after you release the note?** Most plucked string instruments do so (unless you manually mute the note with your hand). Think of the ring of an acoustic guitar or an upright bass. One string doesn't stop ringing when the player moves to another, but it's not a long trailing tail — just a little after-ring. Most ensemble string sounds have this attribute as well. Without it, they'd sound very choppy.

Considering common parameter names

When you understand some of the characteristics and basics of sound, you can get a handle on the tools a synthesizer uses to produce, shape, and modify a tone (including the samples and multisamples I introduce earlier in the chapter). In the following sections, I describe the keyboard parameters that help you manipulate sounds.

Falling for timbre

For a given musical note, many different pitches actually sound, created from the vibrating of the string, wood, column of air, or other part of the instrument that produces the sound. These pitches blend together to form the timbre of the sound. The main pitch that defines the note (whether it's a middle C, an F, a B-flat, or whatever) is called the *fundamental*.

Also sounding at various lower levels are a number of other frequencies, called *harmonics* or *partials*. The order in which these frequencies are produced is a physical phenomenon defined as the *harmonic series*. The lower steps in the series are closely related to the original pitch and sound good with it, producing a pleasing, nonconflicting sound. This type of sound is simpler and less rich (think about a simple penny whistle or a clarinet).

But as you go higher up the series, you get more frequencies that produce a brighter or richer tone and can potentially clash more with the fundamental. These frequencies produce more-complex sounds (think full pipe organ, sax, or trumpet), and even harsh sounds if the conflicting harmonics are loud enough (think of a gong or crash cymbal). The relative strength of each of these frequencies shapes how you perceive its tone and is why you can differentiate one instrument from another. Skilled musicians can hear subtle differences in these harmonics, which is why they can pick out which brand of guitar a player uses or distinguish two different sax players' tones.

Oscillator

The *oscillator* is the sound-producing component. It plays back the sample, multisample, waveform, or digitally produced sound element. A synthesizer may have more than one of these; two, three, and even more oscillators aren't uncommon. You can see the most common analog and virtual analog synthesis waveforms in Figure 14-1:

- ✔ **Sawtooth (or saw) wave:** This waveform is the fullest and richest type offered. It contains all harmonics (described as both even and odd); as they ascend in frequency, they grow weaker in amplitude. A sawtooth wave is often described as bright and buzzy.

- ✔ **Square wave**: A *square wave* is a hollower-sounding waveform. It has only odd-order harmonics, meaning it skips every other harmonic in the series. It's related to the *pulse wave,* which you can think of as a square wave that can be made thinner; its shape can be changed from a square to a narrower rectangle. As it changes, the sound goes from hollow to a thinner, reedier quality. You can continuously vary this width by using an LFO or envelope as a modulator, a process called *pulse width modulation* (PWM). Read more about envelopes and LFOs later in this chapter.

- ✔ **Sine wave:** This waveform has only a fundamental harmonic with no other coloration, so it sounds very simple and pure. It looks like a perfectly rolling wave: all curves.

- ✔ **Triangle wave:** This wave sounds like a darker/duller square wave (because it has less harmonic content). It's very soft but a bit richer than the sine wave.

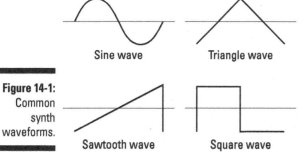

Sine wave   Triangle wave

Figure 14-1:
Common
synth
waveforms.

Sawtooth wave   Square wave

Illustration by Wiley, Composition Services Graphics

Listen to Track 107 to hear examples of each of these waveform types.

The oscillator is also where you choose the pitch or *tuning* of the waveform. And if you want to modulate the pitch, those modulation sources will also be associated with it.

Filter

A *filter* is a tonal shaping device that you run a waveform through. It affects the timbre of the waveform by blocking or letting pass certain frequencies. Think of the tone control of your stereo or TV. You can make the sound brighter by allowing more high frequencies to pass through and darker by blocking them.

The main parameters associated with a filter are the *cutoff,* which is the frequency at which the signal starts to be blocked or allowed to pass, and *resonance* (or *Q*), which emphasizes or boosts the frequencies near the cutoff to produce a sharp tonal bump. High resonance settings are often described as chirpy or peaky and can produce pretty ugly howling sounds under some circumstances.

The most common filter is called a *low-pass,* which allows all frequencies below the cutoff to pass through and gradually blocks the higher ones. A *high-pass* filter does the opposite, allowing only frequencies above the cutoff to pass. A *band-pass* filter allows a certain range of frequencies to pass through and blocks frequencies below and above the band. So it passes on a slice of frequencies. A *band-reject* filter blocks the defined bands, allowing frequencies above and below it to pass. These are not hard cuts; various filter designs reduce the frequencies at different gradations from the cutoff point. Varying the cutoff (commonly called *sweeping the filter*) of each of these types of filters in real time produces a very different sound, and adding some resonance or Q increases the richness of the sweep.

Track 108 offers examples of each type of filter with its cutoff point being swept.

Amplifier (amp)

The *amplifier* controls the level or output of the sound. This level control is usually done individually for each oscillator, so you can mix the various tones as you like. The amp is also where you decide how to *pan* the waveform in a stereo field — that is, decide whether it comes out of both speakers equally or is moved to one side or the other.

Envelope generator

An *envelope generator* (sometimes abbreviated EG) is a modifying device that can change the value of a parameter connected to it over time. It's what a synth uses to change pitch, timbre, or volume over time, and is almost always used to control the amplifier and filter in any given sound. The simplest and most common envelopes are represented as ADSR — attack, decay, sustain, and release.

Two attributes are being changed: the level of the given characteristic (volume, pitch, and so on) at a given point or stage of its sounding and how much time (sometimes called *rate*) it takes to move from one level/stage to the next. So in the basic ADSR envelope (shown in Figure 14-2), the vertical axis is called the *envelope amplitude,* or the level of the sound or modulation. The horizontal axis represents time because the amplitude or modulation amount can change over time. You can translate the stages as follows:

- ✔ **Attack:** The rate from lowest value (off) to maximum level. This maximum is usually defined by a parameter called *envelope depth*, which determines how much affect the total envelope shape will have over the chosen characteristic (pitch, volume, timbre).

- ✔ **Decay:** The rate from the maximum level down to the next stage.

- ✔ **Sustain:** The level the sound stays at until you take your finger off the key. The time from the moment you press down the key until you release it is called the *gate time.* This term is a holdover from analog synthesis days, when a voltage was produced during the time a key was held to both trigger and sustain a note. So the gate represents the playing, sustaining, and releasing of the key. Think of a gate in a fence: You play a note, which opens the gate to let something pass through, and it stays open until you finish passing through (letting go of the key), when the gate closes again.

- ✔ **Release:** The rate from the sustain level back to no value (off).

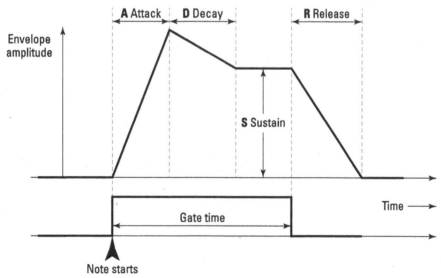

Figure 14-2:
Basic ADSR envelope shape.

Illustration by Wiley, Composition Services Graphics

As synthesizers developed, more complex envelope generators were developed, especially when digital synthesis and virtual analog came along. More steps were added, with the parameters being clearly presented as separate rate and level controls.

In Track 109, you can hear examples of the process of varying the basic envelope shape of a synth sound.

LFO (low frequency oscillator)

This special-purpose oscillator operates below the frequency of human hearing, so it's only used to modulate other parameters in the system. For example, when routed to the pitch of the oscillator it produces vibrato. When routed to the filter cutoff, it produces a sort of wah effect. When routed to the amplifier output, it produces *tremolo,* a fading in and out of the sound (think surf and spaghetti western guitar sounds). The tuning of the LFO (called the frequency) determines the rate of this modulation; the higher the frequency, the faster the rate of modulation. The modulation shape is determined by the waveform chosen for the LFO. (Refer to Figure 14-1 for the most common waveforms.)

Track 110 offers examples of LFO-modulated vibrato, wah, and tremolo.

Trying Some Common Sound Edits

Sometimes you play a sound and you like most of what you hear and how it responds to your playing, but you wish you could change some small characteristic. Maybe the sound is a little too dark or too bright, or it rings on too long after you release the key. In most keyboards, you can fix that without becoming an expert in synth terms and tools or creating a sound from scratch. Just follow the suggestions in the following sections, and you can start to personalize your sounds and achieve the results you want.

Varying the basic timbre (waveform)

The fastest way to create a new sound is to simply change the waveform of an existing sound.

1. **Go into the sound or program edit mode of your keyboard.**

2. **Find the oscillator parameter or page.**

3. **Select a new waveform or multisample.**

4. **Save the new sound.**

   Don't forget to give it a new name and save location; otherwise, you'll lose your first sound!

The sections that follow have some common applications for making this type of edit.

Trying a slight variation of the current sound type

Many sample-playback keyboards offer more than one multisample or waveform of a given type of sound. But the sound they offer for each one has been greatly changed to present you with the most sonic variation. So you may have two electric piano sounds, but the second one has completely different effects, is more distorted (for a heavier rock sound), and is less dynamic to your touch. That's a lot of things to try to edit to make the sound you want, right? No worries; just edit the first sound (which you liked) to use the second electric piano multisample, and then save it to a new location.

Here are a few other ideas:

✔ Take an electric bass sound and replace the waveform with a synth waveform. Voilà! Instant synth bass.

✔ I like to make more synth lead sounds from the onboard waveform selection. Find a lead synth sound you like, go into edit mode, and try out many of the different synth waveforms. Very few keyboards deliver so many closely related lead sounds, but often all you need is a different waveform to add more lead sounds to your arsenal.

✔ When you have a sound that's a *layer* (two sounds on top of each other — say, acoustic piano with strings), you can make some cool variations by changing the waveform for the layered part (the strings). Many times, going to a mellow synth or vocal multisample yields another great sound without much effort.

Track 111 demonstrates some slight variation edit concepts.

Using similar amp characteristics to make a different sound

If a sound plays right (meaning it attacks, sustains, and decays a certain way), you can change it to another type of sound by swapping the multisample. Figure 14-3 shows some common EG amp shapes.

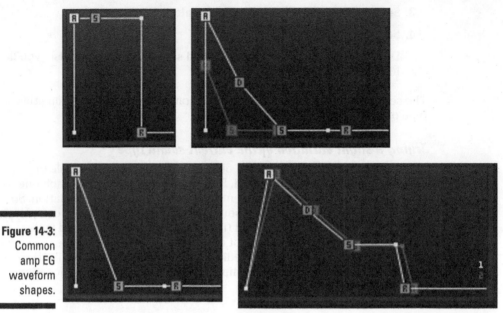

Figure 14-3:
Common
amp EG
waveform
shapes.

Illustration courtesy of Jerry Kovarsky

Try some of these possibilities:

- ✔ Change a bass guitar sound to a synth wave and then raise the pitch an octave or two. Now you have a new lead synth sound.

- ✔ Take a sound that attacks quickly but also decays quickly, like a marimba, xylophone, or plucked string. Change the waveform, and you have all sorts of new short sounds that work well for percussive parts or for arpeggiated patterns.

- ✔ Change the waveform of an organ sound to make a good fast synth sound for playing choppy chord parts.

- ✔ Swap out multisamples to make nice synth pad sounds from sustaining string and vocal sounds.

Track 112 offers examples of making new sounds using EG shape concepts.

Changing the brightness (filter)

This common sound tweak is sometimes just a small adjustment to darken or brighten a sound; that can be all you need to go from "not quite" to "perfect." For example, this edit is the first thing many players like to do to acoustic piano sounds. What sounds good playing alone at home (warm and darker) doesn't end up cutting through the sound of a full band when you play in a club, at church, or wherever. So brighten up the sound a little! The easiest way to change the brightness one way or the other is to simply alter the level of the filter cutoff. If you don't see a front-panel control labeled Filter or Filter Cutoff, do the following:

1. **Go into the sound or program edit mode of your keyboard.**
2. **Find the filter parameters or page and locate the filter cutoff parameter.**
3. **Raise or lower the value to change the sound.**

   To darken the sound, lower the value; to brighten it, raise the value.

4. **Save your new sound.**

   Be sure to give it a new name and save it to a different location so that you don't lose your first sound!

Many keyboards have a front panel knob dedicated to controlling the filter cutoff as you play, which means you don't have to go into edit mode to sweep the cutoff (a popular thing to do, especially for synth sounds). Some synths have a ribbon controller with the filter cutoff assigned to it. And many small performance synths that don't have this dedicated knob assign filter cutoff to the mod wheel for easy filter sweeps.

You may not be able to darken the sound by this simple edit if the sound is using an envelope generator to vary the filter cutoff over time. An easy clue you're in this scenario: The filter cutoff is very low, yet you still find the sound is bright. In this case, you need to lessen the effect the envelope has on the attack section of the shape in order to darken the filter. Look for the envelope depth parameter (it may be called Filter EG) or for an envelope being used as a modulator assigned to filter cutoff and lower the modulation amount.

If your keyboard doesn't have a Filter EG parameter but has the more advanced rate and level envelope generators I discuss in the earlier section "Envelope generator," lower the attack level value. Doing so causes the envelope to not go as high before moving to the decay stage, which darkens your sound.

Finally, some sounds use velocity to modulate the filter cutoff or how much the filter EG affects the cutoff. When you play this type of sound, a very soft touch produces a dark sound, and harder hits produce a brighter sound. If you reduce the velocity control over the filter EG or velocity modulation amount routed to the filter cutoff, you can darken the sound. Yes, it will still get brighter the harder you play, but not as bright. (Note that the softer touch will now be even darker, but often that difference isn't an issue. If it does bother you, raise the filter cutoff just a few numbers.)

Don't forget that EQ is also a type of filter control; you can lower the high EQ level to darken your sound some and raise the high EQ level to brighten it.

Adjusting the amp parameters (volume over time)

Changing the attack and release of a sound is another common, very effective tweak to make. Many good sounds that have some release after you let go of the key can sound sloppy when you're playing faster phrases.

To fix this issue, just follow these steps:

1. **Go into the sound or program edit mode of your keyboard.**

2. **Find the amp parameters or page, locate the amp envelope generator, and lower the release or release rate/time parameter.**

   This step lessens or tightens up the ringing after you let go of a key.

   Note: Most synthesizers have dedicated front panel knobs for the amplifier envelope (likely labeled ADSR), so you can make this change without looking through menus or pages.

3. **Save your new sound.**

   Give it a new name and save location so you avoid losing your first sound.

Likewise, a too-slow attack makes a sound hard to play quickly. To adjust the attack, repeat Steps 2 and 3 in the preceding list, substituting the attack rate parameter for the release parameter in Step 2. To speed up the attack, lower the value.

A quick tip is to take a quick on/quick off sound such as an organ and slightly slow up the attack and lengthen the release. This process turns the sound into a different type of pad sound, great for dreamier background chords in a slow song.

Some more-advanced envelope designs offer a start level and then a second stage for the attack level and rate. To get a quicker attack, check to see whether the start level is very low or very high. If it's quite low, try raising that level to the same level as the attack in the second stage. To slow down an attack, a high start level may get in your way. If so, lower the start level back to 00 before working on the attack time.

Adding modulation

Here are some simple edits that you can do to fix common situations you may encounter with LFO-based modulation. (Flip to the earlier section "LFO [low frequency oscillator]" for details on this tool.)

Tweaking the filter envelope

When changing attack/release significantly on a sound, you may expose the filter envelope movement because it's now different from your amp envelope shape. Say you speed up the attack of the amp and now hear the filter slowly opening up at the start of each new note, or you lengthen the release of the amp and now hear the filter closing too quickly while your sound is fading away. The filter envelope used to match or follow the amp envelope shape closely, but now it stands out. In these cases, you want to go to the filter envelope and make similar edits to its attack and release times as those explained in the nearby section "Adjusting the amp parameters (volume over time)." Some synths even offer the ability to tweak the filter and amp envelopes at the same time, presented as a single/grouped parameter in a quick edit or performance edit page.

The following examples all discuss finding modulation at a specific parameter page. Some synths (both hardware and software) have a Modulation Matrix page or section where you can pick sources of modulation (an LFO, an envelope, or a hardware controller like a wheel or pedal) and assign them to destination parameters (oscillator pitch, filter cutoff, amp level, and amp panning). This setup is a very open and flexible way to create modulation routings, and it brings them all onto one page or screen for easy viewing. So you may need to look there to make your edits.

✔ **The vibrato rate is too slow/too fast when I move the mod wheel forward.** Routing an LFO to the oscillator pitch produces vibrato. To locate which LFO is being used to produce the vibrato, push and leave the mod wheel forward a bit so you're hearing constant vibrato. Go into sound/program edit mode, find the LFO page, and change the rate. If you hear the vibrato changing, you know you have the right one. Increasing the rate speeds up the vibrato; lowering the rate slows it down.

✔ **I hear too much/too little vibrato when I move the mod wheel forward.** Lower or raise the amount of LFO modulation the mod wheel produces from the pitch modulation page. Sometimes it's on the LFO page itself, presented as a Pitch Mod Depth parameter. Sometimes it's presented on a Controllers page as the range the mod wheel puts out (000 to 127). Lowering the value lessens the amount of vibrato produced.

✔ **My sound is panning from one speaker to another, and I need to adjust or remove that.** This effect is produced by an LFO modulating the amp output pan parameter. Go into sound/program edit mode and find this modulation assignment in the amp parameters. You can increase the modulation value to deepen the effect or lower it to reduce or even turn it off. If you want to change the speed of the panning, go to the LFO page and adjust its rate up or down.

Sometimes panning is produced by an effect, not by an internal modulation routing. So look to your effects if amp pan modulation isn't the answer. (I cover effects in Chapter 9.)

✔ **I want my sound to produce a tremolo effect.** Tremolo is produced by an LFO modulating the amp output or level parameter. Go into sound/program edit mode and find the output parameter in the amp parameters. Does it offer a place to assign modulation to it? If so, assign an LFO with a medium depth (for now) so you can hear it. Then go to that LFO page and adjust the rate to taste. Now you can go back to the amp page and readjust the modulation amount to your desired depth.

Note: In some systems, this setup may be on the LFO page, presented as amp modulation depth. Set the amount of tremolo depth here and then go back to the LFO page to adjust the rate.

Personalizing the touch response of a sound

A common issue I hear from owners of keyboards is that they like a sound but it doesn't "feel" right to them. It gets loud too easily or is too hard to control when playing quietly. Playing harder and softer does switch between waveforms, but getting the hardest velocity layer to sound consistently is difficult. The following sections present a few easy edits to make to correct this problem. These types of edits are easy to do and can often be the most satisfying fix to make.

Customizing a sound's dynamics

Dynamics refer to how loudly or softly you play a note and are usually controlled by your touch on the key. All keyboards offer a touch curve or touch setting that affects dynamics. This parameter translates your playing force into instructions for how a sound will respond. If a sound isn't feeling quite right, go to the touch curve or velocity curve parameter first. You most often find it in the Global or Settings mode of a keyboard.

You can also manipulate how your touch affects the dynamics by routing velocity to the amp output. Increasing this amount of modulation makes your soft touch produce an even quieter sound, so you'll need more force to get the sound louder. Often velocity will be routed to modulate the amp envelope amount so you need to locate that parameter and increase its value as well.

If your sound gets too quiet and then too easily gets way loud, you need to reduce the amount of velocity modulation of the amp or amp envelope output. Your sound will get louder overall, so you'll need to lower the amp output to compensate. Be sure to check whether any velocity is routed to filter modulation; if so, you want to lessen that as well.

Not all keyboards allow you to do this level of editing. Certainly, synths and workstations, advanced arrangers, and perhaps a more advanced stage piano do, but otherwise you may be limited to the touch curve method.

Another cool way to make a sound seem more dynamic is to add or increase the amount of velocity controlling the filter cutoff. When you do so, your soft touch causes the filter to be darker, which makes a sound seem quieter. If you're first adding this amount, you need to lower the filter cutoff to give the velocity some room to move. Try starting with the filter cutoff all the way down to 00 and then adjusting the velocity modulation amount and the cutoff until it feels right. *Remember:* This change should be subtle; you're looking to get a sense of volume change, not a drastic filter sweep. If a sound is already using velocity to modulate the amount of filter envelope control, increase this modulation amount and work with it and the filter cutoff value until it feels right. If you find that your sound gets too bright with more forceful playing, you're modulating it too much!

Matching velocity switch points to your touch

Sample-playback keyboards often use different multisamples of a keyboard, recorded at softer and harder touches, to make a sound more realistic and expressive. All the better sampled acoustic and electric piano sounds do, for sure. Although this method is a great approach to re-creating these sounds, the programmed velocity values for when to switch to the next multisample may not match your touch. Basically, what you perceive as a touch to dynamics or brightness problem may actually be a problem with when the keyboard switches to a different multisample. If you have a synth, workstation, or more advanced stage piano or arranger, you may be able to access the multisample switching to see whether it's the issue before you go to the amp and filter parameters. Here's how:

1. **Go into sound/program edit mode.**

2. **Find the oscillator page(s) and look to see whether multiple waveforms or multisamples are arranged to be switched by velocity values.**

   On some instruments, this info is all presented on one oscillator page, but on others it's another part, tone, or layer that is a complete sound element set to be triggered by a certain velocity range.

3. **Check the velocity values.**

   Look at the velocity values used for each multisample or part. MIDI velocity ranges from 001 to 127, so you'll encounter several subranges for an oscillator or multisample — maybe 001 to 32, 033 to 070, 071 to 100, and 101 to 127. Notice that the numbers all run consecutively, with no range overlapping.

4. **Adjust the value of the appropriate layer(s).**

If the top layer is coming in too easily for you or producing too bright a sound, you want to move its start value to a higher velocity number, making it take even more force to trigger it. Set the range to 112 to 127 and see whether that feels better. Remember, though that you can't leave a hole between two layers. With your change, nothing is sounding from 100 to 111, so you have to go back to layer three and raise the top threshold so that the range covers 071 to 111. Now the full range of values will produce sound.

To make a sound softer and more dynamic at low velocity levels, increase the range of values that the lower layers occupy, only bringing in the upper layers at the highest values. To make a sound brighter and more aggressive, increase the range that the upper layers use, spreading them across the majority of the range and only using the lower layers for the lowest numbers.

If you want to get to hear the character of each multisample, you can go to an initialized sound location in your keyboard (if it has one) and assign this multisample to that "raw" sound. It won't sound perfect, but you can hear the true character of the recording and can better judge what each waveform sounds like.

Chapter 15

Teacher Included: Using Onboard Learning Systems

In This Chapter

▷ Getting familiar with your keyboard's built-in songs

▷ Walking through the lesson features of Casio and Yamaha

▷ Playing with some fun instructional features

*P*laying an instrument is a wonderful activity, and being able to express yourself through music is both satisfying and actually good for your long-term health and well being. Learning to read music and develop your technique involves hard work; there are no magic shortcuts to developing your skills, no matter what those Internet ads and online courses may promise.

However, many portable keyboards today offer some great features to help you get started, guide you through proper practice routines, and make the study of music into a fun game for kids of all ages.

In this chapter, I take you through the educational features and helpers built into many of the Casio and Yamaha keyboards. Many people find the included manuals a bit cryptic, so I explain both how and *why* you want to do things. Even if you don't own one of these keyboards, you'll find this chapter interesting and helpful when shopping for a new keyboard.

Working with Built-In Songs

Most electronic keyboards have some built-in demo songs, which the store uses to show off the instrument's sounds and sonic capabilities. But this class of portable keyboards, along with many digital pianos, usually also has a library of simple folk songs, holiday favorites, popular classical selections, and instructional songs to help you in your studies. *Tip:* Look on the front panel for a button labeled Song (Yamaha) or Song Bank (Casio) to confirm that your keyboard has songs built-in, not just a few in-store demos.

Some of these tunes are simple two-handed piano playing, others use the onboard auto-accompaniment, and some are orchestrated to sound like a full production. No matter what the style, you can listen and learn from them.

Selecting a song

First, you need to choose a song. On most low-end models the song names, or at least the categories, appear on the front panel, as shown in Figure 15-1.

⊞ 110 SONG BANK

001~045 WORLD	046~050 EVENT	053 JE TE VEUX	091~110 EXERCISE
001 TWINKLE TWINKLE LITTLE STAR	046 SILENT NIGHT	067 ODE TO JOY	EXERCISE I
007 AMAZING GRACE	051~090 PIANO/CLASSICS	071 RÊVERIE	EXERCISE II
020 GREENSLEEVES	051 MARY HAD A LITTLE LAMB	074 FÜR ELISE	

Figure 15-1:
Front panel
song list.

Image courtesy of Casio America, Inc.

1. **To select a built-in song, press the Song or Song Bank mode button.**

   You'll also see the word *Demos* on the front panel; usually, it means you have to hold down two buttons to bring up a special playback mode of all the built-in songs. That's not what you're looking for in this step; that function plays through all the songs like a jukebox gone mad. You need to be able to select one specific song of your choosing for this process.

2. **Use any of the data entry controls (+/−, up/down, numeric keypad, value wheel/slider, or whatever applies) to select the song you want to listen to.**

3. **Press Play or Start/Stop to listen to the song.**

4. **While the song is playing, press the Pause button (see Figure 15-2) to stop the song but keep it at the current location.**

   To resume play from where you left off, press Pause again. If you press Stop, you stop the song and relocate to the beginning.

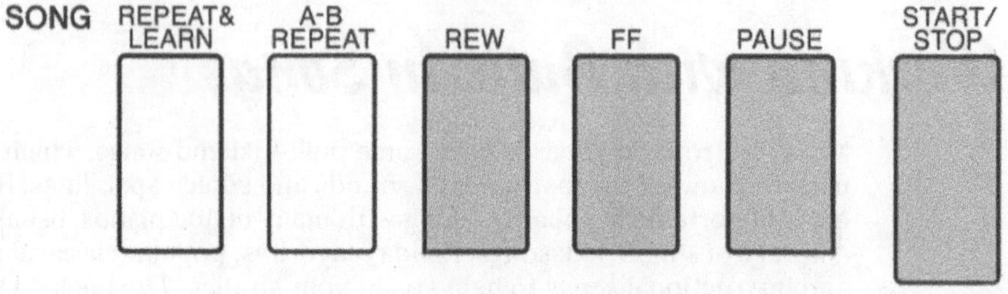

SONG | REPEAT& LEARN | A-B REPEAT | REW | FF | PAUSE | START/ STOP

Figure 15-2:
Front panel
transport
controls.

Image courtesy of Yamaha Corporation of America

5. **Press the Fast Forward (FF) button to move ahead through the song while it's playing and the Rewind (REW) button to scroll back to an earlier section of the song.**

On many keyboards, if you press FF or REW once, the song moves one measure in the chosen direction. Holding down the button causes the keyboard to speed through the song until you let go. Then it resumes playing.

Note: A couple of other buttons — Repeat & Learn and A-B Repeat — also appear in Figure 15-2. These buttons come into play in the later section "Repeating small sections."

Slowing down the tempo

You've found a song you like, and now you want to attempt to play it for yourself. Your keyboard may come with printed music for the included songs as part of the manual, or you may want to figure it out by ear. Whatever method you choose, the first step should be slowing down the song so you can hear it at a slower tempo, good for learning and playing along with. Learning a song at a comfortable (meaning slow) tempo before attempting to play it at the final, correct tempo is important. Work slowly and gradually increase the speed as you get comfortable.

Your keyboard has two buttons labeled Tempo — an up control and a down control (as shown in Figure 15-3) — or a tempo knob or slider. You can use these to adjust the tempo as desired.

I prefer using a Tap Tempo feature if it's available; see Figure 15-3. This function is the ability to tap on a marked button at the speed/timing you want to set the tempo to. When setting the tempo with Tap Tempo, you need to tap at least three times to give the keyboard a clear indication of the tempo you want.

Figure 15-3:
Front panel
tempo
controls.

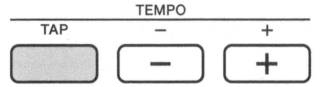

Image courtesy of Yamaha Corporation of America

Turning off one of the parts (RH or LH)

Many keyboards that offer piano pieces as part of their learning systems have a feature for turning off one of the hands or parts. This functionality is a good way to be able to listen to and focus on one part at a time without being distracted by the other part. After you've learned one of the parts, you can turn it off, turn on the other part, and play a duet with the system, each playing one hand.

Look on the front panel of your keyboard for a button labeled Part Select or buttons labeled Part 1 and Part 2 or RH/R (right hand) and LH/L (left hand). Figure 15-4 shows some examples. These buttons turn off a selected part, toggling it on and off with each press. Look at your display for visual feedback of what you're doing with each button press.

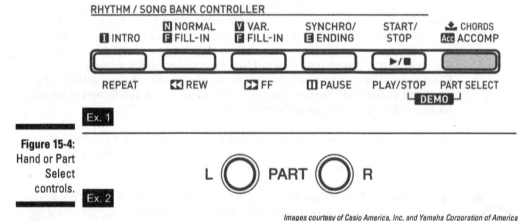

Figure 15-4: Hand or Part Select controls.

Images courtesy of Casio America, Inc, and Yamaha Corporation of America

You may need to be in Lesson Mode to turn off parts on some models. I discuss lesson modes later in the chapter.

Repeating small sections

As you start to learn a song, you want to limit the playback to small sections at a time. Dividing a piece into small phrases is an essential part of practicing that allows you to concentrate on each section and work on it over and over again. Plus, working on small phrases helps when you're trying to figure out a song by ear. (I give guidance on playing by ear in Chapter 16.)

The easiest way to create these smaller phrases is to press a button to mark the start and end locations you want while the song is playing. On Casio keyboards, this button is labeled Repeat; on Yamaha, it's often A-B Repeat (see Figure 15-2). On both brands, setting up these repeats is easy to do:

1. **Select and start the song playing.**

2. **As you come to the measure you want to start repeating from, simply press the Repeat or A-B Repeat button to set the start marker.**

3. **When you reach the end of the phrase you want to use, press the same button again to set the end marker.**

   If you're having trouble setting the right measures, try slowing down the tempo while you set the markers. Then you can raise it back to the speed you want. If you miss the bar you wanted, you can just press the REW button to move back one measure with each tap.

   Now when you play the song, it will start with a count-in to get you ready and then play the same selected range of measures over and over. While it's playing, you can still use the FF, REW, and Pause buttons and adjust the tempo.

4. **To turn off these repeat markers, simply press the Repeat or A-B Repeat button again.**

   Doing so clears those markers so that your song plays fully from beginning to end.

Introducing Casio's Step-up Lesson System

You're not on your own to learn the onboard songs; a patient electronic teacher is waiting to help! Each system is a little different; the following sections get you up to speed on the Casio version.

Following the steps: Listen, Watch, and Remember

The Casio teacher takes you through three levels of learning and practice:

✔ **Listen:** Sit back, let the song play, and get familiar with it. The song plays in small phrase sections, and the display shows you what notes to play and what fingers to use.

✔ **Watch:** Now the system guides you, requiring you to play the notes yourself. The display shows you the notes and fingering. On certain models, the keys even light up to show you the way. Some models talk to you, with the teacher telling you what finger to use. Follow the guides and play through the phrase; timing/tempo isn't important at this stage, only the right notes. If you make a mistake, the system will wait for you and guide you with the right answer.

✔ **Remember:** Now the helpers are turned off, and hopefully you've learned what to do. But not to worry; the helpers come back when you get stuck! Play the song in time, still in the smaller phrase context.

You can play each phrase section as many times as you want and at any tempo, so you can master them all no matter how easy or difficult you find each one. You can stay on each of the teaching modes for as long as you like.

When first learning a song you should work each phrase through the system (Listen, Watch, and Remember) instead of trying to absorb too many phrases in a row.

Getting started: Picking what to work on

Your first step is to choose a song you want to work with. I suggest you consider a song you've heard before if this is the first time you're trying this feature. Here's how it works:

1. **To select a built-in song, press the Song Bank mode button.**

2. **Use any of the data entry controls (+/−, up/down, numeric keypad, or whatever) to select the song you want to learn.**

3. **Choose where to start.**

   If you're just starting out with a new song, you want to begin at the beginning. But if you want to work on a different phrase, press the Next button to advance through them. Watch the screen to find the phrase number you want.

   You can also use the FF and REW buttons to move back and forth through the phrases.

You can (and should!) work on new songs one hand at a time. To select which hand to work on, press the button labeled Part Select. (The label appears under the button; above the button is the label for Chord/Accomp On/Off.)

Each press of the button toggles from one hand to the other to both hands on to both off. As Figure 15-5 shows, the selected hand/part has a faint shadow around it.

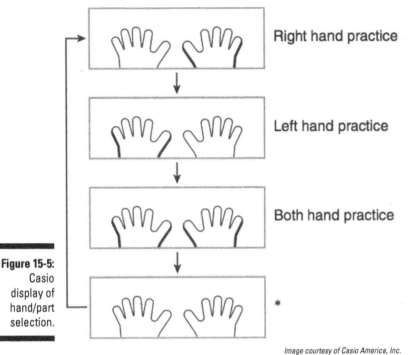

Right hand practice

Left hand practice

Both hand practice

*

Figure 15-5:
Casio
display of
hand/part
selection.

Image courtesy of Casio America, Inc.

Lesson 1: Listening and letting the teacher show you how

The first step in learning a new song is to listen and let the teacher demonstrate what to do. You've already selected your song and the hand/part to work on, so all you need to do is press the Listen button. (Figure 15-6 illustrates all the Casio lesson controls).

Figure 15-6:
Casio lesson
controls.

STEP UP LESSON

| LISTEN | WATCH | REMEMBER | NEXT | AUTO | MUSIC CHALLENGE |

Image courtesy of Casio America, Inc.

After a short count-in, the song starts playing. If the song has an introduction before your melody comes in, the display will show "Wait" and then "Next" as it moves into the first phrase you need to learn. When the phrase starts, the display shows you two things (as shown in Figure 15-7):

✔ The keyboard graphic indicates the proper note.

✔ The hand graphic indicates the correct finger.

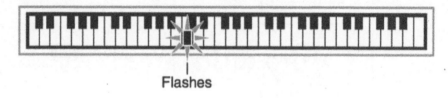

Flashes

Lights

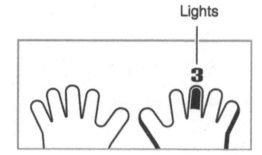

Figure 15-7:
Onscreen display of current note and finger.

Image courtesy of Casio America, Inc.

The phrase will keep repeating over and over. You should listen to get familiar with the music, first for the rhythm of the notes — when do they play, and for how long? Then pay attention to the screen to see the notes and fingerings. Try to memorize both the notes and the fingerings; I like to play air keys just above the notes to start to get a feel for what will happen when I play for real.

Note you'll hear the parts for both hands, not just the one you selected. Your part selection determines only what the keyboard displays, so be sure to listen closely to the hand you've chosen to work on.

When you feel comfortable with this step, press Listen again to stop the phrase play. You're ready to move on to Lesson 2 (described in the following section).

Lesson 2: Playing and watching the display for guidance

When you have the phrase in your ears and the notes and fingerings somewhat memorized, you can move on to trying to play the phrase:

1. **Press the Watch button (see Figure 15-6); you get a count-in, and then the phrase starts to play.**

2. **Follow the instructions and play along.**

   The display shows you each note to play as it comes up, blinking the note until it's time to play it, at which point it turns solid. The display indicates which finger to use by highlighting it on the hand graphic. If you pause, the teacher's voice will tell you which finger to use.

   Listen to Track 113 to hear an example of the onboard teacher helping out.

   The phrase will keep repeating over and over; at first, you should concentrate on playing the right note with the right finger. You don't have to worry about your timing for now, although it's good to try to be in rhythm. If you make a mistake, don't worry; the music will sit and wait for you until you play the right note. If you play the right note quickly, the music will advance to match what you do. As you get comfortable, work on playing the notes with the right rhythm/timing.

3. **When you're finished, press Watch again to stop the phrase play.**

   You can also use the Stop button to turn off the phrase play.

Lesson 3: Progressing from Watch to Remember

The third mode, Remember, is the way of testing whether you've really learned Lessons 1 and 2. The music plays with no guidance from the teacher, and you must play the right notes in the right timing to succeed.

1. **Press Remember (see Figure 15-6); the system gives you a count-in to get ready.**

2. **Start to play, being sure to play with good timing.**

If you get stuck or play a wrong note, the helpers will come back to point you back on track. The note will sound and show on the display, and the teacher will tell you the correct finger. After you've played the right note, you're back on your own until you have a problem.

When you've played through the whole phrase, the system will give you a reaction like "Do it again" or "Bravo!" Either way, the lesson will repeat over and over until you press Remember or Stop.

When you've mastered the chosen phrase, you can go back, pick another phrase (as outlined in the earlier section "Getting started: Picking what to work on"), and start the process again!

As you get comfortable with a song, you can use the Auto-Lesson mode (see Figure 15-6), which steps you through each phrase for the currently selected hand. Each lesson type is demonstrated once (watch) and then the remember phase is repeated three times. Then you have to play from the beginning, so the farther you get into the phrases, the more of the song you have to play. This mode is best when you've already worked through the phrases individually; it makes for a great practice routine after learning a song.

Turning off some of the helpers

You don't have to use all the helpers all the time; you can turn each one off if desired. Here are a few suggestions:

- ✔ **Press the Auto button (see Figure 15-6) to turn off the phrase repeats.** Now each section only plays once and then goes to the next. This option is best for when you've gotten comfortable with each phrase.

- ✔ **You can turn off the voice that guides you for the fingerings.** Here's how the process works for some models:

    1. **Keep pressing the Function button until you get to Speak = On.**

    2. **Press – on the numeric keypad to turn it off. Press + to turn it back on.**

    For other models

    1. **Press the Function button.**

    2. **Scroll using the right arrow button (6 on the numeric keypad) or left arrow button (4 on the numeric keypad) until you get to Lesson.**

    3. **Press Enter (the 9 button).**

    4. **Scroll until the display shows Speak; press – on the numeric keypad to turn it off and + to turn it back on.**

🖊 **You can turn off the note guide that sounds the note when you get stuck.** Some models use the following process:

1. **Keep pressing the Function button until you get to NoteGuid=On.**

2. **Press – on the numeric keypad to turn it off; press + to turn it back on.**

For other models

1. **Press the Function button.**

2. **Scroll using the right arrow button or left arrow button until you get to Lesson.**

3. **Press Enter.**

4. **Scroll until the display shows NoteGuid; press – on the numeric keypad to turn it off and + to turn it back on.**

🖊 **You can go through any lesson level without the song being divided up into smaller phrases.** This exercise is good when you think you've mastered the whole song but still want some guidance. For some models, you

1. **Keep pressing the Function button until you get to Phrase Ln=PrE (preset).**

2. **Press – on the numeric keypad to turn it off and + to turn it back on.**

For other models

1. **Press the Function button.**

2. **Scroll using the right arrow button or left arrow button until you get to Phrase Ln.**

3. **Press Enter.**

4. **Scroll until the display shows Phrase Ln; press – on the numeric keypad to turn it off and + to turn it back on.**

Playing the whole song yourself

When you've mastered all the lessons, you can play the song from beginning to end with no helpers and no pauses. This approach works best for songs that have some additional backing; it's not helpful for a solo piano piece. Do the following:

1. **Press the Part Select button (see Figure 15-4, Ex. 2) until both hands are shadowed in the display.**

This move stops the keyboard from playing the parts; it's all up to you!

2. **Press Start to begin the song playing.**

   It will play from beginning to end with no reaction to what you play. The display still shows you the notes and fingerings if you want to use the guide, but it doesn't wait for you or say anything.

You can have some fun with this level of playback because you can add some extra notes or even improvise over the backing. Have a good time and be creative!

Exploring Yamaha's Educational Suite Lesson System

Yamaha calls its lesson system the Yamaha Educational Suite (Y.E.S. for short). It has various implementations, meaning some keyboards offer more and deeper educational features than others. I go over the basic aspects that are common to all of them in the following sections.

To select which hand to work on, press one of the buttons labeled L or R (see Figure 15-4, Ex. 2 earlier in the chapter) near the Lesson section of the front panel. Pressing both buttons lets you choose two-hand playing.

If you need to, use the REW button to move back a few measures to try a part again. Even better, Yamaha has a dedicated Repeat & Learn button (see Figure 15-8) that moves you back four measures and then keeps repeating that phrase over and over until you press the button again. If you want to keep practicing a specific phrase within the song, you can use the A-B Repeat button to set the start and end of the phrase. Then the phrase will play, stop, count-in, and then play again, over and over. You can change the number of bars it jumps back by pressing a number on the keypad (1 through 9) just after pressing the Repeat & Learn button. This function works in any of the lesson modes. In any lesson mode, you can also always stop the song by pressing Start/Stop.

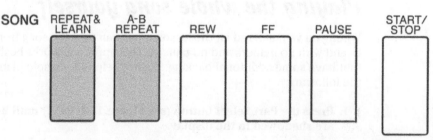

Figure 15-8: Yamaha options for repeating measures in a song.

Image courtesy of Yamaha Corporation of America

Following the steps: Listening, Waiting, Your Tempo, and Minus One

The Yamaha teacher takes you through three levels of learning and practice — Waiting, Your Tempo, and Minus One — but I add a fourth (Listening) to these instructions:

- ✔ **Listening:** You start the song and listen as it plays to get familiar with it. The keyboard displays the note(s) being played, both on a music staff (notation) and with an indicator over the graphic of the keys. You're on your own for fingering. (If you're unfamiliar with music notation, check out Chapter 5.)

   Most of the Y.E.S.-based keyboards don't show this mode (Listening) from the front panel, but you can easily get them to play their songs with the visual guidance. Just select a song and press Start/Stop.

- ✔ **Waiting:** The keyboard displays the note you need to play the same as it does for the Listening step. It waits until you play the correct note to move on to the next. As with the Listening phase, it doesn't show you fingering.

- ✔ **Your Tempo:** In this level, the song keeps playing, and it's up to you to play the right notes with the right timing. If you make mistakes or miss the timing, the backing band slows down and makes things easier for you.

- ✔ **Minus One:** Now you're on your own. You choose which hand(s) to play yourself, and you play the part while the band accompanies you. The display still shows you the notes to play (both on a staff and on the graphic of the keys) but the keyboard doesn't wait or slow down or anything. Use this mode when you think you've got the song down.

Starting off by deciding what to work on

The Yamaha keyboards have a number of songs built in, and not all are good for the lesson function. The manual covers this topic, but basically you want to use the Piano Solo, Piano Ensemble, Piano Accompaniment, Classical, and Traditional Melodies for the lessons.

1. **To select a built-in song, press the Song mode button.**

2. **Use any of the data entry controls (+/–, up/down, numeric keypad, or whatever) to select the song you want to learn.**

A very cool feature of most Yamaha Y.E.S.-equipped keyboards is the ability to load in songs downloaded from the Internet or shared among friends in the Standard MIDI File (SMF) format. Yamaha has a large library of popular songs, classics, and more available to use with its lesson system. Visit www.yamaha musicsoft.com to see all the offerings.

Listening to an automated teacher

This step isn't the first that Yamaha presents in its system, but it's how I recommend you get started. The first thing you should do when learning a new song is to listen and let the teacher show you what to do. You've already selected your song and the hand/part to work on, so all you need to do is press the Start/Stop button.

After a short count-in, the song will start playing. When the main melody starts, the display indicates the required note(s) on the music staff and the key(s) to be played on the keyboard graphic, as shown in Figure 15-9.

The song plays from beginning to end. Listen first for the rhythm of the notes, and then watch the screen to see and start to memorize the notes.

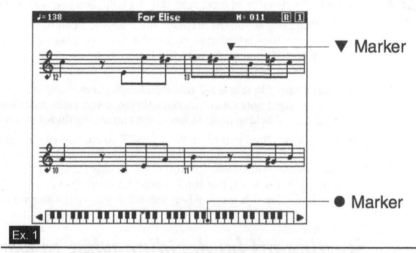

Figure 15-9: Onscreen display of current note.

The notation and key positions of the model melody are shown in the display.

Images courtesy of Yamaha Corporation of America

The keyboard will play both parts even though the one you selected is the only one displayed. Be sure to listen closely to the part you're working on.

You can use the FF and REW buttons to move through the song measure by measure as it plays. I often use this method to go back a few bars and relisten to a section a few times.

When you feel comfortable with this step, you're ready to move on to Lesson 1 in the following section.

Lesson 1: Waiting and watching the display as you play along

When you've gotten familiar with the song from the listening phase, you can move on to trying to play it. Yamaha calls this step Lesson 1: Waiting. Here's how to do it:

1. **Press the Start button in the Lesson section of the front panel (shown in Figure 15-10).**

   Each press of the button toggles between the teaching modes, so be sure you've selected Wait. The song will start to play.

2. **Follow the instructions and play along.**

   The display shows each note you should play as it comes up. You don't have to worry about your timing for now, although you want to try to be in rhythm. If you miss a note, the music will pause until you play the right one.

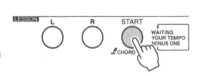

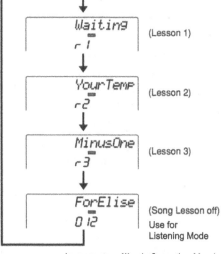

Figure 15-10:
The Lesson controls on the front panel.

Images courtesy of Yamaha Corporation of America

The song plays to the end, and you get a grade for your performance. The choices are Excellent, Very Good, Good, and OK. Nice positive reinforcement!

Lesson 2: Leading the band with Your Tempo

The third step, which Yamaha calls Lesson 2, is called Your Tempo (see Figure 15-10). Now you must play the right notes in the right timing, but the backing parts will slow down, to help you get more comfortable, if you're missing notes or timing. Play well, and the song will gradually speed back up to the proper tempo. In other words, the system will keep pace with you but won't stop and wait. Follow these steps:

1. **Repeatedly press the Start button in the Lesson section until you've selected Your Timing; the song will start playing right away.**

2. **Start to play, keeping an eye on your timing.**

   The display still guides you with the right notes/keys. If you get stuck or play a wrong note, the song slows down a little; hopefully, this easier pace helps you play more accurately. As you get back on track, the song gradually speeds back up to the proper tempo.

If you mess up a few bars and want to drill them for a little while, use the Repeat & Learn button to go back.

Lesson 3: Becoming the star with Minus One

The fourth step, which Yamaha calls Lesson 3, is called Minus One. Now you pick what part you want to play, and it's up to you to play well. The part you select won't sound, so you're free to play the part as you want. Play it as intended or have some fun and add notes or take a solo. Go wild if you want to! Here's how it works:

1. **Select which part you want to play (see Figure 15-4, Ex. 2 earlier in the chapter): the right hand (R), the left hand (L), or both (press both buttons at the same time).**

2. **Repeatedly press the Start button in the Lesson section until you've selected Minus One.**

   The song starts playing right away.

3. **Start playing with good timing.**

   The display still guides you with the right notes/keys but doesn't sound the selected part.

Chapter 16

Sitting In with the Stars: Playing Along with Recordings

*P*erhaps, like many people, you've decided to play keyboard because a performer, a group, or a song caught your attention and made you wish you could do that. So you get an instrument and the first thing you want to do is play that song to relive that initial dream. But you find out that to learn an instrument, you first have to do all this other stuff: develop technique through exercises, learn to read music, read a *For Dummies* book to figure out how to . . . hey, wait a minute!

I used to teach a lot of music lessons, and I never forgot that early desire to learn that turning-point song and to be that artist. So I believe that in the mix of the things that you need to study to become a good player, you should have the chance to get what you want from playing music. I always approached it as, "If you do what I say you need to do, then I'll help you do what you want to do!" Learning to play by ear and to figure out music from recordings is the way to learn those all-important first-influence songs and is an important part of good musicianship. Every good musician masters these skills along with technique, reading, and style studies.

In this chapter, I discuss the pros of playing with recordings and working out your favorite songs from them. I help you get your music player and keyboard connected so you can hear both from the same headphones or speakers. And I provide a lot of the methods and tips that the pros use to break down a song and easily play all the elements of it.

I also acquaint you with some computer-based tools that make figuring out a song easier than it was when I was growing up and first learning and that I use every day in learning new songs for my gigs.

Exploring the Advantages of Playing Along

No doubt about it: Playing an instrument by yourself at home can be a bit lonely at times. Sure, it feels good to express yourself, to celebrate when you feel happy, or to cheer yourself up when you don't. But after a while everyone craves the company of others. At first, you may not feel good enough to play in front of people. And your early learning steps can sound kind of plain and often lack the full punch that a band or ensemble of musicians can provide.

An easy answer to this dilemma for the beginning musician is to play along with your favorite artists through their recordings. You don't need to play a lot because you're not replacing any member of the band (just yet!). You can add your part to the recording, whether that's playing along with the melody, finding your own simple countermelodies, or just holding down some simple chords. Being part of that wonderful noise that is your favorite band or backing band will feel good.

Playing along with recordings as part of your musical development has other, tangible benefits:

- ✔ **It helps your time-keeping and feel.** Being able to keep a steady beat is an important part of making music sound and feel good. You can learn how to count and you can play with a metronome, but to really get the feel of a piece or style of music, nothing beats playing along with musicians who are experts at it.

- ✔ **It's easier for a beginner.** If you don't read music especially well, just poking around while a recording is playing can help you start to learn a song (and I help you even more throughout this chapter).

- ✔ **It helps your musical ear.** Musicians study something in school called *ear training,* which is the ability to hear notes, *intervals* (the distance between two notes), and chord qualities (major, minor, and so on) by ear. And the best practice for ear training is (wait for it) figuring out songs by playing along with recordings!

- ✔ **It gives you a more-complete version of the song.** Printed music is often a simplified reduction of a song. Notating the actual feel of the rhythm would make it unnecessarily complicated, and parts are often simplified to make a songbook version easy to follow. Listening to and playing with the original recording can help fill in those instructions so you can feel and understand the music better. True story: A very famous jazz pianist was once presented with a detailed transcription of his playing, and he reacted by saying, "I can't play this stuff; it looks too hard!" Yet it was something he had performed with ease by ear, experience, and feeling.

✔ **It's fun!** If it's a song or band that you love, why wouldn't you want to be a part of it? You only need to play a little bit; let the original artist do the heavy lifting, and you'll sound great and have a blast. Part of your music-making should always be having fun!

Connecting an Audio Device to Your Keyboard to Hear Both Together

To play keyboard alongside your favorite song, of course, that song has to be playing on something. Many electronic keyboards have inputs for running another device (such as another instrument, a microphone, or a music player) into them. This setup simplifies your cabling and connections and lets you listen to both devices at the same time through headphones. The following sections help you figure out how to hook up your music player of choice (or another audio device) to your keyboard so you can jam with the greats.

I prefer being able to use headphones for playing along to and figuring out music. You want to be able to listen to the song very intently, and that's best done with headphones on. If you're going to be figuring out a song, you'll be repeating sections of it over and over (and over), which can get pretty annoying to other members of your household who can't help but hear what you're doing.

For the basics on mono and stereo and male and female cables and such, take a look at Chapter 4.

Finding a line input and getting connected

Take a look at the back panel of your keyboard for a jack (or two jacks) labeled Line In, Audio In, Aux In, and so on. If your instrument has this kind of jack arrangement, then connecting an audio player to it is no problem. If it doesn't have the appropriate jack(s), skip to the next section.

With the jack located, you need to determine the right type of cable to use. Most portable CD players and all MP3 players have a stereo ⅛-inch (actually mini 3.5-millimeter) jack for the output. If your keyboard has a single jack labeled for input, you need a cable with a stereo 3.5 millimeter male plug (shown in Chapter 4) on each end. This size plug is the most common one found on mobile phones, media players, and most earbud headphones. It's available in mono and stereo versions, so be sure you have the stereo version, indicated by dual black rings near the tip of the plug.

WARNING!

The 3.5 millimeter plug makes a good connection, but can be a bit fragile. Always be careful not to tug on the cable or put pressure on this connection.

If your keyboard has dual inputs (shown in Figure 16-1), they likely use ¼-inch phone plugs.

This size is the most common plug used in musical instruments, mixing boards, and instrument amplifiers. It's the largest plug used and makes a great connection because of its long shaft. It's available in mono and stereo versions, so be sure you have the mono versions, indicated by single black rings near the tip of the plug.

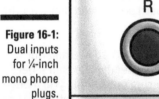

Figure 16-1:
Dual inputs for ¼-inch mono phone plugs.

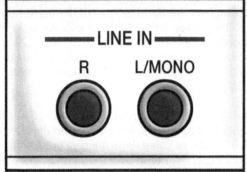

═══ LINE IN ═══

R   L/MONO

Illustration by Lisa Reed

To connect this kind of jack to your device, you need a cable that has a male 3.5 millimeter stereo plug on one end and splits out into dual mono ¼-inch male plugs on the other. You can find this *Y cable* in some electronic stores and online. (*Note:* There are other ways to hook your device up to dual inputs with more-common cables, but they require more connections and the use of adapters. Ideally, you don't want to have extra points of connection because they can separate and can add noise to your system.)

Finally, if your keyboard has dual RCA inputs, you'll need a cable with a male 3.5 millimeter stereo plug on one end and dual RCA male plugs (shown in Chapter 4) on the other.

This plug is commonly used in home stereo and home theatre audio/video products. It makes a great connection because its metal ring/shield fits securely over the jack on the device you're plugging into.

With the music player connected, you should check your owner's manual for instructions on setting the levels for the inputs and test out your connection by listening to some music through your keyboard (ideally on headphones).

No input? No worries: Moving forward with a mixer

If your keyboard doesn't have dedicated inputs to connect your music player to, you need to use a device called a *line mixer* or *mixer.* A mixer combines multiple sources of audio and allows you to hear them all from a single set of outputs, such as headphones. Your music player likely has a stereo 3.5-millimeter output that needs to connect to the mixer; the keyboard probably has dual ¼-inch or RCA outputs. Or you can use the single stereo headphone output (either 3.5-millimeter or ¼-inch) to connect the keyboard to the mixer.

Mixers have inputs called *channels,* and these are usually mono. Because your device and keyboard have stereo outputs, your mixer needs two channels to connect your music player and another two channels for your keyboard. Therefore, you need a four-channel mixer. Some mixers have stereo channels (two inputs for one channel) or have stereo tape or aux inputs, so you can get by with fewer channels in these cases. I even found a cool two-channel micro mixer that has a stereo 3.5-millimeter input for one channel and dual RCA inputs for the other channel, which would also covers your needs. Bottom line: You have some options when it comes to mixer setup. As of this writing, I found six or eight models, each less than $60 U.S., that would work with most standard keyboards and music players. Just be sure that the mixer has a headphone output (it may just be a 3.5-millimeter or ¼-inch stereo jack; it may not specifically be labeled "headphones"). Figure 16-2 shows a small audio mixer that can be used to connect both a keyboard and an audio player device.

The cables you use to connect your keyboard and audio player to the mixer have male plugs on both ends, though what kinds of plugs those are depends on your specific equipment.

Figure 16-2:
Audio mixer
for connect-
ing both a
keyboard
and an
audio player
device.

Photograph courtesy of Alto Professional

Getting In Tune

You may not realize it, but not every song is going to be perfectly in tune with your keyboard. Some older recordings were recorded a little bit slow or fast, and sometimes artists intentionally change the speed of a recording because they like how it makes their voice(s) sound. Fans of the Beatles are well aware of this fact; the band often played with playback speed to make its voices sound younger, deeper, or just different.

When you first pick a song to play along to, you may find that your keyboard sounds a little off. That's a sure sign you need to adjust the tuning, which is almost always a small adjustment.

Look for a parameter called Master Tune or Fine Tune. You can find this setting in the Global (Korg), System (some Roland), Setting (some Casio), Function (Casio, Kurzweil, Roland, and Yamaha), or Utility (some Yamaha) mode depending on your brand and model. This function allows you to slightly adjust the tuning of your keyboard up or down in very small in crements. The tuning always defaults to A = 440.0 hertz, which is the agreed-upon tuning standard in most parts of the world. It means that the A note above middle C is pitched to 440 hertz frequency. You can raise it to 440.1, 440.2, and so on and lower it to 439.9, 439.8 — you get the idea. You should find a note that you know is correct in the song and then repeat it over and over as you change this value until things sound better.

Don't forget to reset this value back to 440.0 when you're done playing along with that particular recording!

Figuring Out a Song You Don't Know

For some people, playing a new song is an easy process. They can sit at a keyboard, hunt and peck around for a bit, and quickly find the notes of a melody. Some even have *perfect pitch,* where they just know what note a pitch is and can find it effortlessly. They recognize whether something is in perfect tune (and are greatly bothered when it isn't).

Good for them. This section isn't for that lucky minority; it's for everyone else. I had to work very hard in my music studies to get good at hearing pitches and chords and figuring out songs by ear. It's a skill, so those not naturally inclined to it can still pick it up through practice. Of course, the more you know about scales, chords, and music theory, the easier this process becomes, but the following sections help you get started without much of that knowledge. (I cover scales and chords in Part II, and you may want to check out *Music Theory For Dummies* by Michael Pilhofer and Holly Day [Wiley].)

Training your ear by trial and error

A good exercise to start developing your skills is to pick out simple nursery rhymes, holiday songs, and well-known melodies by ear. Just start at middle C on the keyboard and try to find the notes of some tune you know the sound of. Play the C and then figure out whether the next note of the song goes up or down from there or stays the same. If it moves, does it seem to be very close or very far? When you've figured one tune out, move to another starting note — say, the G above middle C — and try the same song again. Same melody, different keys on the keyboard.

Ready to move on to recordings? I still recommend that you pick really simple songs in the beginning. You need to develop some skills and gain confidence, so don't start with tunes that are very long and complicated or require a level of technique that you're not ready for. I want you to have a lot of small victories during your development; this positive reinforcement feels good and motivates you to move forward.

When you've picked out a song you want to learn, I suggest you first listen to it over and over and immerse yourself in it. Listen without touching the keyboard or trying too hard to analyze the song. Get familiar with it so you can hum/sing the melody, tap out the groove on your steering wheel or desk, and recognize and anticipate the various section changes.

Next, just let it play a few times while you hunt and peck around the keys. Try to find a note or two that sound good for the beginning of the song. This step can help you to figure out what key it's in and what scale fits the best. I discuss scales in Chapter 5. When you've found something pleasing, try playing a major triad based on that note and then a minor triad from it (refer to Chapter 7). Which sounds more right? Major keys often sound happy, and minor keys sound sadder; do you get either feeling from the music?

Listening to a phrase to learn it

After you get a basic sense of the key or tonality of the song, your best bet is to break it into smaller chunks so you can focus in on it in greater detail.

All music can be divided up into *phrases,* which are complete musical "thoughts" that have a beginning and end. These phrases can be easy to hear and feel; in vocal music, just follow the lyrics. Perhaps each sentence is a phrase, or you hear a couple of sentences and then a pause. The goal here is to work on these smaller segments one at a time.

I suggest that you work on only a few bars of the tune at a time — certainly no more than eight.

As you play the short phrase over and over, you need to listen to one aspect of the music at a time. The main choices are as follows:

- ✔ **Rhythm:** This aspect can be the rhythm of the chords, the melody, or even the drums. You're not worried about any notes yet; you just want to pay attention to how the notes/chords move around. How many chords occur per bar? Do the chords change only every few bars? How *busy* is the melody (how many notes per bar does it have)? What you're doing is identifying targets that you're going to figure out while playing, and you want to know how many you have and when they happen.

- ✔ **Bass notes:** Working out the bass notes is the first step I always take when it comes to notes. Finding the low notes, usually played by bass guitar or a pianist's left hand, creates the building blocks of everything that comes later. In most music, the bass notes are the *roots,* or names of the chords being used, so finding them exposes a lot about the song. If you prefer starting with the melody, that's perfectly fine, too.

A really good tip is to sing the note you're looking for. Sing the bass note along with the recording and stop the music right after the note while you keep singing the tone. Then you can search on the keyboard for the note you're singing. You don't have to be able to sing well — just well enough to match the pitch from your recording. Believe me, I sing horribly, but I use this technique all the time. Just try not to sing too loud if you're around others. Your headphones may contain the music from your keyboard and recording, but anyone within earshot will hear your singing!

✔ **Basic chords:** After you know the bass notes, try playing them as triad chords. Listen to hear whether a major or minor triad is the right choice. Some songs use a note other than the root of the chord in the bass, so if the root-based triad doesn't sound right, think of the bass note as the fifth of a triad and try that. Still not right? Try it as the third of a chord.

If major or minor doesn't sound right, don't forget the fancier triads I discuss in Chapter 7, like the diminished and augmented chords.

If I'm having trouble hearing a chord, I try to find one note that sounds good, like it's part of the chord. Then I look for another and then another so I build up the chord one note at a time.

✔ **Melody:** Because the melody is the most memorable part of a song, many people like to start with it. After all, most people can sing along with a song without knowing anything about chords and bass lines. Just sing the first note, find it at the keyboard, and you're off and running!

Another thing that may help you break down phrases is to find other versions of the same song. If you have the album/studio version, go look for a live version; it may have some of the parts more exposed because it has less studio production. Maybe you can find cover versions of the song by other artists. They may change parts of the song to make it their own, but a cover can be a good reference to better understand the song.

After you've figured out one phrase, move on to the next. When you've picked up all the phrases that make up the first part of the song, try to play them all together. Then start working on the chorus or main hook of the song. Keep working in these small sections until you've progressed through the whole song.

I've found that you need to step away from a song after working for a while and refresh your ears and your brain. Don't force it. Put it away for a day or a few days and then come back to it. You'll often find that you hear something more clearly and can finish a section that had been causing you endless frustration.

Hey, I know that tune: Practicing intervals

When learning melodies or bass lines, being able to identify where the next note goes is a good skill to nurture. Identifying that it goes up or down is the easy part; the real skill you want to work on is "How far did it go?" The distance between two notes is called an *interval*. A good approach for training yourself to recognize intervals is to associate them with a well-known song melody. As an example, the distance from C to G is called a *perfect fifth*. Trying playing it on the keyboard; does it remind you of a

song? Maybe the theme from *Star Wars* or *2001: A Space Odyssey?* The distance from C to C-sharp is called a *minor second*. Play it three times in succession. Thinking about a great white shark, perhaps? Yup, that's the theme from the movie *Jaws*. Making these types of associations between intervals and well-known melodies can help your pitch recognition a lot. I've posted a good listing of reference songs at www.dummies.com/extras/keyboard for each interval.

Using your computer to help

Playing the music file on a computer rather than a CD player or MP3 player is easy and has some real advantages. Simply hook up the audio output of your computer to the inputs of your keyboard or to a mixer as I discuss in the earlier section "Connecting an Audio Device to Your Keyboard to Hear Both Together;" it's no different than using those other devices, so you can still work with headphones. Here's where computers have the upper hand:

- ✔ **Repeatedly relocating to a section:** Whatever music player application you use, it will have better controls for relocating to a specific spot in the tune than a physical player does. I find that computer applications that have a timeline/progress bar make moving my mouse to a visual location easy to do.

- ✔ **Emphasizing a frequency range with EQ:** Most music player apps have some form of EQ built in, and you can use it to help hear parts more clearly. Boost the low frequencies when you're figuring out the bass notes; you can even lower the high notes to help further remove them from your attention. When you're figuring out chords, you can boost some mid-range frequency to help you hear the harmony better. Try one EQ band at a time to find the one that helps emphasize the chords the most.

  Many times what you want to do is get the drums out of your way, so lowering some frequency bands can help. Lower highs to remove cymbal noise, lessen the lows to remove a strong bass drum, and so on.

- ✔ **Using special audio applications:** *Audio applications* are programs for recording or editing speech and music. They often let you *loop,* or repeat a section of the song over and over. You can set when to start and when to loop back, so you can play however many bars you need to work on over and over without have to manually reset the player every time. Audio applications often can set several of these markers, so you can set up loops for the verse, the chorus, the bridge, the solo section, and so on of the song and easily jump to them with a single keystroke.

Some audio applications allow you to slow down the speed of a piece of music without changing the pitch. This function is called *time-stretching,* and it can be the best tool you ever invest in for learning songs. It's like asking the band or your teacher to play the song for you very slowly so you can watch and listen to what she's doing. I use this function all the time. Slowing down a song by around 25 percent or so sounds pretty good; any further than that and it starts to sound funny (though you can still tell the pitch of the notes). Time-stretching is invaluable in helping you to figure out fast passages and riffs in the music; check out Chapter 17 for some options.

Finally, some applications are specifically designed for learning songs from recordings. This process is called *transcribing,* which is the act of committing a live performance or recording to musical notation. These applications offer a simple interface for playing music files and include time-stretching capabilities, EQ, and easy-to-use location markers. (Chapter 17 has more details.) They're well worth the small cost for all they bring to this activity.

Another way you can use your computer to help: Search for videos of people teaching the song on the Internet! With resources such as YouTube, you can often find other musicians teaching how to play popular songs. It may be a guitar lesson, but the player will still name the chords and talk about the melody. It's not cheating to get some help!

Chapter 17

The Computer Connection: Using Software to Enhance Your Music Making

In This Chapter

▶ Understanding how MIDI works

▶ Linking your keyboard with your computer or Apple iPad

▶ Enhancing your sound with music software

Computers play an ever-increasing role in daily life. And so it is with music; you can integrate a computer or tablet device into your musical study, performance, and enjoyment in innumerable ways. In this chapter, I break down the basics of how something called MIDI works, help you to connect your keyboard to your computer or iPad, and expose you to the many types of software that you can use to enrich your music making, learning, and fun.

Getting Acquainted with MIDI

Every keyboard made since the mid-'80s has a connection on the back called MIDI, the Musical Instrument Digital Interface. This round jack with five pin connections revolutionized keyboard playing and music making by providing a way for all keyboards to "talk" to each other. First developed as a way of layering keyboards together, the MIDI language sent messages between the connected devices, so when you played one keyboard the same notes and performance gestures were sent to another keyboard for instant triggering.

From this humble beginning, MIDI grew into a more detailed language that enabled musicians to use computers for storing the settings for sounds from their keyboard, editing those sounds by using a larger graphic interface, recording and editing the MIDI-based performances, mixing music, controlling stage lighting, and many other activities. MIDI forever changed the way music is made, and its inventors received a Technical Grammy Award in 2013 for their achievement. Every company making electronic musical instruments uses MIDI in some way; when you see MIDI listed as a feature on a product, you can be guaranteed that it will work with other MIDI devices and with various types of music software.

How MIDI works: Explaining common MIDI messages

MIDI sends various messages that describe what you're doing at the keyboard. Play a note, and it transmits which note you play, how hard you play it, how long you hold it, whether you use the sustain pedal to hold the note, whether you move any other controllers on the keyboard (the mod wheel, a slider, a switch), and more. Without getting too technical, here are the main types of messages that MIDI represents:

- **Note Number:** *Note Number* is the pitch or note you're playing. MIDI allows for 128 possible notes — many more than are even found on a piano keyboard! Each octave of a keyboard has a number, so notes are represented like C4, F3, A0, E♭5, and so on. The range goes from C1 to C9.

- **Note On/Note Off:** These two commands indicate when you start a note and when you let go of the key. Taken together, they define the length of time you held the note for.

  Just like on a piano, a note can keep ringing after you let go of a key if you're holding down a sustain pedal. MIDI accounts for this situation as well, so a sustain pedal message will override a note off command when necessary, keeping the note ringing until you let go of the sustain pedal. This function is one of the control change messages I discuss later.

- **Velocity:** *Velocity* indicates how hard you play the note. It's called velocity and not force (for example) because it measures the time the key takes to leave its top point of contact and reach the bottom point of contact. That speed or timing translates into a dynamic because playing more forcefully moves the key to the bottom more quickly than playing more softly does.

- **Control Change:** *Control Change* is a broad selection of messages that define some other modifying action. These controllers can represent a continually moving motion (like moving a wheel, knob, or slider) or a single status, like the toggling of a switch on or off. A number of these messages are strictly defined; for example, Control Change (CC) #7 always represents volume, such as the volume knob or slider on an audio device or mixer. *Note:* Pitch Bend and aftertouch are considered special messages and aren't within the Control Change range of messages.

- **MIDI channel:** MIDI offers 16 channels of communication, so a single output can send different messages to different devices at the same time. Only the keyboard(s) set to listen to a given channel respond to those messages, so multipart music can easily be transmitted and reproduced. A keyboard that can listen to multiple MIDI channels at once is called *multitimbral.*

- **MIDI port:** To further increase the size of the MIDI network or group, a keyboard can have more than one MIDI port to communicate on. Each port adds another 16 channels to communicate on. These can be physical inputs and outputs on a device or software ports all available over the same USB port. They're usually named A, B, and so on.

- **Program Change:** This message is used to call up a specific sound on a keyboard or module. It simply represents a memory location in the device; any sound may be stored there. There are 128 possible Program Change values.

- **Bank Select:** To expand the number of programs that can be called up, a group of 128 programs are considered a *bank,* and products can have up to 128 banks. 128 possible banks × 128 program locations = 16,384 sounds. (I hope that's enough for you.) You select a new sound in a different bank from the current one by sending the Bank Select message followed by a Program Change number.

- **System Exclusive:** Keyboards have many things that aren't common and can't be standardized by a specification such as MIDI. These items are most often the parameters of the type of synthesis and other special features. *System Exclusive* messages are defined by each manufacturer to manipulate and store all these individual things. This type of message can only be heard and responded to by that specific brand and model of keyboard. They are most often used for the editing and storage of sounds for a given keyboard.

All these messages are how keyboards and other sound-producing devices, like drum machines and sound modules, talk to each other. MIDI grew into a recording technology as well, so messages also exist for tempo; start, stop, and continue controls for operating a recorder; and many other functions. You can read more about MIDI recording in Chapter 13.

Examining MIDI ports

MIDI connectors on a keyboard are usually objects called *DIN connectors*. You have separate in and out connections; one device transmits via an Out, and another device listens or receives the messages via an In (see Figure 17-1). The hardware looks the same, so be careful when connecting devices. (You won't harm your keyboard if you connect them wrong; it simply won't pass the MIDI signal.)

Figure 17-1:
The MIDI
DIN
connectors.

Illustration by Lisa Reed

You may see a third MIDI port labeled Thru; this port just passes on whatever signal comes to the In. This option is a way of connecting multiple devices in a chain, passing the signal from the first to the second to the third and so on.

More and more modern keyboards are transmitting MIDI over a USB port and may or may not have the traditional DIN ports as well. The USB port is *bidirectional;* it can send and receive messages over the same cable. The port is likely not labeled MIDI; it just says USB and possibly To Host as shown in Figure 17-2. Study up on your keyboard to find out whether it supports MIDI USB functionality.

The most common misconception about MIDI is that it passes the audio signal between devices. People often connect two devices together via MIDI and then are confused when they can't hear them. MIDI only sends control-type messages between the devices; you have to connect the device to a speaker, mixer, or even headphones to hear the sound. It's like the devices are being played in real time, so they need to be monitored the same as if you were playing the keys.

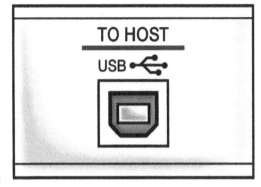

Illustration by Lisa Reed

Figure 17-2:
A USB port
for transmit-
ting MIDI.

Connecting Your Keyboard to Your Computer

You can hook up a MIDI keyboard to any type of computer: tower or laptop, Mac or PC. The main consideration is what type of MIDI jacks your keyboard has. If they are the round DIN connectors, you need to use a MIDI interface; if they're USB, you need only the right cable. (See the preceding section for more on connector types.)

If you're trying to connect to a computer that doesn't offer USB, I have a suggestion for you: Get a new computer! USB became popular in the late '90s, which is considered the Stone Age for computer technology. I don't think you'll find any MIDI/music software that's supported on such an old system, so getting connected will only be the beginning of your troubles.

Using a direct USB connection

This setup is the simplest situation; all you need is a common *USB device cable,* as pictured in Figure 17-3. (It's the standard connection cable most USB devices use.) It has the USB Type B square connector on one end, which gets plugged into your keyboard, and the small, rectangular USB Type A connector on the other end, which connects to your computer.

Smaller USB connectors called USB MiniB or MicroB connectors are often used for digital cameras, smartphones, and small devices like e-book readers and some tablets. These connectors are only used by small, portable MIDI controller products.

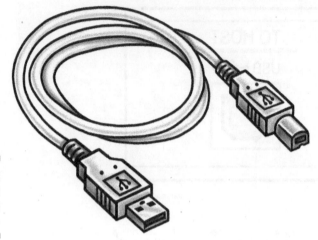

Figure 17-3:
A common
USB device
cable.

Illustration by Lisa Reed

Utilizing a MIDI interface

If your keyboard only has traditional DIN jacks, then you need some sort of MIDI interface. A *MIDI interface* is a box that offers a USB port to connect to your computer (the USB Type B/To Host connector, so you can use a USB device cable) and some number of DIN-based MIDI In and Out ports. The simplest MIDI interface is actually a cable that has DIN-based MIDI In and Out plugs on one end and a USB Type A plug on the other, as shown in Figure 17-4. This setup is fine to use if you have only one keyboard to connect to your computer. Just be sure to measure how far away the keyboard is from the computer because these cables are usually only available in 6-foot to 10-foot lengths.

If you have more than one keyboard (or device) or you think you'll be adding more later, buying a MIDI interface with more than one set of In and Out ports makes sense. Smaller interfaces may offer two In ports and two Out ports (such as the one in Figure 17-5), and larger ones commonly supply more outputs than inputs — for example two In and eight Out. Unless you're planning a large home studio with a lot of hardware synths and keyboards, you probably can get by with a two-In, two-Out interface.

Some MIDI interfaces get their power through the USB connection on your computer, which is fine if you don't have a lot of USB devices (printer, mouse, QWERTY keyboard, webcam, and so on). However, if you do rack up a lot of USB usage, consider getting an interface that has its own power adapter, especially if you use a laptop. Another option is to get a powered USB hub. Simple USB hubs can give you a few more ports to connect devices to, but they still rely on the computer to power them all, and often it can't. A powered hub is the only solution.

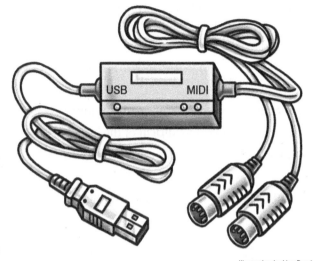

Figure 17-4:
A MIDI
interface
with built-in
cables.

Illustration by Lisa Reed

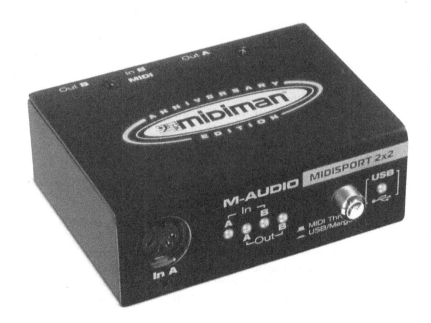

Figure 17-5:
A basic
MIDI
interface
with two
Ins and two
Outs.

Photograph courtesy of M-Audio

Many *USB audio interfaces* (used for recording audio into your computer, as I discuss in Chapter 13) also include MIDI ports, so if you're planning to add one of those as well, you can save money and clutter/hassle by getting these two functions in one box.

After you've gotten your MIDI interface, the cable connections are simple:

- ✔ USB device cable between interface and computer
- ✔ MIDI Out of your keyboard to MIDI In of the interface
- ✔ The matching MIDI Out of the interface back to the MIDI In of your keyboard

So that's three cables needed: one USB and two MIDI.

Working with drivers and plug-and-play

It would be nice if, after you connected cables and devices, things just worked. But life, especially technology, just doesn't work that way. You need to take a few steps to finish configuring your system before you can start using music software and having fun. They are different for each operating system, as you may expect.

Here are a couple of hints that apply to both Mac and PC hookups:

- ✔ I recommend you always go to the manufacturer's website and look for the latest driver there. Often the materials packed in the box are old and usually don't get revised until the company runs out of the pressed CDs. So the version in the box may be very old indeed! The newest drivers are always free for download.

- ✔ To test whether the interface I've installed is working, I use helpful test applications you can download. On a Mac, I like a free utility called *MIDI Monitor;* for PC, I like the free utility *MIDI-OX.* (I say they're free, but please consider donating some money to the authors for their hard work.) Search for these programs on the web; they're easy to install and show you whatever MIDI messages are coming into the computer and what is going out. They're perfect for quickly confirming that things are working without running a music application and are great for learning what messages your keyboard is transmitting.

On a Mac

If you're using an Apple computer, you likely don't need any other special software to make the interface work. But check the technical documents that came with your keyboard; some companies do have special MIDI drivers for the Mac that need to be installed.

Next, you need to run a utility that comes as part of OSX called *Audio MIDI Setup*. Look for it under Applications⇨Utilities. If you have everything connected and powered on when you run this application, it will scan your system and locate and identify all the devices connected. Figure 17-6 shows my setup in the application, with both a dedicated audio/MIDI interface with nothing currently connected to it (AudioBox 22VSL) and a Casio stage piano connected directly via USB. With a direct USB device you don't need to do anything else; after the system scans and finds it, your keyboard will be available to work with any application you run.

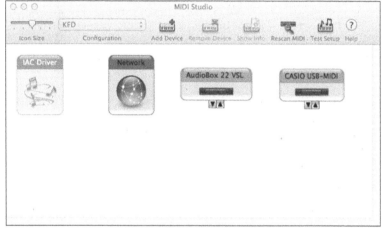

Figure 17-6:
A simple MIDI setup with a direct USB connected keyboard.

Apple Audio MIDI Setup screenshot courtesy of Jerry Kovarsky

If you're using a MIDI interface, the scan will show it. If a keyboard is connected to it via regular MIDI cables, it will likely work but won't show up as an icon and won't be fully configured. If you do nothing else, things will work, but your MIDI software won't show your keyboard by name when choosing a new track to record, for example. You can click on the Add Device icon at the top of the screen and manually configure your keyboard to fix this issue. Double-click on the *new external device* icon that was created, give it a name, and see whether it's already supported in the drop-down lists for Manufacturer and Model. Then connect the keyboard icon to the interface icon by dragging from the arrows to create virtual cables (as shown in Figure 17-7), and you're set.

Apple Audio MIDI Setup screenshot courtesy of Jerry Kovarsky

Figure 17-7:
A keyboard connected to a MIDI interface in Mac OS X Audio MIDI Setup.

On a PC

If you're using a PC/Windows-based computer, you need to install drivers. A few things to keep in mind (and I speak from experience):

✔ **Don't believe it when your computer just tells you it "installed" the device after you plug it in.** This function is the so-called plug-and-play that products promote, but it never works for MIDI interfaces or keyboards. Be sure to read the documentation that came with your keyboard about installing the software drivers and follow the steps carefully.

✔ **Don't connect the MIDI interface before installing the drivers.** The installation process will prompt you when to connect it; read and follow the instructions carefully.

✔ **Always put the MIDI interface on the same USB port you used when installing the drivers.** Thousands of hours of customer support and customer confusion have been caused by this little known fact: Any device drivers installed on a PC work only for the port used during the installation. So if you unplug the device and later plug it into a different port, the device won't work.

Hooking Up to Your iPad

The Apple iPad has a growing number of music applications available and is becoming a favorite tool and toy for musicians around the world. To connect your MIDI keyboard to it, you have a few choices.

As with most technology, a new edition of the iPad seems to come out every five minutes, so you may be working with one of several versions. If you have the original or second or third generation iPad, you have a 30-pin connector on the bottom edge of the device. You need an Apple Camera Connection Kit, which plugs into that port and provides a USB jack. Plug in and you're ready to go.

If you have the fourth generation iPad or the iPad Mini (or even newer models), you have what is called a *Lightning connector.* These models already come with a cable in the box to connect USB devices to the Lightning jack, so you're all set.

If your keyboard has only DIN connectors, you need a MIDI interface to use your iPad. (Flip to the earlier sections "Examining MIDI ports" and "Utilizing a MIDI interface" for details on DIN connectors and general purpose MIDI interfaces, respectively.) But for the iPad, you need a special MIDI interface that supports the unique connectors the tablet uses. A number of companies make dedicated iPad interface cables that support the 30-pin connector of the older models, with MIDI In and Out plugs on the other end of the cable. For the newer, Lightning-based models, you can buy an adapter cable with the 30-pin jack on one end and a Lightning connector on the other. Then you can use any of the available iOS interfaces. (*iOS* is Apple's mobile operating system.)

You can find a smaller adapter that converts the Lightning jack to a 30-pin jack, but this option leaves you with two bulky connectors hanging off your iPad. That setup is risky, both in terms of coming disconnected and of straining or even breaking the connector on your expensive toy. Better to get the cable instead.

No drivers or other setup software is required to use MIDI keyboards and music apps on the iPad. Plug in your keyboard and start up an app, and you're ready to play and have fun!

Exploring Popular Types of Music Software

Music software has been commercially available since the mid-'80s and provides all sorts of cool things to enhance your music making. In the following sections, I divide these options into easy-to-understand groups to give you a brief peek into the wonderful possibilities that await you.

Sequencer/MIDI recorder

This category, commonly called a *digital audio workstation* (DAW), is a recording studio in a box. MIDI is the language you'll likely be using to play into these applications, but they all actually record audio and cover editing, mixing, and outputting final files that you can make CDs from, post files to the web, and share for fun or profit.

They come in many different designs. Some DAWs are designed to emulate the linear tape concept, with tracks that you record from beginning to end. Others take a more modular or chunk-style approach to music making, where you create small sections or patterns and then arrange them in any order you like. This method is often used in a live performance like when a DJ cues up different songs. Some DAWs combine these two approaches.

Many of these titles include software instruments and sounds, so you can get new sounds, often using technologies that your keyboard may not offer. Getting a DAW is like buying additional keyboards along with your recording studio. Some companies offer entry-level versions of their programs, which you can later upgrade up to the fuller-featured versions when you're ready for more. If your keyboard offers no recording function or only limited features, this category is a great one to consider and explore.

Popular DAW computer titles include

- Ableton *Live* (Mac and Windows)
- Apple *GarageBand* (Mac only) — good for beginners as well!
- Apple *Logic Pro* (Mac only)
- Avid *Pro Tools* (Mac and Windows)
- Cakewalk *Sonar* (Windows only)
- Cockos *Reaper* (Mac and Windows)

✔ Image-Line *FL Studio* (Windows only)

✔ MOTU *Digital Performer* (Mac and Windows)

✔ PreSonus *Studio One* (Mac and Windows)

✔ Propellerhead *Reason* (Mac and Windows)

✔ Steinberg *Cubase* (Mac and Windows)

✔ Steinberg *Sequel* (Mac and Windows) — good for beginners as well!

Popular iPad titles include the following:

✔ Apple *GarageBand* — good for beginners as well!

✔ Beepstreet *iSequence*

✔ *FL Studio Mobile*

✔ 4Pockets *Meteor*

✔ Intua *Beatmaker*

✔ Steinberg *Cubasis*

✔ Xewton Music Studio

✔ Yamaha Mobile Music Sequencer

Another type of software is *play along* or *backing tracks,* where you give the software a chord progression and it generates backing parts (drums, bass, chords, and so on) so you can play along with it. Some DAWs have this type of functionality. The most popular software with this capability is PG Music's *Band-In-A-Box* (Mac and Windows).

Educational/learning software

A number of software titles can teach you how to play piano/keyboards (or even guitar or drums). You can study reading music, learn music theory, work on your ear training, study the works of famous composers, and much more.

The beauty of this kind of software is that it's always ready to go when you are and is infinitely patient; you can move at your own speed. As a former teacher, I won't say that working with a human doesn't have its benefits, but I will say a lot of good things for educational software as a companion to traditional studies and lessons. The market has too many titles to list here, but look for software from the following companies and programs as a start:

✔ Computer titles

- Adventus
- Alfred Publishing
- Ars Nova
- Harmonic Vision
- Piano Marvel
- Playground Sessions
- Sibelius

✔ iPad/iPhone titles

- Electric Peel *Note-A-Lator*
- Karajan *Beginner*, *Pro Music,* and *Ear Trainer*
- Musictheory.net *Theory Lessons* and *Tenuto*
- *My Rhythm HD*
- Nitrovery *Rhythm*
- *Polyrhythm*
- *Rhythm Sight Reading Trainer*

You can find a number of metronome apps that run on the iPad or your smartphone — very handy! *Metronome Plus* is very full-featured for a free app. The Pro (paid) version of *ProMetronome* is really great.

In Chapter 16, I mention computer software tools for transcribing songs you want to play along to. These applications are handy because they can slow down the speed of the music without changing the pitch, repeat sections you choose, and make many markers in the song file for easy location of your favorite parts. My favorite titles include Roni Music's *Amazing Slow Downer* (Mac, Windows, and iPad), and Seventh String Software's *Transcribe!* (Mac and Windows). A newer website, `http://jammit.com`, offers the real backing tracks, which you can isolate or remove to learn how to play songs from the site's ever-growing library.

Music notation software

Gone are the days when a composer dipped his quill pen into ink and wrote out his music on manuscript paper. Well, okay, quill pens were gone by the early 1900s, but with the advent of the computer, preparing a musical score or a simple pop tune has never been easier. Just as the computer took over printing and publishing, it has become the de facto standard for music engraving.

Many music notation programs can record MIDI and instantly convert it to notation; though not perfect, this process can be much faster than placing notes one at a time onto a staff. After you enter notes, you can edit and manipulate them with the same flexibility that you do letters within a word processor. Notation software often has sounds built-in so you can hear your music played back from the computer with no other instruments connected. Many of the available packages are designed for the serious composer and arranger and may seem far too deep at first glance for the casual player. But even those programs have "lite" versions or offer easy templates to work from. The main notation computer titles are as follows:

- ✔ Avid *Sibelius* (Mac and Windows)

- ✔ Avid *Sibelius First* (Mac and Windows)

- ✔ DG Software *MagicScore Maestro* (Windows)

- ✔ DoReMIR *ScoreCleaner* (Mac and Windows)

- ✔ Lugert Verlag *Forte* (Windows)

- ✔ Make Music *Finale* and *Finale Notepad* (Mac and Windows)

- ✔ Make Music *Print Music* (Mac and Windows)

- ✔ *MuseScore* (free; Mac and Linux)

- ✔ Notion Music *Notion* (Mac and Windows)

Popular iPad titles include Gargant Studios *Reflow* and Notion Music *Notion*.

Digital sheet music

Digital sheet music is a subset of notation software; these programs are for viewing music scores or buying sheet music/songbooks, not creating them. You can just view scores as graphic files (like a JPEG, TIFF, or PDF), but a dedicated program can offer easier viewing (better page turning, for example) and more features. This activity is well covered by the music notation programs on the computer (see the preceding section), but it's a growing field for the iPad and tablet computers. Popular iPad titles include

- ✔ Avid *Scorch* (only works with Sibelius and PDF files)

- ✔ Deep Dish Designs *DeepDish GigBook*

- ✔ Leoné *MusicReader PDF* (also available as Mac and PC software)

- ✔ Make Music *Finale Songbook* (free; only works with Finale files)

- ✔ MGS Development *forScore*

- ✔ UnReal Book

Some of the online songbook/sheet music sites use their own proprietary viewers for their files, so I'm not listing them here.

Additional instruments/sounds

This field is huge in both computer and iPad development. Software synthesizers are at the forefront of synthesis development and technologies, offering both models of classic synths from years gone by and new, powerful designs. Software sample-players have the largest memory (often reading the samples off the drive in real time, virtually eliminating the need to worry about memory size), and the most advanced feature sets and designs. Most of the major advancements in sample-playback technology happen in the software instruments, and many companies create sounds libraries for these players.

Most major DAWs include some software synthesizers and often a sample-player engine. The main software sample-players for computers are as follows; all are compatible with both Mac and Windows unless otherwise noted:

- Ableton *Sampler*
- Apple Logic's *EXS24* (included in Logic Pro – Mac)
- Avid Pro Tool's *Structure*
- IK Multimedia *SampleTank*
- MOTU *MachFive*
- Native Instrument's *Kontakt* and *Battery*
- Propellerhead Reason's *NN-XT* (included in Reason – Mac and Windows)
- Steinberg *Halion*

Some of the companies that make sound libraries offer their own player engines, but these players are usually only able to play sounds from that company. Examples include East West's *Play* engine, Garritan's *Aria* player, and Best Service's *ENGINE*.

On iPad, the choices are more limited because memory is much smaller. Top titles include the following:

- Akai *iMPC*
- Bismark *bs-16i*
- IK Multimedia *SampleTank*
- *Samplr*

Software instruments are commonly called *virtual instruments* or *VIs*. You can divide software instruments into a few general categories:

- **Re-creations of classic synths:** These VIs are accurate emulations of famous synths, often analog legends from the '70s and '80s. Most are modeled, but some are digital synthesis, and some are based on sample-playback technology. (Chapter 2 has details on digital synthesis, sample-playback, and other kinds of sound production.)

- **Models/emulations of well-known acoustic and electro-mechanical instruments:** This category includes most sampled pianos; modeled tonewheel organs; clavs and electric pianos; and modeled guitars, brass, and woodwinds.

- **Imaginative new synths:** This broad area includes fuller-featured versions based on classic analog synthesis, as well as hybrid technologies and completely new and fresh forms of synthesis.

Plenty of titles are available both for computers and for the iPad — more than I can possibly list here.

Essential online resources

In this chapter, I largely talk about computer software and apps for the iPad. But a whole world of resources on the web can aid in your music discovery, studies, and fun! I obviously can't list them all, but here are a few of my favorites:

- `http://acqweb.org/pubr/music.html`: A good directory of most print and electronic delivery music publishers.

- `www.allmusic.com`: My favorite resource to read reviews of artists' recordings, find their credits, and learn about their careers.

- `http://imsta.org`: Info on the ethics of software use and piracy — do the right thing!

- `www.midi.org`: More about MIDI and how it's used.

- `http://pianochorddictionary.com`: A great resource for learning chords of all types.

- `http://pianolessons.com` and `www.true-piano-lessons.com`: Nice resources for online lessons and study.

- `www.pianoworld.com/forum`: A forum for all things piano and keyboard. It's not about synths and not too tech-y.

- `www.promusicapps.com`: A resource for all things musical on the iPad.

- `www.sfcv.org/learn/composer-gallery`: A wonderful online listing of most classical composers with some bio and reference information.

- `http://sonicstate.com/news`: My go-to site for all news releases, reviews, and so on for music tech products. You can click on filters like software, virtual synths, and iPad/phone to see news about specific categories. (This one's for the more tech-minded readers.)

Part V
The Part of Tens

For lists of ten great songs for a variety of keyboard types, check out `www.dummies.com/extras/keyboard`.

In this part . . .

✔ Get ready to go shopping for your new keyboard. You want to maximize your trip to the store by having a game plan.

✔ Make the most of your entry into the world of keyboards by seeking out other musicians and, yes, committing to practicing.

Chapter 18

Ten Tips for Keyboard Shopping

In This Chapter

▶ Coming prepared

▶ Taking the keyboard(s) for a proper test drive

*Y*ou've decided to buy an electronic keyboard. That's great; you're going to have a lot of fun playing it (or watching your child play it). If you already know exactly what you need and where you're going to get it, then put the book down and get going!

Still here? No worries; you have a lot of decisions to make before committing to a purchase. In this chapter, I guide you through ten tips I've developed from my many years of marketing and selling keyboards and from buying lots of instruments myself.

I advise always going back home, gathering your thoughts, and sleeping on any large-ticket decision. If it's worth having, it's worth a little extra consideration.

Know What Type of Keyboard You Want

Your first step is to narrow down the category of keyboard you want: Is it a digital piano, a portable keyboard, a synthesizer, or an organ? Here's some help to decide:

- ✔ **Read Chapters 2 and 3.** They contain lots of good information to make your choice clearer.

- ✔ **Ask a friend or relative who plays keyboards well (if she seems qualified and you trust her opinion).**

- ✔ **Look online.** Some music magazines and retailers have helpful articles and information on their websites. Of course, they're trying to sell you something, but that doesn't mean they won't inform you along the way. They often use independent industry experts to write these articles.

Don't walk into a store without having narrowed down this all-important question. If you're lucky, the salesperson will be knowledgeable, but that depends on the store, who's working that day, and other factors. Having a few categories in mind is perfectly fine, but you should have a shortlist of possibilities.

Determine Your Price Range

You encounter many choices in whatever category you're looking in, so setting a budget can help you narrow down the options and reduce potential confusion. The old maxim "you get what you pay for" doesn't hold true for keyboards. My experience is that you get a lot more than you pay for, and that's a good thing! Setting a budget may be the factor that helps you decide what category of keyboard you end up with. The higher-end portable may be the better choice for the features you want while still costing less than the lower-end digital piano for example.

Do Your Research

When you have a shortlist of keyboard options (see the earlier section "Know What Type of Keyboard You Want" and Chapters 2 and 3), get online and do some homework! Lots of keyboard info is available on the Internet; try these resources:

- ✔ Check out manufacturers' websites for specs such as size and weight and the inclusion of the right connectors and features you're looking for. Be sure to watch their video demos and also take note if the brand is running any promotions or rebates.

- ✔ Examine the manual to get a feel for how the product operates. If the manual is way confusing, odds are the instrument will be as well. Your manual may be more than one document: a simple guide and a more-detailed one.

- ✔ Search for user groups for the brand(s) you're interested in; they help you find out many things that only a current owner of the product can know. You can also search the site for topics and questions you may have and even ask questions directly of the users. Best of all? No one is trying to sell you anything!

- ✔ Look for user groups for the general category you're interested in (digital pianos, arrangers, synthesizers). They are a great resource for reading about many similar models, and you may find direct comparisons of the keyboard you're interested in with other top choices.

- ✔ Read reviews for the model(s) you're interested in.

Make the Most of Your Trip to the Store

Be sure before you leave the house that your trip will be productive:

- ✔ **Look up the various music stores in your area.** They may be music-specific chain stores or mass-market retailers that carry some keyboards. Find out what brands they carry; not all stores carry all brands. Some manufacturers have dealer listings or dealer locaters on their websites to help.

- ✔ **Call the store and ask whether it has your specific model(s) in stock and whether you can try it/them out.** Many of the large chain stores don't stock every model of a given brand in all their locations. If the store is sold out of the model, you need to wait for a new shipment to come in.

Bring Your Own Headphones

Take some headphones with you to the store so you can try all the products under the same conditions. Different speakers, amps, and locations in various stores can color your perception of the keyboard's sound. Using the same headphones or speakers can help equalize that perception.

Using headphones also helps you tune out the noise in the store and lets you really concentrate on what you're hearing. And if you're a bit shy, you can try sounds out and not worry what other people think about your playing.

This tip works only if you have a good pair of closed/over-the-ear headphones, of course. How good? The best you can find; you're using them to make a critical purchase decision. Cheap earbuds aren't going to do a good job. If you don't own a good set of headphones, see whether a friend or family member can loan you a pair. (You can read about headphones in Chapter 4.)

Ask for a Damper/Sustain Pedal

You should use a damper or sustain pedal if you're trying out acoustic or electric piano sounds. These pedals are rarely attached to the floor model units because they can be stolen easily and get in the way. So be sure to ask a salesperson whether she can hook one up for you to try.

Listen to the Built-In Demos

Even if you've already heard the demos online, checking them out in-person is a good first step. Turn the volume way down when they start to play and then bring it up slowly until it's comfortable to listen to. The instructions should be on the front panel or perhaps a card attached to the instrument; ask for help if you can't figure out how to get them playing.

Get Your Hands on the Keyboard

Reading about and watching videos of a product are passive experiences and can only tell you so much. I strongly feel that you should try a product in person before buying it if at all possible. No one can describe the touch of the keys in a way that truly tells you what they feel like. No reading can fully explain whether you'll find the operations confusing. Therefore, the best way to shop for a keyboard is to actually play it.

Here's a quick checklist of things to explore:

- ✔ **Sounds:** Be sure to listen to all the sounds that are important to you. This list may include single sounds, multisounds, splits, and layers,

- ✔ **Key feel:** Is the keyboard too light/easy to play, too hard/tiring to play, or just right? See whether the keyboard has different touch curves to adjust this sensation. Ask for help in changing them if you need it.

- ✔ **Modes:** Check out any special modes of operation: auto-accompaniment, arpeggiators, drum rhythms, and so on.

- ✔ **Weight:** Try to lift the keyboard to get a sense of what it will be like to move. Digital grands excluded!

- ✔ **Connectors:** Look around the back to see how easily you can read and access the various connectors.

Compare Models

The beauty of visiting a store in person is that you can go from model to model and compare them while the sound and feel of each instrument is fresh in your ears/fingers. Take your time, and don't be afraid to go back and forth a few times. I do so all the time when judging the feel of a keyboard and when comparing the critical sounds such as the acoustic and electric pianos.

Find the Best Deal

Notice I didn't say the best *price*. Price shopping is easy enough to do. You can do web searches and figure out prices with tax and shipping, but the lowest price may not be the best deal. What is seller's return policy if you have buyer's remorse later? Many of the lowest-priced outlets charge a restocking fee, so you should research that upfront.

Is a store offering extra items bundled with the keyboard (pedal, stand, books, cables)? It's worth asking for some even if they aren't marked. Will the store help you if you have questions after the sale? Does it offer lessons? These factors all contribute to the overall deal value.

I worry about shipping large and/or heavy keyboards, which can get banged up in transit, so I prefer to buy these large objects locally (versus over the Internet) if at all possible.

Chapter 19

Ten Ways to Enhance Your Playing Experience

A number of things can make your playing time more enjoyable and productive and something you look forward to. In this chapter, I help you set the stage for great playing and suggest ways to explore the social nature of music making and find sources of inspiration.

Set the Right Mood

I like to play in a room that isn't too bright. Harsh lighting is a buzz-kill for me and can provide unwanted distractions. Try darkening the room a bit (close the curtains) and making the main light source a lamp near the keyboard to help you see the panel and your music. This setup focuses you on the keyboard and your playing, not the rest of the room.

Stretch and Warm Up Before You Play

Warming up your muscles before you use them for any physical activity is a good idea. Playing keyboard involves your back, shoulders, arms, wrists, and fingers, so you want to get those muscles ready. These quick warm-ups get the blood flowing to all these areas and loosen you up:

- Stretch the fingers of both hands outward as far as is comfortable, hold them there for a few counts, and then contract them back into a tight fist. Hold that for a few counts and then repeat.

- Shake your hands and wrists vigorously for a minute or so. Let them be very loose and limp as you do to get the blood flowing throughout.

- Roll your head around slowly, concentrating on your breathing as you do. Don't strain your neck; just let the muscles stretch a bit to get rid of any tension or kinks.

- Raise your arms over your head and stretch upward a few times. Concentrate on gently stretching your upper arms and shoulders as you do.

- Put your palms together in front of you, like you're praying. Lift your elbows up and down slightly, moving your shoulders at the same time.

- With your elbows fully bent and held to your sides, hold your forearms straight up in front of you, palms outward. Rotate your palms until they're now facing you, without moving your arms. Return to the starting position and repeat. Then with the palms facing outward, lower your hand so your fingers point outward and then down, concentrating on gently stretching your wrists.

Watch Your Posture

The most important physical issue when playing a keyboard is keeping good posture, especially regarding your lower back. Sit upright and keep your back straight. Never slump while sitting or playing; this positioning can cause back pain and problems that will follow you for years. I discuss proper posture in more detail in Chapter 6.

Set Up a Practice Routine

Spending time just playing and having fun is completely okay. Playing an instrument shouldn't be a chore that you have to do. But when you want to develop your skills, you need a more organized and purposeful practice plan.

Think about dividing up whatever time you can afford to spend practicing into specific sections devoted to tasks and goals such as the following (and check out Chapter 6 for more info on making the most of your practice time):

- Doing warm-up exercises, including scales
- Practicing specific songs or pieces you're working on, from beginning to end and in smaller sections
- Studying new chords, voicings, inversions, chord progressions, and so on
- *Sight reading* through some music you've never seen before to develop your reading skills or to pick up a new song
- Listening to and figuring out new songs by ear
- Studying features of your keyboard

Pay attention to the time, and be sure you devote some time to each activity you want to work on. Get up and take a little break between activities to clear your head. Just be sure to come back to work; don't go surfing the web or checking to see what's on TV!

Use a Real Damper Pedal If You Play Piano/Electric Piano

Many keyboards don't come with any pedals. Your dealer may have thrown one in, but it's often the small, flat, square pedal that really is just a flat switch (called a *footswitch,* although sometimes it is mistakenly called a sustain pedal because it can be used for that function). I strongly recommend you get a pedal that is the same shape as a real piano's damper pedal (also called a sustain pedal, named correctly this time, in my opinion); check out Chapter 6 for a visual. That way, you get a feel for the true mechanism that you'd encounter on a real piano and in other setups.

Find a Music Buddy

Hanging out with another person who is at the same level as you are can be a wonderful experience. You can share what you're working on or just like to play. He can watch you and point out anything funny in your posture or playing. You can take turns trying to play new exercises and songs. You can listen to music together, turning each other on to your favorite artists and songs or explore features of your keyboard or his to discover things together. In short, you can share the experience of learning and enjoying playing an instrument with a peer.

Where can you find your music buddy? Perhaps at school, at church, through the local music store, through online user groups for your instrument (be careful to get to know them well online first!), or through family and neighbor referrals. Look around; they're out there.

Play Music with Other People

This idea is an extension of the previous section. Making music with others is fun. Here are a few ideas:

- ✔ Form a garage band with some friends or neighbors. You can pick easy songs, just have some laughs, and share a bonding experience.

- ✔ Get involved in the music at your church.

- ✔ Go to a local nursing home; you may find a retired musician there with plenty of time (and knowledge!) on his hands.

- ✔ Ask your local music store for some help finding other players. Be upfront and honest about your skill level so you don't get in over your head.

- ✔ Find a good singer and work on some songs together. Lots of people sing well but can't play an instrument. Team up!

Listen to Recordings for Inspiration

I find that I play differently (and often better) if I sit down to play right after listening to a song or recording I like. If you want to play in the style of an artist or genre you like, listen to a bunch of recordings and then sit down at your keyboard and see what happens. I'm confident that something will have rubbed off. You can do more serious analysis and study later. First, just listen and absorb the influence.

Spend Time Studying on YouTube

You can find an amazing amount of quality instructional material for free. Whatever style of music you like to play, searching for some lessons on YouTube will bring up great results. Type "learn to play xxx" where xxx is a song name, a style of music (jazz, funk, reggae, and so on), or an instrument (piano, organ, and so on). Want to know more about synthesis and editing sounds or effects? Search away; it's all out there!

Get Yourself a Teacher!

I saved the best for last. After some period of time just enjoying yourself and working on your own, you should investigate taking some lessons from a skilled teacher. He can help you develop your technique, improve your reading skills, teach you more about chords and music theory, and much more. Think about what you want to learn and talk about that with the teacher. He should be willing to help you explore what you want to learn while teaching you what he knows you need to learn. Make sure that he accepts the keyboard you own as your practice instrument (some teachers spurn products that don't have a piano feel).

Appendix

Discovering What's on the Audio Tracks

. . . .

So much of this book is about sounds and music. Reading about that topic is nice, but it doesn't come alive and become real until you hear it. Wherever you see the Play This! icon, you find references to audio tracks that demonstrate the sounds of various instruments, exercises you can play, and your interaction with the features of your keyboard. I've recorded these audio examples because I know that hearing is believing!

If you've purchased the paper or e-book version of *Keyboard For Dummies,* you can find the tracks — ready and waiting for you — at www.dummies. com/go/keyboard. (If you don't have Internet access, call 877-762-2974 within the U.S. or 317-572-3993 outside the U.S.) Table A-1 provides you with a handy list of all the audio tracks referenced throughout the book.

Table A-1		Audio Tracks
Track Number	*Chapter Number*	*Track Title or Description*
1	Chapter 2	Acoustic piano sound example
2	Chapter 2	Harpsichord sound example
3	Chapter 2	Clavichord sound example
4	Chapter 2	Celeste sound example
5	Chapter 2	Pipe organ sound example
6	Chapter 2	Rhodes suitcase electric piano MK1 sound example

(continued)

Table A-1 *(continued)*

Track Number	Chapter Number	Track Title or Description
7	Chapter 2	Rhodes suitcase electric piano MKII sound example
8	Chapter 2	Rhodes suitcase electric piano MKV sound example
9	Chapter 2	Wurlitzer electric piano sound example
10	Chapter 2	Hohner Pianet sound example
11	Chapter 2	Hohner Clavinet sound example
12	Chapter 2	Yamaha CP-70 electric grand piano sound example
13	Chapter 2	Hammond B3 organ sound example
14	Chapter 2	Mellotron tape player keyboard sound examples
15	Chapter 2	Vox combo organ sound example
16	Chapter 2	Farfisa combo organ sound example
17	Chapter 2	Moog synthesizer sound examples
18	Chapter 3	Examples of a small memory sampled piano with small loops compared to a larger memory sampled piano
19	Chapter 3	Demonstrations of a single layer sampled piano, a multilayer version with obvious switching points, and a well-constructed multilayer sampled piano
20	Chapter 3	A demonstration of release samples on a sampled acoustic piano
21	Chapter 3	A demonstration of the damper resonance effect on a sampled piano instrument
22	Chapter 5	The first counting exercise (Figure 5-25)
23	Chapter 5	The second counting exercise (Figure 5-27)
24	Chapter 5	The third counting exercise (Figure 5-27)
25	Chapter 5	The exercise in Figure 5-30 played
26	Chapter 5	The exercise in Figure 5-31 played

Track Number	Chapter Number	Track Title or Description
27	Chapter 5	Demonstrations of metronome counting exercises
28	Chapter 6	Figure 6-6 played
29	Chapter 6	Figure 6-7 played
30	Chapter 6	Figure 6-8 played hands alone and then together
31	Chapter 6	Figures 6-10 and 6-11 played
32	Chapter 6	Figure 6-12 played
33	Chapter 6	Figure 6-13 played
34	Chapter 6	Figure 6-14 played
35	Chapter 6	Figure 6-15 played
36	Chapter 6	Figure 6-16 played (major scales)
37	Chapter 6	Demonstration of playing with and without the damper pedal
38	Chapter 7	Figure 7-1 played (various intervals)
39	Chapter 7	Figure 7-2 played (major triad)
40	Chapter 7	Figure 7-3 played (three chords)
41	Chapter 7	Figure 7-4 played (minor triad)
42	Chapter 7	Figure 7-5 played (diminished triad)
43	Chapter 7	Figure 7-6 played (augmented triad)
44	Chapter 7	Figure 7-7 played (suspended chords)
45	Chapter 7	Figure 7-8 played (major scale tone triads)
46	Chapter 7	Figure 7-10 played (blues chord progression)
47	Chapter 7	Figure 7-11 played (doo-wop chord progression)
48	Chapter 7	Figure 7-12 played (chord inversions)
49	Chapter 7	Figure 7-13 played (blues progression using inversions)
50	Chapter 7	Figure 7-14 played (doo-wop progression using inversions)

(continued)

Table A-1 *(continued)*

Track Number	Chapter Number	Track Title or Description
51	Chapter 7	Figure 7-15 played (left hand blues figures)
52	Chapter 7	Figure 7-16 played (left hand doo-wop figures)
53	Chapter 7	Figure 7-17 played (two hand blues chord playing)
54	Chapter 7	Figure 7-18 played (two hand doo-wop chord playing)
55	Chapter 8	Various sounds played below their natural limits
56	Chapter 8	Various sounds played above their natural limits
57	Chapter 8	An acoustic guitar sound played with "bad" piano voicings and then more naturally
58	Chapter 8	A distorted guitar sound played with "bad" piano voicings and then more naturally
59	Chapter 8	Demonstrations of layered sounds
60	Chapter 8	Demonstrations of split keyboard sounds
61	Chapter 9	Reverb effect demonstration
62	Chapter 9	Delay effect demonstration
63	Chapter 9	Chorus, flanging, and phase shifting effects demonstrations
64	Chapter 9	EQ effect demonstration
65	Chapter 9	Distortion effect demonstration
66	Chapter 9	Rotary speaker effect demonstration
67	Chapter 9	Filter effect demonstration
68	Chapter 9	Wah-wah and auto-wah effect demonstration
69	Chapter 10	Casio rhythm variations
70	Chapter 10	Yamaha rhythm variations
71	Chapter 10	Korg multiple rhythm variations

Track Number	*Chapter Number*	*Track Title or Description*
72	Chapter 10	Casio drum fills
73	Chapter 10	Korg multiple drum fill variations
74	Chapter 10	Korg Break feature used within various styles
75	Chapter 10	Korg drum fills switching to different style variations
76	Chapter 11	Various styles being played using a simple C triad
77	Chapter 11	A demonstration of each element within a style/rhythm
78	Chapter 11	An accompaniment pattern played with different chord types
79	Chapter 11	A simple chord progression with accompaniment (Figure 11-6)
80	Chapter 11	Common chord progression played in a variety of music styles
81	Chapter 11	Another common chord progression played in a variety of music styles
82	Chapter 11	A third common chord progression played in a variety of music styles
83	Chapter 11	Casio accompaniment variations
84	Chapter 11	Yamaha accompaniment variations
85	Chapter 11	Korg accompaniment multiple variations
86	Chapter 11	Accompaniment intros demonstrated
87	Chapter 11	Accompaniment endings demonstrated
88	Chapter 11	Changing accompaniment patterns within a song
89	Chapter 11	Mixing the levels of tracks within an accompaniment pattern
90	Chapter 11	Varying the reverb levels within an accompaniment pattern
91	Chapter 11	Changing the sounds for various tracks within an accompaniment pattern
92	Chapter 11	Demonstrating right hand ensemble/ harmony settings

(continued)

Table A-1 *(continued)*

Track Number	Chapter Number	Track Title or Description
93	Chapter 11	Demonstrating the pad feature
94	Chapter 12	Chords played in an arpeggiated fashion on the piano
95	Chapter 12	Figure 12-1 demonstrated
96	Chapter 12	Figure 12-2 demonstrated
97	Chapter 12	Demonstration of changing chords and using space to vary a simple arp pattern
98	Chapter 12	Varying the octave range of an arp pattern
99	Chapter 12	An arp pattern played against a drum rhythm
100	Chapter 12	Demonstration of swing timing feel
101	Chapter 12	Note duration/gate demonstration
102	Chapter 12	Demonstration of a chord sustaining while an arp pattern plays beneath it
103	Chapter 12	Filter sweeps while an arp plays
104	Chapter 12	Sound panning while an arp plays
105	Chapter 12	Delay effect used with an arp pattern
106	Chapter 12	Leaving space while using delay with an arppegiator
107	Chapter 14	Demonstration of various analog synthesis waveforms
108	Chapter 14	Demonstration of various filter sweeps
109	Chapter 14	Varying the ADSR envelope of a sound
110	Chapter 14	Demonstrating LFO-produced vibrato, filter wah, and tremolo
111	Chapter 14	Demonstrating slight edit concepts to produce new sounds
112	Chapter 14	Demonstrating varying the waveforms in similar amp envelope shaped sounds to produce new sounds
113	Chapter 15	Listen as the onboard teacher tells you what fingers to use

Index

• F •

• T •

● X ●

About the Author

Jerry Kovarsky has been playing piano since the age of 8 and got his first electronic keyboard (a rare Gibson organ) a few years later. Those parallel paths continue to this day as he divides his time among the acoustic piano, the organ, synths, and anything that makes cool sounds. After studying music at Manhattan School of Music, the University of Miami, and William Paterson College, he hit the road playing music of every shape and style in clubs, concert halls, and catering halls around the world.

A chance encounter with the client at a recording session led him to start demonstrating Casio keyboards in the early '80s, and he found a new career path, joining the company as a product manager. Thirty years on, he has worked for Casio, Ensoniq, and Korg as a product developer, brand manager, marketing director, and much more. This career enabled him to be part of the teams that introduced hundreds of award-winning and now legendary instruments to the world. That work continues to this day as he consults with a wide group of companies. He writes a monthly column on synthesizer soloing for *Keyboard* magazine and does select interviews with some of the biggest names in keyboards.

Actively playing piano and keyboards in his new home on the island of Maui, Jerry remains on top of all the trends and developments in electronic keyboards and enjoys sharing that knowledge with others.

> *If anyone knows anything about keyboards, it's Jerry Kovarsky. He does it all here, except to explain how to stick knives in keyboards and spin around on them.*
>
> —*Keith Emerson*
>
> Composer/keyboardist
> (The Nice, Emerson, Lake & Palmer)

> *Jerry is that rare combination of a technologist mixed with the soul of a musician. I've known him for over 25 years and I can think of no one better equipped to guide the reader through the myriad of possibilities that electronic keyboards offer. I know he's certainly helped me on my journey!*
>
> —*Herbie Hancock*
>
> Pianist, keyboardist, bandleader,
> and composer

Dedication

I dedicate this book to my parents, who woke me up as a young child to see the Beatles on Ed Sullivan, an event that defined my life moving forward. They supported me in my musical development even though they did not play instruments or even listen to much music in the home. Until I came along. They never questioned my love of music and desire to make music my calling. All kids should have such unconditional love and support.

Author's Acknowledgments

Thanks to Stephen Fortner at *Keyboard* magazine for putting me in touch with the good folks at Wiley. And David, Chrissy, Alissa, and Megan at Wiley for believing in me and whipping my words into shape. Plus my dear friend Geary Yelton, who helped me clarify the deeper technical matters I discuss.

Thanks to all my contacts at the various manufacturers who provided me with loaner products, images, and support to be able to make this book the best it could be. To Bob Larsen from Casio for providing me with my first job in the music products industry, and to Mike Kovins and Chairman Katoh for providing me with the best gig for all those years at Korg. You are both missed.

Thanks to all my artist friends and influences for giving me the motivation and the path to follow in my never-ending pursuit of playing music. And all my fellow musicians for the joy of playing together. Endless thanks to my wife, Jackie, and daughters, Jessica and Dara, for making my life whole and full of meaning and love.

Publisher's Acknowledgments

Acquisitions Editor: David Lutton

Senior Project Editor: Alissa Schwipps

Copy Editor: Megan Knoll

Technical Editor: Geary Yelton

Art Coordinator: Alicia B. South

Project Coordinator: Sheree Montgomery

Supervising Producer: Rich Graves, MBA

Illustrator: Lisa Reed

Cover Image: ©iStock.com/Tatiana Morozova

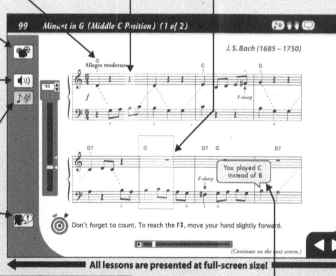

Math & Science

Algebra I For Dummies,
2nd Edition
978-0-470-55964-2

Anatomy and Physiology
For Dummies,
2nd Edition
978-0-470-92326-9

Astronomy For Dummies,
3rd Edition
978-1-118-37697-3

Biology For Dummies,
2nd Edition
978-0-470-59875-7

Chemistry For Dummies,
2nd Edition
978-1-1180-0730-3

Pre-Algebra Essentials
For Dummies
978-0-470-61838-7

Microsoft Office

Excel 2013 For Dummies
978-1-118-51012-4

Office 2013 All-in-One
For Dummies
978-1-118-51636-2

PowerPoint 2013
For Dummies
978-1-118-50253-2

Word 2013 For Dummies
978-1-118-49123-2

Music

Blues Harmonica
For Dummies
978-1-118-25269-7

Guitar For Dummies,
3rd Edition
978-1-118-11554-1

iPod & iTunes
For Dummies,
10th Edition
978-1-118-50864-0

Programming

Android Application
Development For
Dummies, 2nd Edition
978-1-118-38710-8

iOS 6 Application
Development For Dummies
978-1-118-50880-0

Java For Dummies,
5th Edition
978-0-470-37173-2

Religion & Inspiration

The Bible For Dummies
978-0-7645-5296-0

Buddhism For Dummies,
2nd Edition
978-1-118-02379-2

Catholicism For Dummies,
2nd Edition
978-1-118-07778-8

Self-Help & Relationships

Bipolar Disorder
For Dummies,
2nd Edition
978-1-118-33882-7

Meditation For Dummies,
3rd Edition
978-1-118-29144-3

Seniors

Computers For Seniors
For Dummies,
3rd Edition
978-1-118-11553-4

iPad For Seniors
For Dummies,
5th Edition
978-1-118-49708-1

Social Security
For Dummies
978-1-118-20573-0

Smartphones & Tablets

Android Phones
For Dummies
978-1-118-16952-0

Kindle Fire HD
For Dummies
978-1-118-42223-6

NOOK HD For Dummies,
Portable Edition
978-1-118-39498-4

Surface For Dummies
978-1-118-49634-3

Test Prep

ACT For Dummies,
5th Edition
978-1-118-01259-8

ASVAB For Dummies,
3rd Edition
978-0-470-63760-9

GRE For Dummies,
7th Edition
978-0-470-88921-3

Officer Candidate Tests,
For Dummies
978-0-470-59876-4

Physician's Assistant Exam
For Dummies
978-1-118-11556-5

Series 7 Exam
For Dummies
978-0-470-09932-2

Windows 8

Windows 8 For Dummies
978-1-118-13461-0

Windows 8 For Dummies,
Book + DVD Bundle
978-1-118-27167-4

Windows 8 All-in-One
For Dummies
978-1-118-11920-4

e **Available in print and e-book formats.**